THE INSTITUTIONAL FOUNDATIONS OF PUBLIC POLICY IN ARGENTINA

The authors have two purposes in this book, and they succeed admirably at both. They develop a general model of public policy making focused on the difficulties of securing intertemporal exchanges among politicians. Their model enables them to derive a series of empirical propositions about the conditions under which policies are likely to be volatile, rigid, or high quality. They combine the tools of game theory with Williamson's transaction cost theory, North institutional arguments, and contract theory to provide a general theory of public policy making in a comparative political economy setting. They also undertake a detailed study of Argentina, using statistical evidence when and where it is available to complement their nuanced account of institutions, rules, incentives, and outcomes. They manage to make comprehensible the reasons for Argentina's seeming inability to design and implement high-quality public policies over a sustained period of time. If the book does nothing else (and it does a lot more), it would be required reading based just on the empirical material and its interpretation.

Pablo T. Spiller (Ph.D. in Economics, University of Chicago, 1980) is the Jeffrey A. Jacobs Distinguished Professor of Business & Technology at the University of California, Berkeley, and Research Associate, National Bureau of Economic Research. He has held academic positions at the University of Pennsylvania, Stanford University, and the University of Illinois at Urbana-Champaign. He has published several books and more than ninety articles in the general area of political economy and industrial organization. He is the coeditor of the *Journal of Law, Economics and Organization* and associate editor of the *Journal of Applied Economics, Regulation* magazine, and *The Utilities Project*. He has been a special advisor to the Federal Trade Commission's Bureau of Economics, and he was an elected member of the Board of Directors of the American Law and Economics Association.

Mariano Tommasi (Ph.D. in Economics, University of Chicago, 1991) is Professor of Economics at Universidad de San Andres in Argentina. He is past President (2004–5) of the Latin American and Caribbean Economic Association. He has published articles in journals such as *American Economic Review; American Journal of Political Science; American Political Science Review; Journal of Development Economics; Journal of Monetary Economics; International Economic Review; Economics and Politics; Journal of Law, Economics and Organization; Journal of Public Economic Theory; Journal of International Economics;* and *Journal of Institutional and Theoretical Economics.* He has held visiting positions in Economics, Business, and Political Science at Yale, Harvard, UCLA, Tel Aviv, and various Latin American universities. He has received various fellowships and awards, including a Guggenheim Fellowship in 2006. He has been an advisor to several Latin American governments and to international organizations such as the World Bank and the Inter-American Development Bank.

POLITICAL ECONOMY OF INSTITUTIONS AND DECISIONS

Series Editor

Stephen Ansolabehere, Massachusetts Institute of Technology

Founding Editors

James E. Alt, Harvard University
Douglass C. North, Washington University, St. Louis

Other Books in the Series

Alberto Alesina and Howard Rosenthal, *Partisan Politics, Divided Government and the Economy*

Lee J. Alston, Thrainn Eggertsson, and Douglass C. North, eds., *Empirical Studies in Institutional Change*

Lee J. Alston and Joseph P. Ferrie, *Southern Paternalism and the Rise of the American Welfare State: Economics, Politics, and Institutions, 1865–1965*

James E. Alt and Kenneth Shepsle, eds., *Perspectives on Positive Political Economy*

Josephine T. Andrews, *When Majorities Fail: The Russian Parliament, 1990–1993*

Jeffrey S. Banks and Eric A. Hanushek, eds., *Modern Political Economy: Old Topics, New Directions*

Yoram Barzel, *Economic Analysis of Property Rights*, 2nd edition

Yoram Barzel, *A Theory of the State: Economic Rights, Legal Rights, and the Scope of the State*

Robert Bates, *Beyond the Miracle of the Market: The Political Economy of Agrarian Development in Kenya*, 2nd edition

Charles M. Cameron, *Veto Bargaining: Presidents and the Politics of Negative Power*

Kelly H. Chang, *Appointing Central Bankers: The Politics of Monetary Policy in the United States and the European Monetary Union*

Peter Cowhey and Mathew McCubbins, eds., *Structure and Policy in Japan and the United States: An Institutionalist Approach*

Gary W. Cox, *The Efficient Secret: The Cabinet and the Development of Political Parties in Victorian England*

Gary W. Cox, *Making Votes Count: Strategic Coordination in the World's Electoral Systems*

Continued on page following index

THE INSTITUTIONAL FOUNDATIONS OF PUBLIC POLICY IN ARGENTINA

PABLO T. SPILLER

University of California, Berkeley

MARIANO TOMMASI

Universidad de San Andrés

CAMBRIDGE UNIVERSITY PRESS
Cambridge, New York, Melbourne, Madrid, Cape Town, Singapore, São Paulo

Cambridge University Press
32 Avenue of the Americas, New York, NY 10013-2473, USA

www.cambridge.org
Information on this title: www.cambridge.org/9780521854740

First published 2007

Printed in the United States of America

A catalog record for this publication is available from the British Library.

Library of Congress Cataloging in Publication Data

Spiller, Pablo T. (Pablo Tomas), 1951–
The institutional foundations of public policy in Argentina / Pablo T. Spiller,
Mariano Tommasi.
p. cm. – (Political economy of institutions and decisions)
Includes bibliographical references and index.
ISBN-13: 978-0-521-85474-0 (hardback)
1. Political planning – Argentina. 2. Argentina – Politics and government.
3. Argentina – Economic policy. 4. Argentina – Social policy. I. Tommasi,
Mariano, 1964– II. Title. III. Title. IV. Series.
JL2029.P64S64 2007
320.60982–dc22   2006021497

ISBN 978-0-521-85474-0 hardback

Dedicated to Addy and Elisheba and to Paula

Contents

Acknowledgments

This book, as most, had a long gestation period. It started in August 1998 when, thanks to the financial support of Fundación Gobierno y Sociedad, Spiller was able to spend a sabbatical year at the Center of Studies for Institutional Development (CEDI) and at Universidad de San Andrés in Buenos Aires, Argentina. The academic year 1998/1999 was the foundational year for this book; much of the research we report here originated and was presented in its early stages in the weekly interdisciplinary seminars at CEDI. In those seminars, we elicited the right mixture of skepticism, criticism, and excitement, which helped us push our agenda forward. Some of the scholars and researchers then at CEDI appear in this book as coauthors of various chapters.

We owe a tremendous debt to our initial *mecenas*, Miguel Angel Broda, who as president and founder of Fundación Gobierno y Sociedad, enthusiastically – at the time we thought blindly – supported our quixotic assault on Argentina's institutional detail. Without Miguel Angel, this book would have never been written.

Within CEDI, we benefited from an amazing intellectual "support network" over several years. Guillermo Molinelli was at the time imbuing his encyclopedic knowledge of Argentina's institutions into a treatise (published in collaboration with Valeria Palanza and Gisela Sin), and he saw as his role not just to correct us, but also to encourage us, and to force us to further our arguments. He was an indispensable member of our support network, and his influence is evident from our liberal citation of his work. His untimely death made this book a much harder undertaking. Mark Jones, one of our coauthors in Chapter 3, was another encyclopedic member of the CEDI support network. His contribution to this book extends well beyond Chapter 3. With his unparalleled knowledge of Argentine provincial politics, he helped us develop much of our general thinking about those issues. Sebastián Saiegh (coauthor in Chapters 3 and 4) and Matías Iaryczower (coauthor of Chapter 5), although graduate students at the time, were full-right partners in the overall effort. Emiliano Abuelafia, Juliana Bambaci, Roberto Bavastro, Paolo Benedetti, Hernán Blejer, Mariana Chudnovsky, Mauricio Drelichman, Nicolás Ducoté, Milagros Nores, Valeria Palanza, Axel Radics, Fabián Repetto, Lucas Ronconi, Marina Sallustro, Juan Sanguinetti, Gisela Sin, and Jorge Streb completed the CEDI support network. Tamara Sulaque, CEDI's manager, was fundamental in keeping the support network happy and organized. Without her, this book would also have been impossible.

Universidad de San Andrés was also a nurturing environment throughout this project. Among the many colleagues there who helped shape and sharpen our theoretical and applied ideas, we must mention Carlos Acuña, Bob Barros, Marcelo Leiras, and Eduardo Zimmermann. Some parts of Chapter 3 draw on ongoing work with Martín Ardanaz and Marcelo Leiras.

Once the core ideas of this book were developed, we benefited from presenting it at conferences and institutions too many to name. One, though, deserves special mention. Margaret Levi, with terrific timing, energy, and goodwill, organized a full-day multidisciplinary seminar at the University of Washington in Seattle to discuss the book project. That gathering gave us exposure to a number of notable scholars and students, and it was a turning point in helping us organize and shape the book. Margaret herself was a key source of criticism, guidance, and encouragement.

The Institute ATOM at Paris I, as well as Harvard and Yale Universities, also provided enjoyable environments at different points in time while we were working on this book. We owe special thanks to the Leitner Program in International and Comparative Political Economy at Yale University and to its director Frances Rosenbluth for facilitating very productive interactions with colleagues and students in economics and political science.

In the middle of this book's writing, we found a highly receptive ear at the Inter-American Development Bank (IADB). This allowed us to launch, with the leadership of Ernesto Stein, a complementary project on "Political Institutions, Policy-Making Processes and Public Policy" applying our framework to nine other countries in Latin America, using our work on Argentina as a pilot. Some parts of this book draw from our research with Ernesto Stein and Carlos Scartascini on that IADB research project, as well as from some comparative insights we gained from the quality teams assembled for each of the additional nine country studies.

Acknowledgments

Jeff Frieden and Ken Shepsle lent their Research Group on Political Institutions and Economic Policy at Harvard for discussion of our initial paper at one of their biannual meetings, and later for a full-scale two-day discussion of our core ideas as implemented in the IADB project.

Yoram Barzel, Jenna Bednar, Chuck Cameron, Edgardo Favaro, John Ferejohn, Rui de Figueiredo, Ariel Fiszbein, Edgar Kiser, Fabrice Lehoucq, Mariana Llanos, Matt McCubbins, Vicky Murillo, Roger Noll, Anthony Pezzola, Bob Powell, Jessica Seddon Wallack, Olga Shvetsova, Federico Sturzenegger, Emerson Tiller, Barry Weingast, Erik Wibbels, and Oliver Williamson, among many others, provided encouragement and comments on various versions of our work.

We also would like to thank Mercedes Iacoviello and Laura Zuvanic for allowing us to draw freely from their joint work with Tommasi on the Argentine civil service, as well as for specific input and suggestions for Chapter 6.

We also received financial support from the United Nations Development Program; the Center for Latin American Studies at the University of California, Berkeley; and the Joe Shoong Chair in International Business and Public Policy and the Jeffrey A. Jacobs Distinguished Professor Chair in Business and Technology, both at the Haas School of Business.

Introduction

Argentina's sovereign debt default in December 2001 attracted the attention of scholars and policy makers around the world. A country that had a per capita income comparable to Canada's at the turn of the nineteenth century had become an economic disaster 100 years later, with 50 percent of the population living in poverty. Its inability to produce consistent public policies is, we contend, the cause of its economic misfortunes as well as a puzzle that requires explanation.

Argentina's policies have tended to shift dramatically over time. Its aggregate economic policy stance has moved from highly interventionist to extremely promarket and back. After many years of very high inflation and many unsuccessful stabilization attempts, the government introduced a rigid stabilization mechanism known as *convertibility* in 1991. This mechanism allowed for a reduction of inflation to international standards and resulted in a decade of relative macroeconomic prosperity. But the convertibility regime fell chaotically in early 2002 in the aftermath of the default, leading to one of the worst economic crises in recent world history. Argentine microeconomic policies have also been volatile. The geographical distribution of welfare payments changes as frequently as does the minister in charge of social welfare. Public utility policy moves from promoting private investment in infrastructure to asking foreign investors to leave. And, unlike some of its regional neighbors like Brazil or Chile, Argentina also seems unable to steer a well-defined course in its relations with the rest of the world. This lack of definition and incapacity to maintain commitments is mirrored in other areas such as social policy or environmental policy, which are erratic, fragmented, and ineffective.

Argentina is one (rather extreme) example of the point that policy-making capabilities and the quality of policies differ substantially from one country to another. Modern macroeconomics places great importance on the credibility of economic policies as a determinant of their effects (see, for instance, Pritchett 2004; Drazen 2000; Calvo 1989; Kydland and Prescott 1977). No matter how good a policy looks on paper, it will not have the desired effects if economic and social actors do not believe that it will be implemented effectively. We believe that credibility and many other desirable policy qualities depend on a policy's political micro-foundations – that is, on the extent to which political institutions facili-tate the political agreements necessary to sustain effective public policies. Our concern is not so much with the specific content of policies as with some properties of policies, such as whether they are stable, credible, well enforced, and adjusted in a timely manner when circumstances change. Our conviction of the importance of policies' political microfoundations led us to study political and policy-making behavior and their institutional determinants.[1]

In this book we develop a framework for the comparative analysis of the impact of political institutions on public policies. Our framework combines and develops preexisting insights from several quarters of insti-tutional economics and political science, making use of transaction cost analysis,[2] the theory of repeated games, and positive political theory.[3] We

1. To some extent, we are reopening a partly forgotten discussion about "state capac-ity," which had its high points in works such as Weaver and Rockman (1993), which looks at industrialized countries, and Evans (1995), which looks at develop-ing nations.

2. We borrow from transaction cost economics an emphasis on the importance of intertemporal considerations in exchanges (in this case, political exchanges) as well as a microanalytic approach to the study of transactions and their governance (Williamson 2000).

3. The framework suggested in this book draws extensively on a rich literature relating political institutions to political behavior and policy outcomes. Following William Riker's and Oliver Williamson's usage, several authors refer to this literature as *positive political theory* (PPT) (Amadae and Bueno de Mesquita 1999; Williamson 2000). In a recent review of the origins of PPT, Amadae and Bueno de Mesquita assert that it "represents the attempt to build formal models of collective decision-making processes, often relying on the assumption of self-interested rational action" (1999: 269). It is interesting to complement that definition with the words of Robert Cooter who writes: "American political scientists adopted another label to describe their application of economic models to politics. John Ferejohn, Matthew McCubbins, Ken Shepsle, and Barry Weingast (to name but a few) refer to them-selves as 'positive political theorists.' This label stresses the difference between the positive task of explaining how politics actually works and the normative task of philosophizing about how politics ought to work. Thus, positive political theorists distinguish themselves from philosophers who traditionally dominated political the-ory in American universities" (2000: 7).

view public policies as the outcome of political transactions made over time. Using insights from the theory of repeated games, we identify the conditions that are more likely to foster cooperative, credible, and adaptable policies as opposed to noncooperative, noncredible, volatile, or rigid policies. We then draw on the comparative analysis of political institutions to identify the configurations of political institutions most likely to lead to more or less cooperative policy-making environments.

Using our framework, we argue that political institutions in Argentina induce a noncooperative policy-making process that is unable to produce the political agreements necessary to sustain orderly public policies. As a consequence, policies are erratic over time and uncoordinated at any point in time. Although Argentina has occasionally generated temporarily successful policies, most have eventually been hindered by inherent policy instability, short-sighted political behavior, and lack of adequate policies in complementary domains.

OUR APPROACH TO STUDYING POLICY MAKING

The core of our approach is the idea that public policy is a sometimes explicit, sometimes implicit agreement (or "transaction") among policy makers. Thus, important features of public policies depend on the ability of political actors to work together. Since public policies are not spot transactions, cooperation requires striking and enforcing intertemporal political agreements – that is, agreements that can be enforced over time. In environments that facilitate the creation of intertemporal political deals, policy making will be a cooperative process, leading to public policies that are more effective, more sustainable, and more flexible in responding to changing economic or social conditions. In contrast, in settings where political cooperation is hard to develop and sustain, policies will be either too unstable (subject to political swings) or too inflexible, there will be poor coordination between policy-making actors, and the overall process will be characterized by weak state capacities.

Within this framework, the ability to achieve political cooperation affects not so much the content of specific policies as it does some features of public policies: whether they are stable and predictable, whether they can adjust to changing economic conditions, and whether they are well coordinated, implemented, and enforced. These features, we believe, may have as much of an impact on the long-term expectations and behavior of economic agents as the policies themselves do. In other words, current public policies may not have their expected long-term economic impacts if the policy-making process that creates them does not generate adequate beliefs about their long-term sustainability.

Thus, our central question is how the workings of the policy-making process tend to facilitate or hinder cooperative outcomes in the game of political transactions. The literature on repeated oligopoly games provides useful insights. According to the theory, cooperative equilibria are more likely to exist if the number of actors is small, the actors interact repeatedly, the immediate benefits of deviating from cooperation are relatively minimal, deviations from cooperative behavior are easily observed, and there are credible enforcement mechanisms to penalize those who deviate from cooperation.

Mapping how the abstract variables of repeated oligopoly games affect actual policy making and politics in specific countries is not a simple matter. To some extent, such mapping is as much an art as a science. But there are some possible hints toward empirical implementation. While in oligopoly games the number of actors is associated with the number of firms in the market, in politics it should be associated with the number of relevant political actors – that is, those with substantial influence on the making of policy. Likewise, the discount factor may depend on the expected tenure of the political actors or, if the relevant actors are political parties, on the degree of party institutionalization. The availability of credible enforcement mechanisms may be related to the existence of an independent judiciary or to the characteristics of the bureaucracy.

In trying to understand these characteristics of the workings of political institutions, we follow the insights of positive political theory and look into the basic features of the institutional environment, such as whether the government is presidential or parliamentary, what electoral rules are in place, what rules govern interactions between the executive and the legislature, what structure the federal system has, and whether the judiciary is independent.

We believe that the behaviors and outcomes we are interested in are not the result of a single factor but of the interaction of many factors. Thus, we take a systemic approach to studying the connection between institutional variables and the policy-making process. Because we feel it is misleading to characterize countries by a small number of institutional characteristics identified a priori, we proceed backwards from identifying relevant outcomes – the characteristics of public policies, our dependent variable – to characterizing the policy-making process that led those outcomes and then to identifying the institutional and historical reasons the policy-making process operates as it does. This "archeological" approach requires a deep immersion in the workings of politics and policy making in each country studied.

This book is a preliminary step in a broader comparative agenda. We develop here a pilot case, studying the workings of political institutions, the policy-making process, and policies in Argentina. It is our hope that this work will stimulate other researchers to join the effort, applying and extending its framework to other countries. Structured comparison of several countries along the lines suggested here is the natural next step.[4] Cross-sectional econometric analysis may have to wait for further case-based digging and theoretical development.

OVERVIEW OF THE BOOK AND OUR ARGUMENT ABOUT ARGENTINA'S POLICY MAKING

Chapter 1 lays out a sketch of the analytical framework (more formally presented in Chapter 2), summarizes the implications in terms of policy characteristics and their effects on the relevant economic outcomes, and warns against naively technocratic approaches to policy and to institutional reform.

Chapter 2 uses the theory of repeated games to argue that efficient and effective policy making requires an environment that provides for political cooperation over time. If that is not the case, political and policy actions will be characterized by short-term horizons, inflexible rules, the inability to implement efficient policy changes, and underinvestment in capacities, all leading to low-quality policies. The chapter also identifies various elements that affect the capacity to create efficient intertemporal exchanges. These elements include the number of political actors with power over a given decision, their intertemporal linkages (how long they are in office), the characteristics of the arenas where they undertake their political exchanges, and the availability of enforcement technologies, such as an independent and capable bureaucracy or an independent supreme court.

The rest of the book applies this framework to Argentina and argues that *the workings of political institutions in Argentina lead to short-sighted policy making, and this, in turn, to low-quality policies.* Part II

---

4. For some progress in that direction, see the project "Political Institutions, Policymaking Processes, and Policy Outcomes in Latin America" at the research department of the Inter-American Development Bank, *http://www.iadb.org/res/ network_study.cfm?st_id=82.*

of the book analyzes the workings of the main institutions of the policy-making process in Argentina. Chapters 3 to 6 provide details of the workings of key political institutions and arenas, while Chapter 7 describes the impact of those workings on policy making and the characteristics of policies in several policy areas.

The book shows that political practices in Argentina do not facilitate policy consensus, policy coordination, the development of consistent policies over time, or the accumulation of policy-making knowledge and expertise.

One of the most noticeable features of Argentine politics and policy making is that key political actors tend to have short political horizons. The unusual democratic instability that characterized Argentina for most of the twentieth century has contributed to the shortness of horizons, even after the return to democracy in 1983. Democratic instability has left an imprint through path-dependent behavior in Congress, the courts, the bureaucracy, the federal fiscal system, and the actions and expectations of nongovernmental actors. But, we argue in Part II, a history of democratic instability is not the only factor that contributes to short-sighted policy-making behavior. Electoral rules that transfer power away from Congress and national parties toward provincial political patrons (who are not particularly interested in building a strong national congress) also contribute to the shortening of legislators' political horizons and, in an interactive ("general equilibrium") way, affect the incentives of the rest of the polity.

In addition, weak constraints (constitutional, judicial, budgetary) on unilateral actions by the executive of the day undermine political players' ability to enter into efficient political exchanges. Weak constraints on some moves of the national government (the executive and Congress) on issues that affect the provinces have a similar impact on intergovernmental relations.

The combination of the lack of legislative incentives, the ability of the executive to act unilaterally, and the power of provincial leaders have all moved crucial political and policy bargaining away from the national legislature and into other arenas. Some key policy decisions take place in executive quarters (between the president, a key minister, advisors, and a few businesspeople), in meetings of the president with some governors, or in other closed groups. Not only are those arenas not transparent, they also lack the required institutional stickiness to enforce bargains over time.

Introduction

The shortcomings of the Argentine policy-making process can be summarized by a number of propositions about the behavior of some of the main institutional actors and the characteristics of some of the main institutional arenas:

1. Congress is not an important policy-making arena.
2. The executive tends to have substantial leeway to take unilateral policy action.
3. Provincial political powers (especially provincial governors) are very important in national policy making.
4. There is a symbiotic interaction between national and provincial policy making that operates through political and federal fiscal channels.
5. Given the incentives of the executive of the day, of legislators, and of provincial governors, there is little investment in policy-making capacities in several spheres.
6. Fiscal federalism considerations are a factor in almost every policy issue, adding transaction difficulties and rigidities to policy making.
7. The bureaucracy is not an effective corps to which to delegate the technical implementation of policy bargains.
8. The judiciary does not provide much intertemporal "glue" to political or policy agreements.
9. Nongovernmental actors in the policy process (such as business groups and unions), lacking a well-institutionalized environment for political exchange, usually follow strategies that attempt to maximize short-term benefits and to build in rigidities into future policies.

Argentina, then, has a relatively large number of political actors with the ability to block policy decisions. Many have either short horizons or wrong incentives or both. Some potentially important actors, such as legislators, justices, and key civil servants, have very short time horizons. The powerful (and potentially more long-lived) governors have only marginal incentives to work for the provision of national public goods. Because the executive has had excessive leeway to undo previous agreements, legislators and others have had little incentive to work toward those agreements in the first place. Third-party and other enforcement technologies (such as courts or bureaucratic delegation) have been missing. The interaction of the capacity for unilateral moves, history, and the lack of institutionalization of Congress (and of legislative careers) has moved the center of policy decision making away from the national legislature and into other arenas. Crucial policy decisions are negotiated in informal arenas that are not adequately structured for the institutional enforcement of bargains. (It is worth noting that none of these aspects of the policy-making process provides accountability to the citizens or improves the quality of democratic agency more generally.)

In such a scenario, interest groups such as business and unions will also tend to follow noncooperative short-term strategies, trying to maximize short-term payoffs whenever they have access to state resources. This was clear during the reform experience of the 1990s, in which many reform measures amounted to a front-loading of payoffs to many key actors, such as local business groups favored by privatization, key unions favored by reforms in the health and pension system, and pension funds that charged very high up-front commissions (see Etchemendy 2002; Murillo 1997, 2001, 2002; and Kay 2003b). Thus, not only political actors but also socioeconomic actors undertake short-sighted political strategies. Short-term maximization of political opportunities also shortens their horizons as economic actors. The short-term nature of most policy and institutional arrangements seems well understood by economic agents, who, for instance, did not contribute much to the privatized pension system (see Chapter 7). Some short-term credibility in monetary and exchange rate policy was bought through the extremely rigid (and in the end costly) convertibility system. (See Acuña, Galiani, and Tommasi 2005.)

THE USEFULNESS OF THIS CASE

Even though we selected Argentina for personal reasons, both of us having been born near the (opposite) banks of the River Plate, we believe that looking at Argentina through the new theoretical lens we suggest is useful, and it also makes an interesting case study in its own right. The country's poor and erratic social and economic performance, as well as the policy-making weaknesses of this rather developed less-developed country, are quite notable and have gained recent international attention. The institutional prism we are using is valuable for analyzing Argentina, moreover, because its constitutional structure is very similar to that of the best-studied case, the United States. In several of the later chapters, we follow a principle of minimum differentiation in order to study the interactive effects of small variations in political institutions. In doing so, we contribute not only to the study of Argentina but also to the development of better institutional theories.

To refine institutional theories, it is necessary to move away from the often implicit specificities of the U.S. case, but it is also necessary to conduct the study of other cases with the same level of empirical and theoretical depth. This book constitutes one step toward that broad comparative effort, studying one country, Argentina, in some detail.[5]

5. Books by Ames (2001) and Samuels (2003) provide an integrated view of the workings of the Brazilian political system within eclectic and nuanced institutionalist approaches. See also Ramseyer and Rosenbluth (1993) on Japan, Crisp (2000) on Venezuela, and Londregan (2000) on Chile. For a related effort, see the U.S.-Japan comparison collected by Cowhey and McCubbins (1995).

PART I

An Intertemporal Approach to Policy Making

I

Sketch of the Framework and Implications

A BRIEF SKETCH OF THE FRAMEWORK

We view public policies as the outcome of intertemporal transactions among political actors. Our dependent variable, Y ([1] in Figure 1.1), represents the features of public policies: their stability, adaptability, coordination, and other qualities. The appendix to this chapter discusses these dependent features in more detail.

We explain policies and their features as the outcome of a policy-making game ([2] in Figure 1.1), emphasizing the intertemporal nature of the transactions underlying policy choices and implementation. Formally, let $G: X \times Z \to Y$ denote the policy-making game, played under the rules of the game X over the issues with characteristics Z, in which the characteristics of policies Y are determined.

The transactions that political actors are willing and able to undertake will depend on the political characteristics of the policy issues under consideration ([3] in Figure 1.1). More specifically, we follow the literature on transaction cost politics in emphasizing some transaction characteristics of policy issues, such as the intertemporal patterns of payoffs for different actors. The vector Z summarizes those transaction characteristics. As in transaction cost economics, different political issues can be characterized by a number of properties. These properties are important in determining the ease of implementing a particular agreement. They include the number and cohesiveness of the political actors involved, the degree of irreversibility of the assets involved in the policy, the intertemporal pattern of payoffs to the actors, the duration of the policy exchanges involved, the ease with which performance can be measured, the observability of shocks, the urgency with which the policy needs to be implemented, and the degree to which the policy benefits broad or narrow interests.

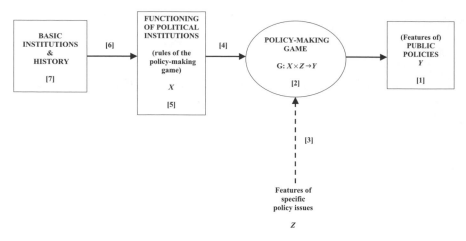

Figure 1.1. The Framework

Formulating policies that provide an immediate benefit (such as food stamps) is not the same as formulating policies that will deliver benefits far in the future (such as reforming the pension system).[1] The hazards of opportunism affecting the latter type of policies are similar to those faced by regulated industries with large sunk investments. These variations in the transaction characteristics of different policy issues will, in turn, induce variations in the resulting policy characteristics in different areas. Public policies with more complex transaction characteristics will require more institutional safeguards to make them effective over time. Without such safeguards, ad hoc governance structures may be necessary to sustain them.

The actions and strategies available to actors in the policy-making game will depend on the rules of that game, X in our theoretical notation ([4] in Figure 1.1). These rules derive from the incentives and constraints faced by policy-making actors, which in turn are derived from the workings of political institutions – that is, from the institutional environment.

---

1. Pension policy has intertemporal characteristics that make it subject to political opportunism. It forces people to part with current income in exchange for money after retirement. It is endangered by the tendency of ex post political coalitions to renege on previous policies (see Iversen and Soskice 2002) and by the political temptation to expand coverage to those who did not pay into the system throughout their careers. Pension systems have been politically and economically problematic in many countries. Those problems might be alleviated in countries where political institutions have a stronger capacity for intertemporal commitment.

In game theoretic language, abstract elements of the policy-making game will affect the types of equilibria that result and hence will affect the nature of the resulting policies. These abstract elements may include the number of players, the timing and observability of their moves, and their discount (or patience) factor. These elements need to be mapped to observable aspects of real-world political institutions. Such mapping will involve answering questions about the policy-making process, such as: Who are the powerful actors in the policy-making game? How many are there? What is the nature of their incentives? Do they have long or short horizons? Do they have access to technologies to enforce their agreements over time?

The answers to these questions will be determined by a further set of questions about the workings of a country's political institutions, such as: Are legislators policy-oriented? Is Congress an important arena of policy making? What is the nature of the party system? Are political parties centralized or fragmented? Is the executive able to "legislate" without Congress? Does the executive have discretion in the implementation of the budget? Is the bureaucracy well qualified and professional? Do key civil servants have long time horizons? Is the judiciary a good enforcer of intertemporal agreements reflected in laws, pacts, and constitutions?

The answers to all of these questions about the workings of political institutions in the country are, in our view, the interactive outcome ([5] in Figure 1.1) of a country's basic institutions, including the constitution and electoral rules, as well as of historical inheritances ([6] in Figure 1.1). By "interactive outcome" we mean a *configuration* or *constellation* of political institutions and historical inheritances that lead to the interrelated political behaviors that characterize the policy-making process.

Given that our approach places heavy demands on uncovering and understanding political-institutional detail, determining each of these data points is cumbersome to say the least. In this book, we concentrate on understanding in detail the set of Xs that characterizes one country, Argentina, and the resulting generic characterization of most policies in that country. That is, we walk the horizontal row of Figure 1.1 for Argentina.[2]

---

2. The connection to the characteristics of each policy issue is presented in a broken line in Figure 1.1 to emphasize the fact that even though cross-issue predictions are important in the general approach, they are not emphasized in the application in this book, in which we characterize the generic properties of all policies in one country and focus on explaining their politico-institutional determinants.

IMPLICATIONS FOR ECONOMIC OUTCOMES
AND FOR POLICY DESIGN

Our framework has nonstandard implications for "policy reform," one of the main concerns in the developing circles associated with the Washington-based financial institutions. Indeed, our framework implies that a given "policy" may induce different economic outcomes, depending on aspects of the country's institutions, history, and policy-making capabilities. Perhaps that is easier seen from the perspective of one policy characteristic that has received substantial attention in modern economic theory: credibility. The effects of policies on the final economic and social outcomes of interest depend on the actions and reactions of economic and social agents, who take into account their expectations about the future of the policies in question before deciding on their responses.

The effects of lack of credibility about the future of policies have been studied in a variety of economic contexts. For instance, in reference to trade reform, Rodrik (1989: 2) explains that

> it is not trade liberalization per se, but *credible* trade liberalization that is the source of efficiency benefits. The predictability of the incentives created by a trade regime, or lack thereof, is generally of much greater importance than the *structure* of these incentives. In other words, a distorted, but *stable* set of incentives does much less damage to economic performance than an uncertain and unstable set of incentives generated by a process of trade reform lacking credibility.

Several formal models of the effects of policies of uncertain duration or of imperfect credibility have been developed in monetary, fiscal, and exchange rate policy. Persson and Tabellini (1994) collect some of the classic articles; Calvo (1996: Part V) collects several important papers by Guillermo Calvo on the subject, and the Drazen (2000) textbook devotes all of Part II to the issue of commitment, credibility, and reputation.

Levy and Spiller (1994; 1996) explore related issues in the field of regulation, with an approach close to the one we develop here. They examine political complexity (that is, transaction hazards) in the regulation of public utilities, where the extent of sunk investments generates the potential for political opportunism: The government may promote investment today but change the rules of the game after the investment is made. They link institutions and regulatory processes to sector performance. Their results are consistent with our view that policy decision-making processes are fundamental determinants of private incentives and hence of economic performance. Indeed, they find that performance can be satisfactory with a wide range of regulatory procedures as long as regulatory credibility can be developed. Without that commitment, they conclude, long-term investment will not take place.[3]

Credibility is only one of a number of features of policies that influence their effect on development outcomes. In the appendix to this chapter, we discuss some of those features, which include *adaptability* (the extent to which policies can be adjusted when they fail or when circumstances change), *coherence, coordination*, and the quality of *implementation* and *enforcement*. These characteristics, in turn, are derived from the complex process by which policies are discussed, decided, implemented, evaluated, and modified. In order to understand the way in which policies influence behavior and hence aggregate outcomes, in order to understand under what conditions some "reforms" are more like to give good fruits, and in order to be more effective in suggesting ways to improve development outcomes, we need to understand the processes within which countries instrument policies. In other words, we need to understand in detail each country's policy-making processes.

Policy reforms uninformed by the nature of a country's policy-making framework, may not trigger the expected response from economic agents. Chapter 7 provides evidence from multiple policy domains of policies undertaken in Argentina over the last several years that did not induce the expected results.

STUDYING THE EFFECTS OF POLITICAL INSTITUTIONS

We have been arguing that those in the business of suggesting to improve development outcomes should pay special attention to institutions and to policy-making processes. In doing so, it is natural to start from a rich previous literature on the effects of political institutions on political outcomes and on policy outcomes.

Political economists have produced studies of the effects of political institutions on economic policy outcomes across countries. Many of these studies tend to be based on careful mathematical modeling of the effects

---

3. In terms of the mapping $X \times Z \to Y$ described earlier, Levy and Spiller hold constant the issue (regulation of telecommunications) with its vector of transaction characteristics (its Z) and vary the institutional endowments X of different countries. From our comparative transaction cost politics perspective, they take the important step of varying the institutional environments across countries while holding constant the properties of the transaction, the regulation of utilities. From there, they endogenize the governance structure of that particular transaction between "the government" and "the firm" to the features of each institutional environment.

of institutions on policy outcomes using highly stylized institutional char-acterizations. One of the best-known lines of work is well summarized in Persson and Tabellini (2003) and references therein. They have identified some empirical regularities, such as that presidential regimes seem to lead to smaller public sectors; that proportional elections lead to higher and less-targeted government spending and larger budget deficit; and that the details of the electoral system, such as district size and ballot structure, influence corruption.[4]

Other strands of institutional analysis have focused on the effects of specific variables or sets of institutional variables on specific political outcomes in a handful of countries, providing more detail and dynam-ics than what could be captured by large-scale cross-country regressions. Some noticeable efforts with emphasis on Latin American presidential democracies include Carey and Shugart (1992) on executive-legislative relations, Carey and Shugart (1998) on executive decree authority, Mainwaring and Scully (1995) on party systems, and Morgenstern and Nacif (2002) on legislative politics.

Several papers focus on aspects of political institutions and politics in specific countries, among them those by Pereira and Mueller (2004), Figueiredo and Limongi (2000), and Samuels (2000) on Brazil; Díaz-Cayeros and Magaloni (2001) on Mexico; Crisp and Ingall (2002) on Colombia; Lehoucq (1996) on Costa Rica; and several pieces on Argentina that we address more extensively later in the book. This literature draws insights from (and generalizes) the well-developed "positive political" lit-erature, which has had a distinctly U.S. flavor due both to its intellectual home in U.S. universities and its focus on U.S. institutions, especially Congress.

In this book we use the rich literature on positive political theory selec-tively, focusing on specific questions that relate to the building blocks of our overall endeavor. We use insights from the PPT literature to under-stand the determinants of some aspects of political behavior and the functioning of political institutions that we consider important to the policy-making process. For instance, later in the book we argue that key political actors in Argentina have short horizons and that intertempo-ral policy bargains are hard to enforce without adequate mechanisms.

---

4. The "regularities" identified and the theoretical and empirical analysis behind them is a subject of healthy debate. Among notable recent criticism and reevaluation, see, for instance, Acemoglu (2005) and Boix (2005).

We relate the shortness of horizons in this presidential system to the fact that in Argentina (unlike in the United States) not only are key members of the executive transient, but so are most legislators. In attempting to understand the determinants and implications of the brevity of congressional careers in Argentina, in Chapter 3 we use (and adapt to the country context) several existing works regarding political career paths, party politics, executive-legislative relations, and congressional organization. We relate the lack of adequate enforcement mechanisms, among other things, to the weakness of the Argentine Supreme Court. In Chapter 5, we draw on studies of the history of the Argentine Supreme Court as well as on strategic models of justices' voting in order to explain why the Argentine Court has not been an adequate enforcer of intertemporal agreements.

IMPLICATIONS FOR POLITICAL REFORM AND INSTITUTIONAL REFORM

One of the messages of this book is that policy-making processes are very complex, as a result of the multiplicity of actors with diverse powers, time horizons, and incentives that participate in them; the variety of arenas in which they play the game; and the diversity of rules of engagement that can have an impact on the way the game is played. Even though the theoretical and empirical (cross-country regressions) literature on the effects of political institutions on political and policy outcomes has been a helpful tool for the analysis, each country's policy-making process is the outcome of a *configuration* of political rules and practices. A focus on a few institutional characteristics (such as whether the country has a presidential or parliamentary system, whether the electoral rules are of the plurality or proportional representation variety, or whether the president has more or less legislative powers) will only provide a very fragmented and unsatisfactory understanding of these processes. To understand them fully, the institutional setup needs to be looked upon as a system.

There is a new wave in thinking about economic policy in developing countries, to which we fully subscribe, that argues against universally applicable policy recipes being pushed for all countries independently of the circumstance, time, and place where they are applied.[5] In the agenda

---

5. See, for instance, Rodrik (2006), Lindauer and Pritchett (2002), Inter-American Development Bank (2005), and Evans (2004).

reflected in this book, we push for a similar logic when thinking about institutional reform. The merits of potential changes in political and institutional rules must be considered carefully, with an understanding of how these rules fit within the broader institutional configuration. Broad generalizations about the merits of different political regimes, electoral systems, or constitutional adjudication of powers among branches are not very useful. Partial equilibrium views that stress the importance of a single institutional dimension may lead to misguided institutional and policy reforms. Understanding the overall workings of the political process and of the policy-making process in each specific country, with its specific historical trajectory, is a crucial prerequisite for developing appropriate policy reform proposals and institutional reform proposals.

Appendix

THE DEPENDENT VARIABLE: OUTER FEATURES OF PUBLIC POLICIES

Most of the political economy literature addresses the content, or "inner features," of public policies, such as whether agriculture is subsidized or taxed, which sectors get more or less protection, or who benefits or loses from income redistribution. Here, we focus on characteristics that we call the "outer features" of public policies. Some of these can, at least for analytical purposes, be discussed independently of their content. These features fit naturally with our theoretical emphasis on cooperation. They include predictability, adaptability to changing circumstances, and consistency across policy areas, among others.

Although the predominant focus of the political economy literature has been on the content of policies (see, for instance, the excellent summaries in Persson and Tabellini 2000 and in Drazen 2000), our focus on the policy-making process and government capabilities has received some attention in economics, political science, and policy analysis. We mention here a few related precedents. Weaver and Rockman (1993) enumerate ten capabilities "that all governments need": to set and maintain priorities among conflicting demands so that they are not overwhelmed and bankrupted; to target resources where they are most effective; to innovate when old policies have failed; to coordinate conflicting objectives into a coherent whole; to be able to impose losses on powerful groups;

to represent diffuse, unorganized interests in addition to concentrated, well-organized ones; to ensure effective implementation of government policies once they have been decided; to ensure policy stability so that policies have time to work; to make and maintain international commitments; and to manage political cleavages to ensure that societal relations do not degenerate into open conflict.

Rodrik (1995) analyzes the implementation of the same policy (export subsidization) in six countries and their varying degrees of success at inducing the desired economic behavior. He relates success to features such as the consistency with which the policy was implemented, which office was in charge, how or whether the policy was bundled with other policy objectives, and how predictable the future of the policy was.

The work of Tsebelis (2002) and of Cox and McCubbins (2001) also focuses on characteristics of policies and the policy-making processes that generate them. Tsebelis is concerned with policy stability, and Cox and McCubbins consider some related properties of policy-making systems, such as their decisiveness (capacity to change policy) and resoluteness (capacity to stick to a policy choice).

The following list of the outer features of policy on which we focus in this book does not include all those that may provide useful insights. We have chosen to focus on those characteristics that pertain to our empirical application to Argentina.[6]

STABILITY

In the framework of this book, we associate stability with intertemporal agreements that allow the preservation of policies beyond the tenure of particular officeholders or coalitions. Our notion of stability is similar to the notion of "resoluteness" in Cox and McCubbins (2001) and is one of the key government capabilities discussed in Weaver and Rockman (1993): "ensuring policy stability so that policies have time to work." Pritchett (2004), in discussing the growth effects of market-oriented reforms, emphasizes the importance of "policy reliability," the fact that the credibility or predictability of future policy actions is one crucial element in generating growth responses.

6. See Spiller, Stein, and Tommasi (2003) for a longer discussion and Stein and Tommasi (2005) for some empirical indicators of these policy properties for eighteen Latin American countries.

ADAPTABILITY

Policies may be more or less responsive to changes in the environment. Although policy changes that follow random political shocks are not necessarily welfare-improving, that is not true of policy changes that follow economic shocks or of technological changes that make a previous policy obsolete, very costly, or inadequate.[7]

The inability of polities to adjust to new circumstances relates to the difficulty of developing patterns of political cooperation that facilitate the implementation of welfare-improving policies. In environments with high political transaction costs, political actors may embed rigidities into policies as protection against future reversals, even if those reversals might be welfare-improving. Political players who want to protect themselves against political opportunism may create rigidities that prevent future decision makers from adjusting to changing economic circumstances or that limit their ability to adjust. A dramatic illustration was provided in 2001 in Argentina, when the rigidities of the convertibility regime combined with the rigidities of the federal fiscal agreement to lead the country into a spiral of crisis and despair while key political actors were unable to agree on adequate policy responses.

Rigidities arise not only from the structures and safeguards imposed to prevent opportunistic political manipulation but also from the inability of relevant players to reach consensus about change (see Tsebelis 2002). As we will explain in more detail later, such circumstances of nonreform can also be understood as "transaction failures." That is, the actors fail to make the compromises and compensations necessary to move policies in directions that would make every relevant political actor better off. Technological or terms-of-trade changes, for example, can make protection of some industries particularly inefficient. When polities have adequate capacities for intertemporal trade, they can stop subsidizing inefficient industries and begin compensating workers and capitalists with sector-specific assets and skills. That is a difficult task even in the most efficient of polities, but the capacity to undertake and enforce the necessary intertemporal commitments varies across institutional environments. If the losers know that they will have the political capacity to enforce compensation in the future, they are less likely to obstruct reforms. The

---

7. The changing underlying circumstances might include the stock of knowledge – for example, learning about the effects of a policy. Hence, what Weaver and Rockman (1993) call the ability "to innovate when old policies have failed" could be categorized under our notion of adaptability.

strength and stability of political parties and of their links with specific socioeconomic constituencies is one characteristic of the polity important for such compromises.[8]

COORDINATION AND COHERENCE

Policies are the result of combined actions taken by multiple actors operating at different stages of the policy process. Sometimes, the overlapping of actors is natural, given the complexity and multidimensionality of policy goals. Consider poverty alleviation. Poverty and underdevelopment are a multifaceted problem: People in poverty tend to face challenges in labor markets, education, health, nutrition, access to the legal system, and many other aspects of life. Dealing with such complex social realities requires intervention by multiple offices and at multiple levels of government.

Given the incremental nature of program creation in government bodies, moreover, their functions overlap. When new programs are added to existing policies, they do not necessarily fall under the same bureaucratic umbrella. Sabatier explains: "In any given policy domain, such as air pollution control or health policy, there are normally dozens of different programs involving multiple levels of government that are operating" (1999: 3–4). Different programs operate at interrelated levels, affecting common regions and individuals; focusing on individual programs may be the correct response for a politician seeking to further his own political interests, but it will probably generate inconsistent, ineffective, or incoherent policies. Lack of coordination among policy makers can also lead to inconsistent or incoherent policies, reflecting the noncooperative nature of their political interactions.

INVESTMENT-RELATED QUALITIES AND CAPACITIES

Many actions by political players have investment-like properties, implying up-front costs and long-term benefits. Some of these benefits are fully internalizable by political actors, while others are not. Consider one example from the legislative realm: Some legislators find learning the intricacies of the budget, environmental policy, or utilities regulation too time-consuming to bother with. Although such expertise may contribute to a more successful legislative process, it does not necessarily improve the

8. For example, Aninat et al. (2004) describe how the strength of Chilean parties and coalitions allowed a president from the center-left coalition "Concertación" to steer some reforms to trade policy that hurt entrenched constituencies of the coalition.

career prospects of the individual legislator. The time a legislator must spend learning technical issues, drafting legislation, and supervising legislative procedures is time not spent on more personally rewarding activities, such as seeking constituency support or speaking to the press. So officeholders may not spend time on substantive legislative issues unless the policy-making environment protects their political property rights (see Weingast and Marshall 1988) or rewards common-good activities (see Krehbiel 1991).

Another characteristic that is hard to handle empirically is the quality of the public policy-making arena (see Nelson and Tommasi 2001). Some countries develop arenas – whether within the government, in political parties, or in exchanges with think tanks, research institutes, universities, or non-government organizations – that provide some "intertemporal technical glue" to the policy-making process. Whether such spaces develop and whether the available scientific knowledge is incorporated into the policy-making process is highly idiosyncratic to each country. History plays a role here, as does the "industrial organization" of research in the country. But fundamentally, the constitution of such spaces depends also on the incentives of the key political actors. These incentives, in turn, are affected by the institutional features of the country in question.

Our knowledge of Argentina indicates that such policy-making spaces function very poorly there. Superficial observations from our own globetrotting suggest that they may operate more effectively in other developing countries. In Chile, political parties and coalitions draw on the technical expertise of ideologically aligned think tanks in a much more consistent and structured manner than in Argentina. Also, Chilean legislators seem to bring technical expertise to their debates more consistently than do Argentine legislators (see Aninat et al. 2004 and Montecinos 2003). Similarly, in Colombia, there is greater capacity in important technical offices, such as the Central Bank (Banco de la Republica) and the National Planning Commission (see Juárez 1995 and Urrutia 1991). Brazil is also reputed to have the capacity to sustain some bases of institutional learning and intertemporal consistency in areas such as its Foreign Office (Itamaraty) and National Development Bank (BNDES) (see Lafer 2002). And the internal organization of some dominant political parties, such as the Liberal Democratic Party in Japan and the Institutional Revolutionary Party in Mexico, has led to the buildup of some technical capabilities over time.[9]

9. See Baron (1996), Grindle (1996), and Rosenbluth and Thies (2000) on Japan. See Lehoucq et al. (2004) and Cornelius (2000) on Mexico. Mexico did not build its

IMPLEMENTATION AND ENFORCEMENT

Argentina is notorious for its poor enforcement of public policies, such as those governing taxation and labor standards. Poor policy implementation may be related to inadequate state capabilities caused by a lack of investment incentives, as the previous point suggests. But it may also be due to the fact that some policy-making actors who cannot prevail legislatively can still subvert implementation. These problems also reflect transaction inefficiencies of the policy-making process: the enacting legislative actors *should* be able to contemplate and compensate for the interests of other actors, and even of later actors, in such a way as to prevent subsequent obstructions to their legislation's enforcement.

policy-making capacities across the board but focused on specific policy areas of interest to the dominant coalition. Something similar happened in Venezuela during a bipartisan power-sharing agreement known as the Punto Fijo Accord, in which important policy-making capabilities were developed in crucial areas, such as by the company running the nationalized oil industry, Petróleos de Venezuela (see Monaldi et al. 2004).

2

A Theory of Intertemporal Political Cooperation

This chapter uses the theory of repeated games to study the determinants of policy-making behavior. It provides a game-theoretical connection between elements of the policy-making game and the nature and characteristics of resulting policies. The abstract elements identified in the theory are mapped to observable aspects of political behavior ([4] in Figure 1.1). After identifying basic characteristics of political transactions, developing our basic model, and discussing its implications, we present some extensions that allow for richer characteristics of the underlying policy issues as well as for richer characterizations of the rules of the political game. At the end of the chapter, we discuss the potential empirical application of the framework for different policy issues and in different political environments.

CHARACTERISTICS OF POLITICAL TRANSACTIONS

A number of fundamental features, several of which are amenable to analysis from a transaction cost perspective, characterize the political transactions surrounding public policies. In this chapter, we provide a model that captures six of those features. They are as follows:

1. *Intertemporal political exchanges.* Politics and policy making take place over time. Decisions are made at different points in time, often by different configurations of actors, and decisions made at any point in time have future consequences.[1]

---

1. This argument is related to the emphasis that the new institutional economics brings to the economic domain: "Institutional economics is to a large degree concerned with deferred exchanges or exchanges that provide for a definite order of performance

2. *The shifting bargaining power of political actors.* Political popularity, coalition formation, and the normal workings of democracy lead to substantial randomness in the power of any political actor over time.[2]

3. *Elements of conflict and of commonality of interests.* Almost any decision made in the public arena has some aspects of a "public good," broadly defined. Indeed, the most extensively articulated explanatory theories of the state are based on the demand for public goods and on the state's capacity to deliver them (Hardin 1997). Also, almost all public policies have a distributional component. Even military defense, which is the quintessential public good, has important distributional (say, regional) components. Similarly, macroeconomic stabilization, another quintessential public good, has distributional components in its implementation: Raising taxes or reducing expenditures has major distributional connotations, which are the source of much conflict (Alesina and Drazen 1991; Drazen 2000).

4. *Changing realities.* Random events require continuous policy adaptations. New circumstances in international markets, policy decisions in other countries, technological changes, diseases, natural disasters, and social and demographic changes are events that present new demands on public policy.

5. *Contractual moments.* Most policies could be characterized by two different decision frequencies or moments: moments of major institutional definitions, which we will call "contractual moments," and regular policy making under those institutions or rules. Consider monetary policy. Fundamental institutions, such as an independent central bank with a given governance and a given mandate, and policy rules, such as an exchange rate regime, are established at specific moments in time. Specific values for policy instruments, such as the

and thus involve the passage of time for their completion" (Furubotn and Richter 1998: 128).

2. This is also true in nondemocratic polities, albeit in different forms. Dixit, Grossman, and Gul put it this way: "In any political system, authority to divide the political and economic spoils rests with the individual or individuals who are 'in power.' This power may derive from electoral success, as in democracy, or from military success, as in many autocracies. In any event, the prevailing rulers can grab everything that is up for grabs: they can decide all ideological issues to their own liking and distribute all economic surplus to themselves and their supporters. Of course, political fortunes may change over time: today's opposition may become tomorrow's rulers. Then the new rulers could use their power to their own advantage, fully undoing the decisions and allocations of the past" (2000: 531).

interest rate or the nominal exchange rate, are then chosen under the given institutional structure or rule.

6. *Incomplete political contracts.* Many of the changing realities described in item 4 are such that it would be impossible for political agreements or policy agreements to cover every feasible future circumstance. Thus, political contracts are necessarily incomplete.

The model we present in the next section captures each of these important characteristics in a stylized manner.

A BASIC MODEL OF POLICY MAKING

We model policy as the outcome of a noncooperative game among political actors bounded by contracting moments. Our basic model is a simple variation of models used before in the literature, such as those by Alesina (1988), Dixit, Grossman, and Gul (2000), Dixit (2003), and de Figueiredo (2002). In terms of the framework presented in the introduction, the model and its solution could be thought of as a mapping $G : X \times Z \to Y$ of rules of the political game X and characteristics of policy issues Z onto characteristics of the resulting policies Y.

Some Modeling Assumptions

We capture in our model, albeit in a very stylized fashion, the six key features of political transactions. The notion of intertemporal exchange is captured by modeling the policy process as a *repeated game*, a class of games in which players face the same *stage game* repeatedly over time. Repeated games are a natural way to model ongoing relationships, and they provide the simplest way of studying self-enforcing arrangements formally (Morrow 1994; Pearce 1992). We capture the fact that political bargaining power changes over time by allowing the location (or role) of each player in the stage game to change, stochastically, over time. The payoff function of players captures the conflict as well as the commonality of interests in public policies. Contracting moments are captured as stage zero, before the repeated game starts, in which players can enter into agreements that bind their later behavior.[3] The incompleteness of political

---

3. In extensions to the basic model, available upon request, we allow for more frequent "recontracting." Such an extension permits, for instance, capturing instances in which periods of high policy volatility are followed by the imposition of rigid rules to avoid that volatility.

contracting is captured by restricting the set of agreements that are feasible and enforceable.

A Game of Political Transactions

The Setup. Imagine a number of political actors[4]: political parties, provinces in a federal country, organized groups, and others. These political actors, the players, have to make collective decisions (under certain rules to be specified) and may also take individual actions.[5] For the sake of concreteness, we focus here on an example with two political players ($i = A, B$) who have to choose a policy y_t at each point in time. Each player attempts to maximize the following utility function:

$$V = - \left[\sum_{t=0}^{\infty} \delta^t E[L_i(y_t, \theta_t)] \right], \qquad (1)$$

where $\delta \in [0, 1]$ is a discount factor measuring patience and $L_i(\ )$ is a loss function that depends on the collectively chosen policy y and the economic shock θ.[6] E stands for the expectation operator, where the expected value is taken over the distribution of the possible realizations of the shock θ.

The shock θ, which is identically and independently distributed over time, with $E(\theta) = 0$, is a common observable but nonverifiable economic shock, which might come from international markets, policy decisions in other countries, technological changes, diseases, natural disasters, or social and demographic changes.[7] It shifts the preferred policies of all players in the same direction, capturing a common interest that players have in policies that adequately respond to shocks.

The subscript i in the loss function denotes the fact that the players evaluate policies differently. For simplicity, let

$$L_i(y_t, \theta_t) = [y_t - (y_i + \theta_t)]^2. \qquad (2)$$

---

4. Readers who prefer to avoid mathematical expressions should skip most of this section and just focus on the results and propositions.

5. A simple example is a confederation in which certain policies are decided collectively while other policies are chosen individually by each constituent unit. More generally, parties to a collective decision also make individual decisions, such as how much to invest in order to build capacities for future policy decision making.

6. Note that in this context, maximizing utility means minimizing the term in brackets, the loss function.

7. The assumption of nonverifiability is a stylized manner of capturing the fact that it is very unlikely that an external party could enforce contracts on future policies.

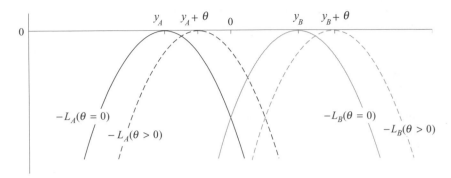

Figure 2.1. Preferences

This means that each player suffers an increasing loss as the policy of the period deviates further from his preferred policy, which in each period is $y_i + \theta_t$. The policy y_i would be the preferred policy of player i when the shock θ has an average value of zero. To account for the fact that different actors prefer different policies, $y_A \neq y_B$ captures the elements of conflict in the policy game. The fact that everyone's preferred policy responds in the same direction to θ captures the common (valence) interest in economic efficiency. As an example of these reduced-form policy preferences, imagine a policy that taxes citizens and uses the money to provide a public good. Richer players will want lower taxes, while poorer players will want higher ones, but everybody's desire for public goods would shift as the price of goods fluctuated.[8] For computational simplicity, we further assume that $y_B = -y_A > 0$; that is, the preferred policy of each of the two players is the mirror image around θ of the preferred policy of the other player. Figure 2.1 illustrates these policy preferences.

In each period, after the realization of θ_t, the policy y_t is decided. The political decision-making process (the collective choice mechanism) constitutes a key aspect of the description of our policy-making environment. In the basic model presented here, we use an extremely simplified decision-making procedure that nevertheless allows us to focus on the intertemporal dimension of policy making and politics (the position of players in this decision-making process changes over time). We capture this last point by introducing a random political shock that shifts the relative political power of each player at each point in time. For simplicity,

8. See Cukierman and Tommasi (1998a; 1998b) and Persson and Tabellini (2000) for other examples that could deliver this type of reduced-form policy preference.

assume that a coin is flipped and that each player gets to be the one-period dictator with probability $^1/_2$. That is:

$$\mu_t = i = A, \ B \text{ with probability } {}^1/_2, \tag{3}$$

and $\mu_t = i$ implies that player i decides y_t in period t. In the extensions later in this chapter, we generalize the probability of party A winning to p between 0 and 1. In that case, $1 - p$ is the probability of B winning.

This model is a simplified version of richer collective decision-making mechanisms, such as those used by Alesina (1988), Baron and Ferejohn (1989), and Dixit, Grossman, and Gul (2000). For Alesina, the probability p of each party winning the election is endogenous to the platforms announced by each party. Dixit et al. have p exogenous, but rather than being constant over time, it varies according to a stochastic Markov process with persistence to capture the usual persistence of political power. (On average, whoever is in power today is also more likely to be in power tomorrow.) In Baron and Ferejohn and in a subsequent work inspired by that paper (Persson and Tabellini 2000), the intraperiod collective decision-making procedure is richer, with an agenda setter chosen at random and the majority voting to accept changes to the status quo. Our model can be seen as an extremely simplified version of the "random recognition rule" of Baron and Ferejohn, in which the agenda setter has full power to decide policy. Alternatively, we could characterize our collective choice mechanism as a stochastic dictatorship. This oversimplification allows us to put all the emphasis on the intertemporal aspects of political negotiation and policy implementation.[9]

We assume, additionally, that there is an initial period (zero) in which, by unanimity, players can make some agreements. This period is the contracting moment, when the parties reach an understanding about how they will restrict their actions in the future. (In the extensions, we allow for more frequent contracting moments.) The set of feasible contracts constitutes an exogenous feature of the institutional environment, which will affect the types of policies that emerge in equilibrium. The set of feasible contracts will also depend on the nature of the issues in question and on the observability and verifiability of the various actions and payoffs.

---

9. This basic specification of the model, if taken literally, could, for example, represent a case in which the fundamentals (for example, electoral rules or underlying social cleavages) are such that there is always a unified government and a stable party system dominated by two major parties that alternate in power. For a modeling strategy very close to the one we follow here and for a useful discussion of the related literature, see de Figueiredo (2002).

First-Best Utilitarian Benchmark

We start by defining a first-best utilitarian benchmark as

$$\text{Min} \sum_{t=0}^{\infty} \delta^t E[L_A(y_t, \theta_t) + L_B(y_t, \theta_t)]^2. \tag{4}$$

Given our assumptions, (4) simplifies to

$$\text{Min} \sum_{t=0}^{\infty} \delta^t E(y_t - \theta_t)^2. \tag{5}$$

It is easy to see that expression (5) is minimized by choosing policy $y_t = y^*(\theta_t) = \theta_t$ for all t. This result characterizes the first-best policy as a function of the realization of economic shocks but is independent from the realization of political shocks.

Result 1: The first-best policy is a function of the realization of economic shocks but is independent of the realization of political shocks.

The utility value for each player of this first-best solution is[10]

$$V^* = -y_B^2(1 + \delta + \delta^2 + \cdots) = \frac{-y_B^2}{1 - \delta}. \tag{6}$$

The Noncooperative Game

We now analyze the solution to the noncooperative game. If instead of being repeated the game were played only once, there would be only one solution. In that unique one-shot Nash equilibrium, the player who gets to decide policy implements his or her most desired policy, ignoring the interests of others. This means $y = y_\mu + \theta$, where the subscript μ will stand for A or B, depending on who happens to be in power.

Turning to the repeated game, the infinite repetition of the one-shot Nash (with $y_t = y_{\mu_t} + \theta_t$) is an equilibrium.[11] If A knows that the strategy of B is always to choose his preferred policy $y_t = y_B + \theta_t$, A's best response is to do likewise and always choose $y_t = y_A + \theta_t$.

Result 2: In the noncooperative equilibrium, unlike in the first-best outcome, the policy chosen in each period depends on the realization of the political shock.

10. That is because with $y_t = \theta_t$, each player will always be at a distance y_B from his or her (ex post) preferred policy $y_i + \theta_t$. Recall also that the sequence $(1 + \delta + \delta^2 + \delta^3 + \cdots)$ is equal to $1/(1 - \delta)$ for δ between 0 and 1.
11. In any repeated game, an infinite repetition of the actions leading to an equilibrium in the stage game also constitutes an equilibrium of the repeated game.

We define as V^N the present value of expected utility for each player from the infinite repetition of the one-shot Nash equilibrium. In such an equilibrium, each party has a chance of one half of choosing policy. If I am the party in power, I minimize my short-term loss function, setting it equal to zero. If the other party is in power, he or she does likewise, which implies that the chosen policy is $2y_B$ away from my favorite. After that, we continue playing the Nash equilibrium, which delivers a *continuation value* of V^N from there on. Thus, we have

$$V^N = -\frac{1}{2}[0 + (2y_B)^2] + \delta V^N = \frac{-2y_B^2}{1 - \delta}. \qquad (7)$$

(The second equality is obtained by manipulating V^N out of the first one.)

Although the infinite repetition of the one-shot Nash is always an equilibrium, players may be able to do better than that in the repeated game. Players could use "the shadow of the future" to enforce more cooperative behavior in the stage game. Technically, repeated games have multiple equilibria; that is, many strategy pairs could constitute equilibria.[12] For brevity, in our exposition we will concentrate on the *cooperative equilibrium* (one that is symmetric and achieves a maximum level of cooperation) sustained by threats of future punishment known as trigger strategies. Hence, our claims with respect to the likelihood of achieving political cooperation will refer to the likelihood of this particular equilibrium. Most of those claims will be valid more generally as comparisons among sets of equilibria.

To simplify the analysis, we focus, then, on the possibility of the most cooperative behavior supported by the punishment strategy of permanent reversion to noncooperation. This is the following trigger strategy for both players $i = A, B$:

$$y_1^i = y^*(\theta_1) = \theta_1 \qquad (8)$$

and

$$y_t^i = \begin{cases} y_t^* = \theta_t & \text{if } y_\tau = \theta_\tau \forall \tau < t \\ y_i + \theta_t & \text{otherwise} \end{cases}. \qquad (9)$$

12. Indeed, there is a result known as the folk theorem, which states that any individually rational and feasible payoff vector could be attained in an equilibrium to the repeated game.

This trigger strategy consists of cooperating (by choosing the first-best policy) as long as the other player also cooperates. The payoff along the equilibrium path of cooperation is

$$V^* = \frac{-y_B^2}{1 - \delta} \tag{10}$$

for both players, which coincides with the value of the loss function in the first-best outcome. In order to verify whether this strategy pair constitutes an equilibrium, we have to consider the value of an opportunistic deviation to $y_{\mu_t} + \theta_t$. Such a deviation would move the game to noncooperation forever, leading the deviant party to the value

$$V^D = 0 + \delta V^N = -\frac{\delta}{1 - \delta} 2y_B^2. \tag{11}$$

Comparing the utility functions V^* and V^D, we can conclude that cooperation can be sustained if and only if $\delta \geq \frac{1}{2}$. The first-best outcome can be attained, through cooperation, for a value of δ that is large enough – that is, when players attach sufficient importance to payoffs in the future.

Result 3: The first-best outcome can be attained through intertemporal cooperation when players have long horizons – that is, when players are patient enough.

More generally, the possibility of sustaining cooperation will depend on several factors, including the number of players as well as the parameters that characterize the details of a richer decision-making procedure than the one we assumed in (3).

The most straightforward extension consists of letting the probability of each party being in power differ from $\frac{1}{2}$. Let p be the probability that A is in power in any given period, with $1 - p$ being the probability of B being in power. It is easy to show that the possibility of sustaining intertemporal cooperation is maximized for $p = \frac{1}{2}$ and that it declines monotonically as p moves away from $\frac{1}{2}$. Formally, as p approaches $\frac{1}{2}$, cooperation can be sustained over a wider range of other parameters (for instance, δ).[13] Figure 2.2 illustrates the range of combinations of p and δ for which cooperative policy making can be obtained. As one party becomes more likely to be in power almost all the time (as p goes to 1 or to 0), this party's incentives to cooperate decline, since the future benefits of cooperation will be reaped only in the rare moments that the other party is in power. In such cases, the player has to place a very heavy weight on the future (δ much higher than $\frac{1}{2}$) in order to be willing to cooperate.

13. See, for instance, Alesina (1988) and de Figueiredo (2002).

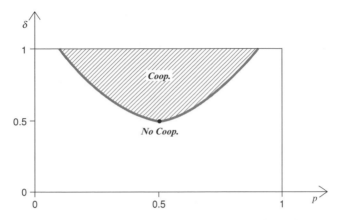

Figure 2.2. Range of parameters for cooperative policy making

Another natural extension consists of having more than two players. In the simplest extension, we can have N players, with each one having a probability $1/N$ of being in power at each point. It can be shown that, in general, the probability of cooperation decreases as the number of players grows.

Richer results in terms of the determinants of cooperation could be obtained by enriching the intraperiod decision-making process away from the extremely simplified stochastic dictator we have used. We return to such extensions later in the chapter. Having analyzed the equilibria of the repeated game, we turn now to stage zero of the game.

The Contracting Moment

The contracting moment is an agreement among the parties that will affect their ability to make decisions at the implementation stage. For a complete description of the game, we need some further specification of the decision-making process at the initial stage. Imagine, for instance, that decisions are unanimous, with a given procedure or bargaining protocol for arriving at consensus. For simplicity, we will assume that the parties bargain efficiently at the initial stage. From now on, we assume that $p = {}^1/_2$, and as a consequence, the Nash bargaining solution implies that the players evenly distribute the gains from the initial stage.

If the parties could specify all possible future states of the world, they could also, at the contracting moment, agree on a policy response for each case; and if they could enforce the agreed-upon policy responses, they would then contract on first-best policies. These conditions, however,

35

violate the basic assumption that contracts are necessarily incomplete, which is at the core of transaction cost analysis.

More realistically, then, the features of the resulting policies will depend on the set of feasible contracts. Suppose, for instance, that agreements can be enforced only with verifiable information and that the realization of economic shocks is not verifiable. In that case, it will not be possible to enforce contracts that are contingent upon the economic state. On the other hand, simple rules that limit the ability of each party to implement its most desired policy can be agreed upon. It is easy to show that, in our simple example, the best such rule is to set a constant $y_t = 0$ for all t – that is, a policy in between the ex ante most desired policies of each player. This will deliver an expected utility of

$$V^0 = - \sum_{t=0}^{\infty} \delta^t E(y_B + \theta_t)^2 = - \frac{y_B^2 + \mathrm{Var}(\theta)}{1 - \delta}. \tag{12}$$

A comparison of (12) and (10) shows that $V^0 < V^*$. Since the rigid policy cannot adapt to economic shocks, its outcome is inferior to the first-best policy for both players. That is, a cooperative equilibrium is preferable to the best available rigid rule. Thus, whenever the repeated game delivers cooperation, a rigid rule will not be utilized. As expected, then, when players are sufficiently patient, they will prefer adapting to economic shocks over setting a rigid ex ante rule.

Result 4: When the repeated game leads to cooperation, the players will not restrict themselves to rigid rules and will instead allow the collective decision-making process to respond to economic shocks that require policy adjustment.

Result 4 has a direct relation to the idea of relational contracts. If the polity works well, then political agreements will have a relational flavor. Parties will be able to informally adapt to shocks without undertaking major political renegotiations. In such cases, political actors will not need to tie each other's hands in order to prevent political opportunism. Polities that work well do not impose a large number of constraints on policy making.[14]

---

14. The discussion in the text is based on a comparison of the two extreme equilibria: maximum cooperation and no cooperation at all. More generally, there may be instances in which full (first-best) cooperation cannot be sustained, but there is enough cooperation to sustain procedural requirements in decision making, delegated discretion, or other mechanisms that would generate outcomes that both players would prefer to rigid rules or unconstrained discretion.

Rigid rules may be useful when the unconstrained game has noncooperation as its outcome. Comparing the rigid rule to the noncooperative case, we find that $V^N < V^0$ if and only if $(y_B)^2 > \text{Var}(\theta)$. Noting that y_B is a measure of the intensity of the conflict of interest and that $\text{Var}(\theta)$ is a measure of the volatility of the economic environment, we conclude that when the parties have a limited capacity to self-enforce cooperative agreements (that is, when δ is low), rigid policy rules will be chosen if the conflicts of interest are large compared with the volatility of the economic environment.

Thus, we find that when the polity has a low capacity to enforce intertemporal political exchanges, policies will be either too volatile (responding both to politics and to the economic environment) or too rigid (set ex ante and not responsive to the economic environment). The choice between rigid rules and discretionary policies pits the relative cost of partisan policy making (related to the heterogeneity of preferences) against not being able to adjust to economic shocks (related to the variance of the economic shocks). Therefore, when enforcement of intertemporal political exchanges is relatively weak, political agreements may be highly volatile or policies highly inflexible.[15]

SUMMARY OF RESULTS FROM THE BASIC MODEL

This simple exercise already contains results that are relevant to the study of the impact of political institutions on the properties of policy outcomes. On the one hand, when self-enforcement of political agreements is feasible, policies will be flexible enough to accommodate changing economic and social realities, but they will not be subject to political opportunism. On the other hand, when the environment does not foster cooperation, there will be excess policy volatility in response to political shocks as well as some policy rigidities built in as protection from political opportunism. Figure 2.3 summarizes these basic results, with $\hat{\delta}$ representing a threshold value of the discount factor above which first-best policies $y^*(\theta)$ can be attained. Below $\hat{\delta}$, first-best policies cannot be attained in equilibrium, so policies will be too responsive to political opportunism (captured by their dependence on μ) or they will have embedded rigidities ($\bar{y}$) depending on whether or not $(y_B)^2 > \text{Var}(\theta)$.

---

15. In an extension of the model in which recontracting is allowed, we obtain the more realistic prediction that some policies will shift back and forth from a volatility regime to a rigid rule depending on the evolution of economic shocks.

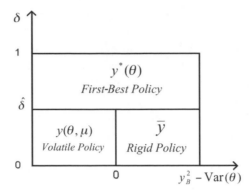

Figure 2.3. Summary of results from the basic model

To summarize:

1. First-best policies are a function of *economic* but not *political* shocks.
2. First-best policies can be attained when players are sufficiently far-sighted.

In the following extensions, we emphasize determinants of intertemporal cooperation other than the discount factor. We use the expression "good transaction environments" to refer to a combination of elements of the game that make cooperation more likely and the expression "bad transaction environments" to refer to the opposite.

3. In bad transaction environments, policies may depend on the realization of political shocks.
4. In bad transaction environments, policy makers may impose rigid rules to prevent opportunism by other parties.
5. As a result, in bad transaction environments, some policies may be too volatile while others are too rigid.

This is a good point at which to compare some of the results of our model (summarized by Figure 2.3) with some of the previous literature in economics and in political science. An important body of work in economics, under the heading "rules versus discretion," suggests that under some conditions imposing policy rules is a way of avoiding some biases arising from policy discretion.[16] This idea originated in monetary policy applications and has been extended to the advocacy of fiscal policy

16. See, for instance, good textbook treatments by Drazen (2000) and Persson and Tabellini (2000).

rules.[17] In terms of Figure 2.3, proponents of rules call for moving due east in the bottom panel of the diagram. But the academic literature has also noted that repeated play could substitute for rules that necessarily imply some rigidity – we want to add the caveat that, whenever feasible, the focus should be put first on the broader determinants of cooperation (that is, on governance), which might allow movement upward rather than sideways in Figure 2.3.[18]

Figure 2.3 also allows us to compare our predictions with those of the veto players literature. That approach emphasizes a trade-off between decisiveness and resoluteness (Cox and McCubbins 2001: 28). A north-south comparison in Figure 2.3 allows us to predict that some polities may be neither too decisive nor too resolute. The answer to whether a given political system will be able to implement policy changes when necessary and to whether it will be able to stick to prior policy decisions in the face of political rotation lies in whether political institutions foster cooperation in policy making.

EXTENSIONS

Let us recapitulate the results so far in terms of our broader theoretical framework ($X \times Z \to Y$). The model has mapped a description of the rules of the political game and a given set of characteristics of the underlying policy issues into characteristics of the resulting policies. A policy (Y) could be adaptable/flexible, as in $y^*(\theta)$ in Figure 2.3; it could be volatile due to political opportunism, as in $y(\theta, \mu)$; or it could be rigid, as in $\bar{y}$.

The rules of the political game (X) assumed so far include a particular intraperiod decision-making process in which one party chooses policy unilaterally in that period, a particular stochastic process (μ_t) for the selection of that "temporary dictator," the specific probability ($p, 1 - p$) that each party has of being selected, and the number of players (in this case $N = 2$). Other assumptions in the model might be features (Z) of the policy issue under consideration: the fact that it is a one-time policy chosen anew every period, for example, or the properties of the economic shock θ_t (including its variance). Some elements of the game could be features of the policy issue in question, characteristics of the political environment,

17. Kopits (2001) provides a summary of fiscal rules.
18. Another reason to focus on the vertical rather than the horizontal axis is that under some circumstances some form of cooperation is necessary even to sustain the implementation of some rules. Braun and Tommasi (2004) provide a critical discussion of fiscal policy rules.

or both. The number of players is usually affected by the characteristics of the institutional environment, while specific policy issues bring particular political actors to the table. Similarly, the information structure of the game (observability or verifiability of shocks) could include the different properties of different policy issues or could relate to capacities of broader institutional actors, such as the bureaucracy or the judiciary, and their potential to act as third-party enforcers of agreements among policy makers.

The modeling assumptions employed so far constitute, of course, an abstraction. We can obtain further insights by relaxing or modifying them. We have selected some extensions that apply to Argentina and that are developed in the rest of the book. We group the extensions into two categories: those that modify the properties of the policy issues or resulting policy features and those that modify the rules of the political game.

Extensions I: Richer Policy Implications

The policy issue of the basic model is a fairly simple one: It is a one-shot policy that is chosen anew, in a collective manner, in each period. We consider two natural extensions: intertemporal policy linkages and individual policy actions.

Intertemporal Policy Linkages. Most policies are not one-shot decisions that are independent of past and future policy decisions and have only contemporary effects. Policies are linked intertemporally for physical reasons (a bridge built today provides service in the future), legal reasons (a law is in place until it is changed), or economic reasons (present fiscal actions have future effects through intertemporal budget constraints). Policies chosen today have an impact on future payoffs, as do investment decisions in the economic realm.[19]

Investment-like reasoning allows us to derive further implications from the characteristics of the transactions environment for the quality of the resulting policies. From transaction cost economics, we know that in poor transaction environments there will be less investment than in better ones. Another possible result from adding intertemporal linkages relates to the sequence of transitional payoffs during a policy reform process.

---

19. In the policy application, investments are actions that raise future policy productivity, such as provincial governments investing in improving tax-raising capacities and legislators investing in acquiring policy expertise.

Some welfare-enhancing policy reforms are not feasible in equilibrium because of time consistency problems. Veto players who benefit from some aspects of reform but are hurt by others may block a reform process at a point when the remaining moves are not beneficial to them; by backward induction, other veto players who would have benefited from the later moves may block the adoption of reform from the beginning. In such circumstances, there would be a no-reform outcome. That result is already known in the literature of the political economy of reform.[20] We are adding the recognition that the likelihood of that result depends on the quality of the transaction environment. If players have instruments with which to enforce intertemporal cooperation, they may be able to implement reforms that imply noncontemporaneous costs and benefits to the various actors. In other words, *the feasibility of welfare-enhancing policy reforms depends on the properties of the environment for political transactions.*

Individual Policy Actions. Another (technically trivial) extension introduces individual policy actions. In bad transaction environments, individual policy actions will be less cooperative and will lead to poorly coordinated policies. This is a basic result of intratemporal cooperation in repeated games in economics. Very low discount factors, for example, lead to noncooperative actions in games that involve simultaneous moves.

Summary. The results so far can be summarized in a proposition relating the properties of resulting policies to the characteristics of the transactions environment. The proposition summarizes links [1], [2], and [3] in Figure 1.1.[21]

> **Proposition 1.** In bad transaction environments (those that make noncooperative policy making more likely), policies will be
>
> - Too volatile (they will change too often in response to political winds)
> - Too rigid (often incapable of adjusting in the face of changed circumstances, such as economic shocks)
> - Poorly coordinated or incoherent

20. See for instance Drazen (2000: Chapter 13), Sturzenegger and Tommasi (1998), and Martinelli and Tommasi (1997).
21. The way in which we group and present the results here is geared toward their application to Argentina. For example, we do not exploit cross-issue (cross-Z) variation as much as the framework allows, and we just emphasize the generic implications of having better or worse political transaction environments.

Polities afflicted by bad transaction environments will also

- Invest insufficiently in capacities and thereby produce low-quality policies
- Be unable to undertake some welfare-enhancing reforms

Proposition 1, then, summarizes some direct implications for the relationship between the extent of political cooperation and the features of the resulting public policies. In the next section, we turn to the effects of different political institutions (different rules of the policy-making game) on the extent of cooperation in policy making.

Extensions II: The Rules of the Political Game

We have argued that several features of public policies depend on the cooperativeness of political interactions. Here, we move in the direction of identifying what aspects of political institutions are conducive to political cooperation. Later in the chapter, we suggest how to relate this abstract listing to actual political variables, and in the rest of the book we build that relation for the case of Argentina. These steps are equivalent to link [4] in Figure 1.1. Next, we list factors that affect the degree of cooperation in equilibrium outcomes, drawing insights from the analysis of repeated oligopoly games.[22]

Intraperiod Payoff Structure. The elasticity of per period payoff to alternative spot actions is an important determinant of whether cooperation is sustainable in equilibrium or not. In repeated games, if the spot payoff from noncooperation is very high, cooperation is less likely. In repeated oligopoly games, this is the case with elasticity to price discounts: If a firm stands to gain very large short-term profits by lowering its price (for example, because there are a large number of competitors from which to attract customers), collusive oligopoly is harder to sustain. In the context of the Argentine federal fiscal system, a province's individual payoff for deviating from a cooperative agreement (for example, by attempting

---

22. See, for example, Green and Porter (1984), Rotemberg and Saloner (1986), Fudenberg and Tirole (1991: Chapter 5), and Mas-Colell, Whinston, and Green (1995: Chapter 12). The listing of the determinants of cooperation does not pretend to be exhaustive but is geared toward the factors identified as relevant in our analysis of the Argentine case. Dixit provides a similar listing (1996: 71).

to get special benefits from the national government) is quite high, and hence the federal fiscal game has noncooperation as its equilibrium outcome.[23]

Number of Political Players. The theory predicts that the larger the number of players is, the smaller will be the set of other parameters for which cooperation obtains. Fudenberg and Tirole (1991: Section 5.1.2) and Fudenberg and Maskin (1986) show that when the set of feasible payoffs is held constant, increasing the number of players reduces the set of equilibria toward less-cooperative ones. This result is in line with traditional assumptions (such as those in Buchanan and Tullock 1962) that the costs of making a decision increase with the number of players. It also relates to the previous point, in that in many common pool situations the intraperiod payoff structure is related to the number of players.

It is important to note that in the empirical implementation our notion of the number of players is different from the number of veto players in Tsebelis (2002). In Tsebelis, the number of veto players relates (roughly) to the number of actors holding institutional veto positions at a particular point in time; in contrast, we refer to the number of "permanent" players, even if they do not happen to be holding specific veto positions at a particular point in time.[24]

Intertemporal Linkages among Key Political Actors. The intertemporal pattern of interactions among specific individuals in formal political positions (such as legislators, governors, and bureaucrats) matters for developing cooperative outcomes. It is not the same to have a legislature in which the same individuals interact over extended periods of time as it is to have a legislature where individuals are drawn at random from given populations (such as parties or provinces) and replaced frequently.

---

23. The relation between actions and payoff in the stage game may represent alternative policy areas (Zs) or alternative policy choices in previous moments (Y_{t-1}, introducing path dependence, as we exemplify in Chapter 4) or alternative intraperiod decision-making rules (X), the focus of this section.

24. In a country with a stable party system dominated by two major parties that alternate in power, for instance, even if one party is out of power at a particular point in time, it is still a player in the intertemporal game. In such a case, we would concur with Tsebelis and with Cox and McCubbins in characterizing such system as *decisive*; whether we concur with them in calling that system *nonresolute* will depend on whether intertemporal cooperation prevents opportunistic short-term policy manipulation.

Cooperation is less likely in the latter case. Historical events such as civil wars, military regimes, or civil unrest may also affect the potential for political cooperation, as will the history of the franchise and the interactions it induces between citizens and their elected representatives. In countries where large groups of citizens do not have a long tradition of democratic participation, clientelistic practices may induce more short-term behavior by both voters and politicians.[25]

Timing and Observability of Moves. Cooperation is harder to sustain if unilateral moves are hard to observe or verify.[26] The ability of political actors to make unobserved unilateral moves depends on the institutional environment. Environments with transparent budget processes limit the government's use of the budget to subvert prior agreements. In the United States, for example, the budget process substantially limits the ability of the executive to transfer budgets from one department to another, or even to move funds within a department. As a consequence, the ability of the executive to undermine previously agreed-upon expenditure patterns in order to obtain new support from other groups is limited. This limit on unilateral actions facilitates intertemporal agreements. In other environments, as we discuss later for Argentina, the budget process grants the executive too much leeway in how it may spend monies appropriated to that branch. As a consequence, the executive will not use this part of the budget to support intertemporal agreements. Instead, this part of the budget will be used to obtain instantaneous support for its preferred policies.[27]

Delegation. Repeated play encourages self-enforcement of agreements, but certain forms of cooperation can be achieved by alternative institutional means. One alternative is to fix policy rules of the type analyzed earlier to prevent future opportunistic behavior. Delegating policy to an independent technical agency is another alternative. It is easy to show that, in the simple model presented earlier, delegating policy forever to an individual with preferences between those of the two parties (with $y_i = 0$) leads to the first-best outcome.

25. According to the World Bank (2001), that may be true in Peru. See also Morón and Sanborn (2004).
26. See Green and Porter (1984), Lehrer (1989), Hungerford (1991), and Bednar (2003).
27. See Alston et al. (2004) for a somewhat different view for the case of Brazil.

More realistically, delegation has its problems, but there are instances in which the cost of those problems is smaller than the cost of partisan policy making. The feasibility of and benefits from such delegation may vary systematically depending on some features of the institutional environment of each country. In our applications, we will focus on the feasibility and desirability of delegating policy implementation to a technical bureaucracy. Although bureaucratic delegation is endogenous to each policy agreement (Epstein and O'Halloran 1999; Huber and Shipan 2002), it is constrained by some general properties of the civil service in the country, such as its professionalism (Huber and McCarty 2001).

Availability of Enforcement Technologies. As in transaction cost economics, intertemporal cooperation is easier to achieve if there is good third-party enforcement. The presence and characteristics of an impartial umpire and enforcer of political agreements, such as an independent judiciary, vary from country to country. As a result, the degree of enforcement of intertemporal political cooperation also varies.

The Policy-Making Arena. Arenas that make cooperation easier to enforce could facilitate the complex intertemporal exchanges required to implement effective public policies. Seminal work on the U.S. Congress debates the role that different institutional arrangements (such as the committee system) have in facilitating legislative bargaining, but it is implicitly agreed that *somehow* things are arranged in a way that facilitates intertemporal cooperation in political exchanges (see, for instance, Weingast and Marshall 1988; Shepsle and Bonchek 1997; and Shepsle and Weingast 1995). Whether the legislature, as the arena where these transactions take place, is adequately institutionalized depends on several factors, including legislators' incentives and capabilities. There are some environments – and we argue that Argentina is one of those – in which legislatures are much weaker than in the benchmark U.S. case. If political exchanges are actually undertaken, they take place in settings that are more informal, more uncertain, and harder to monitor, observe, and enforce.[28]

28. The place where cooperative exchanges take place over time could include arenas other than or in addition to the national legislature. In Japan, for instance, one key arena of the policy-making process has been the heavily institutionalized internal organization of the dominant Liberal Democratic Party (Ramseyer and Rosenbluth 1993; Baron 1996; Rosenbluth and Thies 2000). A somewhat similar picture emerges in some analyses of the experience of Mexico during the decades of PRI domination (Lehoucq et al. 2004).

Summary. Proposition 2 summarizes the preceding discussion.

Proposition 2. Political cooperation leading to effective public policies is more likely if

1. The short-run payoffs from noncooperation are low
2. The number of political actors is small
3. The actors have strong intertemporal linkages
4. Policy and political moves are widely observable
5. Good delegation technologies are available
6. Good enforcement technologies are available
7. The key political exchanges take place in arenas where properties 2–6 tend to be satisfied.

APPLYING THE THEORY

The model presented in this chapter has a number of theoretical implications. With Propositions 1 and 2, we have arranged some of the main results in order to gear them toward the application to Argentina that we develop in the rest of the book. Before moving to that application, we provide some ideas on how this framework could be further developed and applied more generally.

The framework could be summarized as a matrix having sets of political-institutional variables characterizing a country (the Xs) as rows, different policy issues with different transaction characteristics (Zs) as columns, and features of resulting policies (Ys) inside the cells. The framework can be applied to study variations in policy characteristics for a given polity across policy issues or to study variations in policy characteristics across polities for a policy issue with given transaction characteristics.

For any polity, some issues present more challenging transactional features than others. The political implementation of the deals that sustain policies with different transaction complexities will lead to policies with different features. The exercise of comparing those features is the public policy (or political) version of the archetypical exercise in transaction cost economics of understanding different forms of economic governance as a function of the different transactional hazards present in different economic activities, taking as given some characteristics of the institutional environment, such as the quality of the judiciary.

Comparing policy implementation features across polities for a given issue with particular transaction characteristics is an exercise started by Levy and Spiller (1994; 1996) for the telecommunications sector and advanced by others, such as Huber and Shipan (2002). In this work, we take a step in the direction of generalizing and deepening the logic of Levy and Spiller. In particular, we believe that the institutional determinants of public policy go beyond the standard political groupings of some of the previous literature. The homework required to map institutional incentives onto political behavior and policy making is fairly demanding of institutional and historical detail. Such work has not been done for many countries,[29] and what is available has not necessarily been structured with our questions about the policy-making process in mind.

The digging necessary to characterize the policy-making process, its consequences, and its determinants should consist of three parts: (1) a description of the characteristics of policies in the country; (2) a description of the workings of political institutions and the policy-making process in the country, which should help to explain (1); and (3) an analysis linking the country's political institutions and history to the policy-making process.[30] In Part II of this book, we do that for the case of Argentina. Chapters 3 to 6 look at specific pieces of the Argentine institutional landscape that constitute the components for the overall description of the policy-making process and the resulting policies presented in Chapter 7.

29. There is obviously a huge amount of work on the United States, but most of it focuses on narrow strips of the institutional landscape, precisely because many features that are already known can be taken as given. There are some isolated systemic institutional analyses of a few countries; see, for instance, Rosenbluth and Thies (2000) and Baron (1996) on Japan and Ames (2001) and Samuels (2003) on Brazil.

30. These steps are similar to the ones proposed by Cowhey and McCubbins (1995) in comparing Japan and the United States. They refer to *structure* (the formal rules, whether legal, constitutional, or party-derived, that bind political actors and shape their motivation), *politics* (political behavior under those rules), and *policy*.

PART II

The Workings of Political Institutions, Policy Making, and Policies in Argentina

In this part of the book, we analyze in detail the workings of the main institutions of the policy-making process in Argentina. We show here that these institutions do not facilitate the development of consistent policies over time, the development of policy-making capabilities, the accumulation of policy-making knowledge and expertise, or the coordination of policy. In particular, we show in Chapters 3 through 6 that Argentina's key political actors tend to have short political horizons, wrong incentives, or both, and that Argentina lacks institutional arrangements, such as a professional bureaucracy or an independent judiciary that, in the presence of short political horizons of the key players, would provide the missing institutional glue to facilitate intertemporal coordination and the enforcement of agreements. Chapter 7, then, shows that these institutional features indeed translate in uncoordinated, incoherent, at times rigid, and systematically unstable policy making, features that necessarily lead to low-quality policies and a lack of incentives to invest in capabilities, with the consequent implications for general well-being.

Chapter 3 analyzes the Argentine Congress. In this chapter, we show that the structure of the Congress and the behavior of its legislators reflect equilibrium behavior given the incentives faced by the legislators and their political masters – the provincial party bosses. In particular, we show that given the latter's political incentives, Argentine legislators although professional politicians are only amateur legislators. Most of them spend just a single term in Congress, do not specialize, and do not undertake legislative public-good activities, such as controlling the bureaucracy or improving legislative practices. As a consequence, Argentina's Congress does not serve as a source of policy stability or credibility. It is also not the arena where most of the key political decisions are taken. These are taken in other, less transparent and less formal arenas, such as the president's office and informal gatherings with provincial governors. This chapter also explores in detail the origins and the effects of the incentives faced by the provincial party bosses.

Chapter 4 explores the fundamental role of federalism in Argentina. Although a federal constitution provides room for institutional innovation, exploration, and competition, and thus could have strong market-preserving and development-enhancing features (Weingast 1995), we show in this chapter that the many deficiencies of Argentina's federalism, and in particular its fiscal features, are the result of a dynamic game among the national government and provincial governments. We show that this game, involving the distribution of taxes, transfers, and spending responsibilities, permeates national and subnational policy making even for policy areas that do not a have a direct connection to federal (such as intergovernmental and provincial) issues. The incentives generated by the federal fiscal game, in turn, reinforce the institutional weaknesses of the national policy-making arena emphasized elsewhere in this book. The chapter, then, explains the evolution and recent state of the federal fiscal system using and extending the theory developed in Part I of this book.

Chapter 5 analyzes the incentives and constraints facing Argentine justices that make it so that, in general, the Court has not served as a binding constraint on the workings of the Argentine executive. According to the division of power theory, the constitutional political fragmentation of Argentina should have produced a relatively independent judiciary. In fact, legal scholars have argued that this was the case until the first coup d'état in 1930. Political instability, however, seems to have brought about a fundamental change in the relation of the polity to the Argentine Court. The Argentine Supreme Court has had its share of political manipulation, with presidents from the mid-1940s until 1999 and from 2003 on being able to govern with relatively sympathetic Supreme Courts. The current common wisdom, then, suggests a pliable Supreme Court. In Chapter 5, we explore the relation between the polity and the Court and uncover the political and historical sources of its inability to serve as a credibility-enhancing institution.

In Chapter 6, we analyze the factors that have made the Argentine bureaucracy, as the Supreme Court, unable to serve as a commitment device in the Argentine policy-making process. We show that those problems are, again, a general equilibrium result to the nature and incentives faced by Argentina's politicians. In particular, we argue that Argentina's lack of a high-quality and professional bureaucracy and its use of the so-called parallel bureaucracy rather than the professional civil servants for key decision making, are the institutional response to the lack of any relevant political principal interested in providing long-term incentives to bureaucratic actors. Congress, being a marginal policy-making actor, lacks the incentives and ability to provide incentives and to monitor the bureaucratic apparatus. Executives, transient by nature, do not have long-term incentives to build a quality permanent bureaucracy either. Unable to motivate the permanent bureaucracy, they have tended to fill the main bureaucratic positions with transient loyalists, giving rise to the parallel bureaucracy. This practice, in turn, has further reduced the incentives of the permanent bureaucrats and has limited the consistency and coherence of policies.

Chapter 7 comes back to provide the evidence concerning the basic nature of public policies in Argentina, in particular their incoherence, rigidity, and volatility. We do this in two ways. First, using international indicators on public policy, we put Argentina in the international context. Then, we provide direct evidence on the nature of policy making by examining selected policy areas – pension reform, social policies, utilities' regulation, and international trade negotiations.

Part II, then, provides the archeology required by the analytical foundations of Part I. It provides detailed analyses of Argentina's key policy-making institutions and shows that, given the inherent incentives, it lacks an environment conducive to cooperation. We then show that, indeed, public policy is made in a noncooperative fashion, with the consequent implications for the quality of public policies.

3

Congress, Political Careers, and the Provincial Connection

WITH MARK P. JONES AND SEBASTIÁN SAIEGH

Legislatures are critical institutions in the effective functioning of a democratic system and in the policy-making process. In terms of the framework developed in Part I, Congress is the most natural arena for the institutionalized political exchanges necessary to sustain effective public policies. The ability of the congressional arena to play such a role varies substantially from country to country. At the more proactive and constructive end of the spectrum, the U.S. Congress is able to develop its own legislative proposals and has an active role in directing the policy agenda as well as in overseeing policy implementation. Congress itself is institutionalized in a manner that facilitates intertemporal exchanges and that leads to the accumulation of policy capabilities (Weingast and Marshall 1988; Krehbiel 1991). This, in turn, is associated with legislators having the right human capital characteristics to make them productive in those roles (Diermeier, Keane, and Merlo 2005).

The extensive literature on the U.S. Congress provides a detailed and relatively comprehensive understanding of this institution and a set of widely accepted truisms. Members of the U.S. Congress serve long terms in office. They specialize in the topics of committees on which they serve. They play an active role in the policy-making process. As an institution, the U.S. Congress engages in considerable oversight of the public bureaucracy, and it is at the center of policy making.[1]

---

1. On the longevity of U.S. congressional careers, see Polsby (1968) and Ornstein, Mann, and Malbin (1998). On committee specialization and the U.S. Congress's policy-making role, see Shepsle (1978), Weingast and Moran (1983), Weingast and Marshall (1988), Krehbiel (1991), and Londregan and Snyder (1994). On oversight, see Weingast and Moran (1983) and McCubbins, Noll, and Weingast (1989). For a differing view of U.S. presidential powers, see Moe and Howell (1999). For a critical assessment of the "congressional dominance" theory, see Moe (1987).

Most legislatures, however, do not resemble the U.S. Congress in many or even any of these features. That is the case in many of the party-centered systems that dominate the world's democracies (see Shugart and Haggard 2001). As a consequence of its atypical nature, studies of the U.S. Congress, while helpful in generating some general theoretical propositions, are also limited in their usefulness for extending legislative theory. Until quite recently, studies of other legislatures (especially of other presidential democracies) have been rare. This chapter, as well as our previous work, contributes to the newer scholarship on Latin American congresses.[2]

Argentina is a country in which none of the previously mentioned characterizations of the U.S. Congress appears to apply. Argentine legislators are transitory visitors, averaging only one term in office. They do not specialize, they belong to multiple committees, and they do not play an active role in the policy-making process. The Argentine Congress pays little attention to oversight activities. And in Argentina, crucial political and policy bargains are struck in a less institutionalized manner, away from the national legislature. In this chapter, we make progress in explaining why the Argentine Congress diverges so much from the typical portrayal of the U.S. Congress. In doing so, we provide a crucial building block to support our overall description of the Argentine policy-making process, while we also advance scholarly knowledge of the functioning of legislatures in the world, particularly of the relation between electoral incentives, legislative careers, and legislative institutions.

The fact that the Argentine Congress is not an important policy-making arena is the general equilibrium result of a number of factors, including prominently (1) electoral rules and political practices that make legislators weak political actors who are mostly uninterested in public policy, (2) constitutional rules and historical/equilibrium practices that give the executive broad policy-making leeway, (3) lack of judicial enforcement of policy agreements, and (4) the absence of a competent professional bureaucracy to which the implementation of policy agreements could be

---

2. Some of the countries that have received attention include Chile (Londregan 2000), Brazil (Ames 1995; 2001; Figueiredo and Limongi 2000; Samuels 2003; Desposato 2003; Alston et al. 2004), Costa Rica (Carey 1996), and Mexico (Nacif 2002). On Argentina, see Danesi (2004), Jones (2001; 2002), Jones and Hwang (2005), and Jones et al. (2001; 2002). This chapter draws extensively from the last two papers. We want to thank Silvina Danesi and Mariana Llanos for allowing us to draw freely from their work, especially Danesi (2004) and Llanos (2003).

delegated. In this chapter, we focus on the first two factors; later chapters look into (3) and (4).

The idea that the organization of the U.S. Congress reflects the electoral incentives of its members has been a cornerstone of the literature on American politics since the 1974 publication of David Mayhew's *Congress: The Electoral Connection*. The key question for comparative work is whether the assumptions that drive Mayhew-type arguments for the U.S. case contribute to an understanding of legislative incentives elsewhere. In principle, non-U.S. politicians are as strategic in their actions as their U.S. counterparts. The political institutions that shape legislators' incentives, however, vary from country to country; career structure, electoral laws, and party rules can be very different. The question narrows, then, to the incentives of politicians in different contexts.[3]

If party nomination is inconsequential for electoral success, for example, as it seems to be for incumbents in the Brazilian Chamber of Deputies (see Ames 2001), party renomination will play no substantial role in shaping legislators' behavior. In contrast, there are situations, as in closed-list proportional representation (PR) systems, where nomination at the top of a major party list can virtually guarantee electoral success.[4] In the latter case, legislators' behavior will be constrained by the renomination rules but essentially unconstrained by the electoral process (Strøm 1997). In federal countries with closed-list PR electoral systems, the process by which the provincial (district) party lists are formed largely affects which candidates run on each party list, the order in which they appear on the list, and, consequently, their chances of winning a seat in Congress. Hence, the role that electoral rules and political practices grant local party leaders in the creation of the district party list determines whether local party leaders are or are not key determinants of legislators' futures.

In Argentina, where local party bosses dominate the construction of the local party list, legislators' ability to pursue a legislative career independently is substantially curtailed. In this sense, Argentina is different from Brazil and the United States, where the decision to run for reelection lies almost exclusively with the incumbent legislators. Argentine legislators, in order to pursue their desired career paths, must maintain good

---

3. See Morgenstern and Nacif (2002) for a similar perspective in an interesting comparative work.
4. In closed-list systems, individual candidates cannot be added to the party roster either by the candidate or by voters directly.

relationships with their local party bosses. Although challenging the local party boss can sometimes be a good strategy, it is a risky one, and the timing of the challenge must be carefully chosen. Absent a challenge, career progression requires the support of the local party boss.

Local party bosses have a complex political objective. They want to maximize the performance of their party in their province and at the same time safeguard their position in the provincial party structure. The threat of challenge by popular legislators provides local party bosses with a strong incentive to reduce the national and provincial visibility of their local underlings by rotating them among the jobs the provincial party can offer. The electoral risk associated with nominating lesser-known candidates is attenuated by Argentina's electoral rules, especially the use of party-supplied ballots and closed-list PR with provinces as districts. Voters tend to vote for the party list, not for the individuals on the list.

Within this institutional context, legislators have little incentive to work hard to improve their visibility in the eyes of the voters and no incentive to develop legislative policy expertise. A legislator may be marginally aided in his or her career progression by obtaining public visibility. Policy expertise is unrelated to visibility, however, and it is not relevant for the candidate nomination and general election process. The institutional barriers to reelection therefore generate widespread shirking, providing suboptimal levels of effort from both an informational and an institutional perspective (see Krehbiel 1991; Fearon 1999; Ferejohn 1999).

A legislature's organization reflects the incentives of its members. In Argentina, the committee system does not enable legislators to pursue their electoral objectives through constituency service or to develop informational capabilities (see Weingast and Marshall 1988; Krehbiel 1991).[5] Instead, legislators serve on committees mainly to obtain perks and additional resources, as well as to remain in good standing with the provincial party leadership.

The rest of the chapter is organized as follows. It begins by looking at the policy-making role of the Argentine Congress, with a focus on the budget process. The following section examines the organization and

5. This is in contrast to the U.S. system. The U.S.-centered literature has developed two interpretations of the U.S. committee system: the "distributive hypothesis" and the "informational hypothesis." Politics in Argentina is fairly distributive, but this distribution is less focused on constituencies than on local political patrons, and this distribution does not take place through legislation in specific policy areas negotiated in powerful committees but more often in the arena of federal fiscal negotiations, which we analyze in Chapter 4.

institutionalization of Congress, with a focus on the committee system. We then turn to legislative careers, the subnational connection, and the role of provincial party bosses. The final section of the chapter places the Argentine legislature in a comparative Latin American perspective.

CONGRESS AND THE POLICY-MAKING PROCESS: THE BUDGET

The Argentine Congress has a relatively marginal role in policy making. Chapter 7 provides several illustrations of the lack of congressional involvement in areas as diverse as international trade negotiations and antipoverty policies. Chapter 6 provides similar illustrations of the lack of congressional involvement in overseeing the bureaucracy. In this section, we focus on the budget process. Fiscal policy in general and the budgetary process in particular are key areas of public policy. Among other things, they define the size and composition of public spending, they lay down the government's relative priorities for federal programs, they are central in shaping national economic policy, and they can play an essential role in the achievement of important policy outcomes, such as macroeconomic stability. The national budget is generally the most significant piece of legislation adopted each year. For this reason, a look at the actors involved in the process by which the budget is designed, approved, and implemented helps us to show why the Argentine Congress is not an important arena for national policy making. Although empowered with important budgeting prerogatives, Congress in fact plays a weak role throughout the different stages of the budget process.[6]

The Formal Budget Process in Argentina

The budget process as it is formally outlined by the Argentine Constitution and subsequent legislation has four stages[7] The first is formulation. The Ministry of the Economy sets budget priorities and defines investment programs, prepares macroeconomic forecasts, and provides support in the definition of expenditure ceilings. The National Budget Office evaluates the preliminary budget proposals prepared by the agencies and puts together the aggregate proposal. The executive then decides the aggregate

---

6. This section draws heavily on two recent papers on the role of Congress in the budget process: Abuelafia et al. (2005) and Uña et al. (2005). See also Rodríguez and Bonvecchi (2004).

7. This description is taken from the Law of Financial Administration (*Ley de Administración Financiera*) of 1993.

budgetary policy and distributes the expenditure ceilings among the agencies. Congress receives information only about the general guidelines of the budget proposal.

The second stage is approval. The executive submits the proposal to Congress and replies to enquiries (oral or written) formulated by budget committees of both chambers. Congress is empowered to approve or reject the budget proposal, to introduce modifications, and to remove articles. After Congress approves the budget, the executive can introduce line item vetoes into the budget. If the executive uses its veto power, Congress can overrule the vetoes with a two-thirds majority.

The third stage is execution. The executive distributes the expenditure authorizations among agencies and introduces modifications to the project. It cannot introduce modifications that alter total expenditure or debt level. Agency heads distribute the quotas among their agencies' programs and are responsible for recording the details of the programs' physical execution. The chief of cabinet is responsible for providing information regarding budget execution to Congress.[8] At this stage, Congress is the only institution that can modify total expenditure, the debt level, or the purpose and objective of expenditures.

The fourth and final stage is control. The executive coordinates the internal auditing activities and procedures, and the internal auditing units perform the internal audits. Congress, through the National Audit Office, performs ex post controls regarding budget implementation. Additionally, it has to evaluate and approve the *Cuenta de Inversión* (the annual budget execution report submitted by the executive).

The Actual Workings of the Budget Process in Argentina

Despite the official expectation of bureaucratic control of the initial stages of budget formulation, the formulation stage of the budget is in fact conducted within the executive, and the key actor is the president. This stage includes the development of macroeconomic and revenue forecasts. These are theoretically designed to act as a limit on spending and to contribute

8. The chief of cabinet is a figure introduced in the 1994 constitutional reform. In practice, the cabinet chief has acted mostly as a glorified presidential representative and has failed to achieve the coordination role that the 1994 Constitution provided for the office. See Novaro (2000) for an in-depth analysis of the impact of the creation of the chief of cabinet office on the reform of the state process in the 1990s.

to fiscal sustainability. As Abuelafia et al. (2005) and Uña et al. (2005) argue, however, there is a systematic strategic use of macroeconomic forecasts. The strategic overestimation of revenue forecasts, for example, has important implications for the game at subsequent stages. At the approval stage, Congress receives a budget proposal with income and spending levels quite different from the real levels that will be executed later on by the executive.

The role of Congress at the approval stage is twofold: It can exert its influence on the budget by changing its size and by introducing changes in its composition (budget reallocations). Consider the first role – the extent to which Congress actually modifies the budget in terms of total spending. Abuelafia et al. explore these modifications. They show that in most years such changes affect less than 1 percent of the budget. There are some exceptions. In 1997, for instance, Congress made relatively large changes in total spending. Yet these changes were concentrated in an increase in Social Security and in fact were made in response to an agreement between the executive and some provincial governors that the national government would take over the funding of the deficits of provincial pension schemes. This agreement was signed after the executive proposal entered Congress and therefore had to be included at the approval stage. This case suggests the weak role of Congress and points to the role that informal and powerful actors (such as provincial governors) play in budget negotiations even when the budgetary rules provide no formal role for them.[9]

Regarding Congress's second role, budget reallocations, Abuelafia et al. analyze the relative magnitude of changes in spending composition introduced by Congress. They find a rather limited role in all but the exceptional years of 1997 and 2002. Some negotiation does go on in Congress, even if most of the action occurs at the executive level. Provincial governors, ministers, public managers, and private interests who failed to include their budget needs in the planning phase attempt to exert influence on legislators to modify the budget. Furthermore, legislators attempt to increase the allocation of pork to their districts (Rodriguez and Bonvecchi

---

9. During the post–crisis years of 2002–3, changes have also been significant. In 2002, the initial budget proposal was rendered highly inadequate due to rapid changes in macroeconomic conditions. For the first time in a decade, the budget was not approved within the timeframe stipulated by budgetary rules. Yet because the delay in budget approval was a consequence of rapid exchange rate depreciation, we do not consider the changes introduced by Congress in 2002 as an indication that Congress has taken on a role of stronger influence in the budgeting process.

2004; Uña et al. 2005). Yet all in all, Congress plays a marginal role in determining both the total size and allocation of the budget compared to the size of the role granted to that body by the Constitution and budgetary rules (Scartascini and Stein 2005; Uña et al. 2005). Formally, at the execution stage, the executive is simply to implement the allocations approved by Congress; if any significant change has to be made to the size or allocation of the budget, Congress must approve it. In reality, there are three main ways in which the executive changes the budget at this stage. The first is through the use of presidential proactive powers: changing the approved budget by issuing decrees (Urgency and Necessity Decrees, or *Decretos de Necesidad y Urgencia*). In this case, the executive uses – or rather abuses – its formal power to increase the total amount of the budget in case of an emergency. In theory, these decrees are subject to congressional revision: Whenever the executive promulgates this kind of decree, it has to submit it jointly with a justification to Congress. A bicameral committee is empowered to overrule the decree. In practice, though, the bicameral committee set up to review this type of decree has not been constituted, and thus the executive can modify the budget unchecked.

The second way in which the executive changes the allocation of the budget is through the discretional administration of the quota system. In theory, the quota system is the administrative tool by which the budget is implemented. In practice, it is used in years when resources have been overestimated as a de facto way for the executive to decide on budget allocations. By choosing which agencies and ministries receive their full quota and which receive less, the executive can control the actual allocation of the budget. This allocation often differs substantially from the allocation approved by Congress.

Finally, Congress has, over time, delegated to the executive the ability to implement changes in the budget. The rules governing the budget process establish that Congress is the only branch of government entitled to modify total expenditures, total authorized debt level, or the economic classification of expenditures and their objectives and functions. In practice, though, these restrictions are almost never respected, as Congress regularly authorizes the executive to modify the budget. In 2000, 2001, and 2004, the authorizations were granted in the Budget Law itself. In 1998, 1999, 2002, and 2003, the authorizations were established by decrees. In 2002 and 2003, the decrees were based on the Economic Emergency Law.

Congressional oversight of budgetary spending is similarly weak. Control mechanisms are subject to political manipulation by actors who

are able to limit or distort the functioning of the agencies and personnel involved in the process. The Auditoría General de la Nación (AGN)
is the public entity subordinated to Congress charged with oversight and
control responsibilities for the budget. In practice, rather than providing
an independent and fair evaluation and control of public expenditures, it is
used as an additional resource at the bargaining table by political actors.
Thus, only certain events, agencies, or officers are subject to auditing
procedures. Also, the severity of these procedures is determined by politics and changes for no clear reason. If a particular agency, program, or
officer is audited and irregularities are identified, the AGN report may
be used as a bargaining chip before it becomes public (Abuelafia et al.
2005).

Also at issue is the timing with which the audit reports are made public.
Budget rules do not specify a deadline for the presentation by Congress of
its evaluation and approval of the executive's annual report, the *Cuenta
de Inversión*, which details and justifies the last fiscal year's spending. As
a consequence, the AGN runs behind schedule, sometimes postponing
delivery of its report for years. The last *Cuenta de Inversión* approved by
Congress, for example, dates from 1993 (Uña et al. 2005). As a result,
what is evaluated and learned from the process of evaluation is not available to become useful feedback information for the next fiscal year. The
bottom line is that congressional oversight and control mechanisms are
very weak in Argentina's budget process, generating mostly formal compliance with regulations but not acting to enforce efficiency and honesty
in public administration. Furthermore, although Congress has the formal
responsibility of controlling the role of the executive in budget implementation, it does not in fact make use of this formal power, and it lacks both
the technical capacity and the political power to do so.

Conclusion

Analysis of the Argentine budget process provides an excellent example
of the weak role played by the Argentine Congress in the policy-making
process. The so-called power of the purse that drives U.S. congressional
involvement in the budget process is, in equilibrium, a presidential pre-
rogative in Argentina. The actual Argentine budget process demonstrates
the divergence between formal rules and actual practices, the fact that
Congress is not an important policy-making arena, the fact of presidential dominance, and the involvement of informal actors, such as provincial
governors.

LEGISLATIVE ORGANIZATION

The overall aim of this chapter is to evaluate the role of the Argentine legislature in the policy-making process and to show how Argentine electoral rules have reduced legislators' incentives to specialize and to develop strong legislative institutions. Standing committees are among the most important of such legislative institutions. Comparative research has shown their centrality as determinants of legislative outcomes. In this section, we focus on how the committee system in the Argentine Chamber of Deputies works. The purpose of this appraisal is to allow us to test different hypotheses regarding the role of standing committees in the legislative policy-making process. In particular, this section seeks to sort out whether committee members serve particular constituencies (through specialization) or whether other political agents (that is, parties and local party bosses) have the upper hand in the legislative policy-making process.

Standing Committees in the Argentine Congress

We take a look first at the formal and informal practices surrounding the role of standing committees in the legislative policy-making process. As they are in most legislative bodies, committees are the workhorses of the legislative process in the Argentine Congress. Referral to one or more committees is usually a step in the process of adopting a bill in Argentina, and indeed committees may be able to prevent unwanted legislation from being further considered. This gate-keeping power is relative, as bills may also be discharged from the committees and submitted to the floor. But doing so usually entails a special procedure that requires the approval of all the legislative parties' leaders in conjunction with the speaker and the support of a two-thirds majority of legislators. Because such agreement is rare, most bills are discussed and voted on in committees before being sent to the floor.[10]

Committees usually reach decisions by a vote of the majority. In practice, this majority is often not a majority of committee members but rather a majority of a certain minimum number of members present (the quorum). Following the committee review (*dictamen de comisión*), proposed

---

10. In the 1987–8 and 1997–8 legislative periods, for example, only 14 percent and 25 percent of bills, respectively, were sent directly to the Chamber floor (Rossi 1998). Moreover, although there is no formal rule giving the committees the power to submit to the floor legislation that cannot be amended (closed rule), the Chamber approved 70 percent of bills sent to the floor without any amendment (Rossi 1998).

bills are reported to the floor for further debate and voting. The Chamber procedures allow the floor to send amended bills back to their respective committees for final consideration, but this seldom takes place in practice.

All permanent committees in the Argentine Congress have specific policy jurisdictions defined by subject matter. This definition, though, does not parallel the structure of administrative or cabinet agencies. In fact, some committees have far too vast – and others far too narrow – a focus. As a result, bills are referred to multiple committees, and either turf fights or legislative paralysis ensues. According to the chamber rules, whenever a bill is referred to more than one committee, a committee of the whole (composed of all the members of the committees involved) has to agree before a bill can be sent to the floor. This procedure creates multiple veto points. When the Appropriations Committee is involved, the committee of the whole has to make a decision within a month. Otherwise, the lead committee can report the bill to the floor.

Committee Membership

Not only are legislative committees poorly matched with the structure of the cabinet, but their number and size also bear no correspondence to the size of the legislature. Between 1983 and 2004, the number of standing committees increased from 27 to 45, while the number of deputies increased only slightly, from 254 to 257. Danesi (2004) argues that the creation of new committees in this period had more to do with the need to assign a committee chairmanship or other position to some important politician than it had to do with legislative needs. (This fact is reflected in the vague wording used to justify the creation of each new committee.) The Chamber rules regulate committee membership, establishing that each committee must have a minimum of fifteen and a maximum of twenty-five members.[11]

It is clear that too many committees vie for legislators' time and attention. In terms of the legislature's role in the policy-making process, a system with too many committees may overextend legislators, create duplication in their work, or both. The rules and norms governing committee composition and membership are thus important, as the size of a committee may affect its ability to develop expertise and to function effectively. Unlike the U.S. Congress, the Argentine Congress has no such thing as a

---

11. A small number of committees have somewhat larger maximums, which progressively increased, albeit slightly, during the 1983–2004 period.

seniority system. Within both the Chamber of Deputies and the Senate, committee and leadership assignments are made on a partisan basis. The rules of both chambers state that the composition of each committee shall proportionally reflect the partisan composition of the bodies as a whole. Thus, parties have a central role in the allocation of committees in the Argentine Congress. Committee chairmanships are allocated to the party holding the majority of the seats, and committee assignments are decided in each legislative party caucus.

The chamber rules, moreover, do not restrict multiple assignments. Thus, there are currently 675 committee slots in the Argentine Chamber of Deputies. It is noteworthy that there has been a monotonic growth not only in the supply of committee slots but also in the demand for them. The large number of Chamber committee assignments in the 2004 legislative period required every member to fill an average of 2.63 slots. In 1997, the typical Argentine deputy served on 3.5 committees, but by 2004 that deputy served on 4.5 committees.

An Empirical Analysis of Committee Membership

In this section, we try to explain the determinants of this penchant for serving on so many committees. In particular, we analyze whether legislators are led to overextend their participation in committees by their desire to please their constituencies at the expense of specialization. In Jones et al. (2002), we explored this issue and conducted a series of statistical tests using data for 956 legislators between 1983 and 1997.

First, we studied the main determinants of committee participation. We explored the effect of the number of committees in the chamber, party delegation size, and chamber seniority on the number of committees on which each legislator served. The results show that the number of committees in the legislature has the largest effect on the number of committees on which each legislator served. Participation in committees increases by more than 10 percent with the creation of each additional committee. This finding shows that legislators do not substitute committee memberships; rather, as new committees are created, they demand more memberships. Furthermore, legislators are not concerned about running themselves ragged as a result of overparticipation in committees. They seem more concerned about participating in as many of them as possible. This suggests that committee membership imposes few costs on members. Also, because time and effort are limited resources, it means that they specialize less than they would if they participated in fewer committees.

The results of our study also speak to the issue of partisan constraints and seniority effects. They show that legislators from larger parties tend to hold more committee appointments. Small parties do not ask their members to serve on multiple committees simply to increase their committee representation. Seniority in the chamber has a slightly negative effect on committee participation. More experienced legislators tend to participate in a smaller number of committees. This can be taken as supporting evidence for the hypothesis that legislators tend to specialize over time. But this seniority effect, although statistically significant, is politically irrelevant: An increase in tenure of one year reduces committee membership by less than 2 percent, implying an elasticity of just over 1 percent. The brevity of congressional careers, analyzed in more detail in the rest of this chapter, tends to drastically limit legislators' incentives to specialize.

The next step in our empirical inquiry was to analyze the source of Argentine legislators' lack of specialization. In other words, we asked whether committee membership is determined by a legislator's individual preferences or by those of his or her constituents. Using the same sample, we estimated a system of seemingly unrelated logit equations to test the effect of a number of explanatory variables on legislators' participation in the thirteen most important committees of the Argentine Chamber of Deputies. The independent variables in our analysis included the number of committees to which a legislator belonged, party delegation size, Chamber seniority, the number of committees in the chamber, alignment with the governor, and, as attractiveness measures, the legislator's professional background and the regional interests of his or her constituents.[12]

The effect of these covariates on the response variable differs across committees. In general, the number of committees in the Chamber had either no effect or a negligible negative effect on legislators' decisions to participate in each particular committee. This finding is consistent with the results discussed earlier. With respect to committee participation, the results are also consistent with the lack of a substitution effect described

12. We did not employ indices of legislators' issue preferences similar to those used in studies of the U.S. Congress because roll call votes in Argentina happen infrequently and because legislative politics in Argentina are nonideological in nature (Jones 2002; Jones and Hwang 2005). We designed the regional interests variable to capture constituency characteristics related to the jurisdiction of the committee in question. We considered different economic and social indicators as a proxy for regional interests. See Jones et al. (2002) for a complete description of the coding rules for the attractiveness measures.

earlier. The effect of this variable is positive and significant for all committees except the Health and Labor Committees.

We can also interpret this result as a measure of the importance of a particular committee. Most legislators can request to become members of different committees, but only some are able to serve on the important committees (likely because of unobserved personal and political characteristics, but, given the lack of permanency in the Chamber, irrespective of seniority). When we take into account the magnitude of the effect of the committee participation variable, we can conclude that the most important committee is the Appropriations Committee, followed by Foreign Affairs and Agriculture. With respect to the effect of seniority in the chamber, the results show that more experienced legislators have a higher probability of being members of the Appropriations, Foreign Affairs, Defense, and Labor Committees, while less experienced legislators are more likely to be members of the Urban Affairs Committee. The effect of seniority is null for the other eight committees. Hence, it takes slightly more experience to belong to the more prominent committees, such as Appropriations or Foreign Affairs. The magnitude of this effect, however, indicates that the substantive impact of tenure is relatively small.

In the case of the attractiveness measures, we found on the one hand that constituency interest has a negligible effect on the likelihood that a legislator will participate in a given committee for all but the Urban Affairs Committee. On the other hand, the results show that professional background is often a powerful determinant of committee membership. Being a physician increases the probability of belonging to the Health Committee by 67 percent, being a union leader increases the probability of belonging to the Labor Committee by 55 percent, and being an economist or accountant increases the probability of belonging to the Appropriations Committee by 50 percent. The obvious question is whether there are partisan effects involved in legislators' committee membership decisions. The results show that the size of a legislator's party delegation in the Argentine Congress has virtually no effect on the probability that he or she will belong to one of these thirteen committees.

In sum, the results in Jones et al. (2002) led us to reject the distributive hypothesis (Weingast and Marshall 1988) as a plausible explanation of how the Argentine legislature is organized. Although relevant to committee membership, constituency interests are politically insignificant. A casual review of the results may appear to provide support for the informational hypothesis (Krehbiel 1991). A closer examination of the results, however, leads to the conclusion that support for the informational hypothesis is also modest. Even though background may determine committee membership, short tenure and multiple memberships weaken any notion of specialization. As a consequence, informational advantages are not obtained. Additional knowledge of the Argentine legislature gained from extensive interviews with legislators, staffers, and other qualified observers supports this view (see also Danesi 2004). A more compelling explanation of these results is that legislators, required to serve on committees, simply choose those whose topic they find of greatest intrinsic interest and on which they can serve with the least personal cost.

It is important to notice that Argentine legislators do not need to rely on any particular kind of political support to choose the committees on which they would like to participate. A different picture emerges, however, when one looks at committee chairmanships. Obtaining the more prestigious committee chair positions may depend on a legislator's relationship with his or her party leadership or local party leader. To explore this notion in Jones et al. (2002), we also conducted a statistical analysis of the main determinants of being a committee chair for a subset of legislators in the aforementioned sample.[13] We estimated the effect of alignment with the governor, majority party membership, Chamber seniority, committee chair seniority, and the number of chair positions available on the likelihood of being selected to a chair position. The results show that the strongest impact on chair selection is committee chair seniority, while majority party status, gubernatorial alignment, and seniority in the chamber all have a considerable impact as well. The most powerful determinant, chair seniority, is also affected by the behavior of the local party boss.[14] Hence, these results suggest that committee chair appointments in the Argentine Congress, rather than functioning by means of a pure seniority system, are determined largely by a legislator's relationship with his or her local party leaders.

The differential effect of having a powerful patron on committee chairmanship is not surprising. In contrast to serving on a committee as a general member, being a committee chair is highly valued. With few exceptions, every committee chair receives extra resources (mostly for

---

13. We excluded alternates as well as those who cannot serve as committee chairs (the Chamber president and the leaders of the party delegations).
14. Tenure as a chair implies tenure in Congress; given that reelection is largely a factor of the leader's decision to place a candidate on the ballot a second time, the boss thus affects the likelihood of a legislator establishing chair seniority. It follows, then, that another determinant of chair appointment, Chamber seniority, must also be a factor of this relationship.

staff salaries) amounting to approximately 50 percent of the base allocation received by each legislator. The committee chair also controls the permanent staff assigned to the committee. Each committee has access to a secretary, an administrative secretary, and two clerical assistants. These personnel only perform administrative functions, however, and should be seen as a way to compensate loyal legislators with patronage positions rather than as an indication of a chair's predisposition to conduct a committee's business in a professionalized way.

A study of the Argentine legislature conducted in 1993 concluded that its committees lacked skilled staff (see Rundquist and Wellborn 1994). The authors found that most committees had a single nonpartisan staff professional employed by the secretariat, supplemented by party-employed staff controlled by the chamber or committee party leadership. "Rarely do committee (partisan and nonpartisan) staffs number more than a half dozen," they explain (393). Wynia (1995) paints a very similar picture: Argentine legislators keep large congressional staffs, he argues, but these staff members are "under-prepared and inadequately financed" to conduct research on the executive's proposals (79).

To wrap up, the evidence presented in this section indicates that the Argentine legislature is not organized in a manner that maximizes its effectiveness in the policy-making process. Additional evidence of Argentine deputies' low level of interest in legislation is reflected in the allocation of resources within the Chamber. Danesi (2004) presents evidence comparing the Argentine Chamber of Deputies with those of other Latin American countries (Chile, Paraguay, and Uruguay). Argentina ranks lowest in several indicators of the resources devoted to legislative functions. Legislators' lack of interest in strengthening the legislative capabilities of Congress is apparent in the history of the Committee for the Modernization of Congress, which we summarize (from Danesi 2004: Section 4.2) in the next section.

The Committee for the Modernization of Congress: A Brief History

With the return to democracy in 1983, one energetic deputy (O. Bordón) introduced a project for the study and design of a model to introduce structural reforms into the Chamber of Deputies.[15] That initiative was ignored, in spite of its reintroduction in early 1985. But immediately after

---

15. This section is based on Danesi (2004: Section 4.2).

its midterm electoral victory of 1985, the Radical Party (*Unión Cívica Radical*; UCR) took away from the Peronist Party (Partido Justicialista; PJ) several important committee leadership positions in the Chamber. In exchange, and in order to resolve the tensions between the major parties regarding the new distribution of committee memberships, the UCR accepted the PJ's demand for the creation of a new special (that is, temporary) committee within the Chamber: the Committee for the Modernization of Congress (Comisión para la Modernización del Congreso; CMC). In general terms, the committee was created to improve and strengthen the functioning of the Chamber of Deputies. More specifically, the CMC's goals were to study and design a new congressional modernization model that included strengthening the role of Congress; developing coordination and cooperation mechanisms between the Chamber and the Senate, the executive, and provincial legislatures; implementing human resource policies; improving technical institutions within the Chamber; computerizing the Chamber's information system; and introducing reforms regarding Congressional activities.

In the sixteen years from its creation until 2001, the CMC sponsored eighteen bills; 22 percent of them were approved on the floor. Only a minority of the bills approved were directly related to the committee's original goals. The majority were proposals that requested increases in the number of its staff, demands that the committee be granted a permanent status, and other matters unrelated to the committee's goals.

With respect to its own proposals, of the total number of bills (twenty-one) voted on the floor, 71 percent were introduced during the 2000–1 period, and 67 percent were approved. Among those that were not approved, it is important to note the number of bills directly related to the committee's goals that involved substantial reforms of the Chamber's internal functioning and organization, such as a proposal to change the internal rules of the Chamber and a strategic plan to modernize Congress. Moreover, some important bills, although approved on the floor, were never implemented afterward, including a bilateral agreement with the German Parliament, the Bundestag, to develop a system of technological modernization within the Chamber.

The poor performance of the CMC, legislators' indifference toward the committee, and the lack of approval on the floor of key projects regarding the main committee goals are all indicators of legislators' lack of incentive to strengthen Congress in the Argentine policy-making process. As transient visitors, it is not in their interest to do so. We take up this point in the next section.

Table 3.1. *Number of Deputies Elected in Each District (since 1992)*

District	Total Deputies	Number Elected in 1995, 1999, and 2003	Number Elected in 1993, 1997, and 2001
Buenos Aires	70	35	35
City of Buenos Aires (federal capital)	25	12	13
Santa Fe	19	10	9
Córdoba	18	9	9
Mendoza	10	5	5
Entre Ríos	9	4	5
Tucumán	9	5	4
Corrientes, Salta, Santiago del Estero, and Misiones (4 provinces)	7	4	3
Chaco	7	3	4
Jujuy and San Juan (2)	6	3	3
Catamarca, San Luis, La Pampa, Neuquén, and Santa Cruz (5)	5	2	3
La Rioja, Chubut, Formosa, Río Negro, and Tierra del Fuego (5)	5	3	2

Source: Molinelli, Palanza, and Sin (1999).

LEGISLATIVE CAREERS AND THE SUBNATIONAL CONNECTION

The Brevity of Legislative Careers

The Chamber has 257 members, elected from province-wide multimember districts for four-year terms. The deputies are chosen from closed party lists using the D'Hondt method of proportional representation in multimember districts. Deputies are allocated to the provinces based on their population according to the 1980 census, with each province receiving a minimum of five deputies and no province receiving fewer deputies than it held during the 1973–6 democratic period. Half (127 and 130) of the Chamber is renewed every two years, with each of the twenty-four electoral districts, or provinces, renewing half (or a close approximation) of its delegation. Table 3.1 shows the distribution of deputies by electoral district (as well as the number of deputies that renew every two years in each district). Note that the median and the modal district magnitude in each election is 3 and that 75 percent of the districts return four or fewer deputies to the Chamber each election year.

Table 3.2. *Reelection Rates to the Argentine Chamber of Deputies, 1985–2003*

Year	Percentage of Deputies Reelected	Year	Percentage of Deputies Reelected
1985–1987	29.2	1995–1997	14.7
1987–1989	22.0	1997–1999	20.4
1989–1991	18.9	1999–2001	23.6
1991–1993	16.2	2001–2003	15.4
1993–1995	14.2	Average 1985–2003	19.4

Source: Elaborated with data from Molinelli, Palanza, and Sin (1999) and from official records of the Argentine Chamber of Deputies.

Table 3.3. *Congressional Service by Argentine and Costa Rican Legislators*

Number of Terms Served	Number of Legislators	
	Costa Rica (1949–1990)	Argentina (1983–2001)
1	87	85
2	11	11
3+	3	4

Source: Carey (1996: 77) for Costa Rica, and our own elaboration from information in Molinelli, Palanza, and Sin (1999) and in official records of the Argentine Chamber of Deputies for Argentina.

The first thing to note about the careers of Argentine legislators is that they are quite short. As of January 2001, only one legislator had served continuously in the Chamber of Deputies since the country's return to democracy in 1983. Since 1983, the overall stability of membership in the Argentine Chamber of Deputies has been relatively low. During the 1983–2001 period, the average Argentine deputy served only one term in office, and only 20 percent of incumbents were reelected to their seats (see Table 3.2). In contrast, during the twentieth century, the average U.S. House member served between five and six terms (Ornstein, Mann, and Malbin 1998).

The distribution of legislators' number of terms served in the Argentine Congress is almost identical to that of Costa Rica, a country with term limits where legislators are forbidden from running for consecutive reelection. This can be seen in Table 3.3, which shows the number of terms served by legislators in the Costa Rican Assembly from 1949 to 1990 alongside the same information for Argentine legislators from 1983 to 2001.

Political instability played an important role in curtailing congressional careers in Argentina before 1983. Average tenure in the Chamber declined noticeably from around five years in the 1920s and 1930s to fewer than two years in the 1970s (Tommasi and Spiller 2000). With the return to democracy in 1983, the duration of congressional careers climbed back up. Regime discontinuities have resulted in significant shifts in parliamentary composition in other countries, as well. But in most of the countries of Western Europe, turnover rates declined steadily in the period following World War II after approximately three elections or an eight-year period (Best and Cotta 2000). And as regimes stabilized, congressional careers in many Latin American countries, including Venezuela and Brazil, grew longer.[16] But Argentine legislative careers are still quite short in international comparison, even after many years of sustained democratic rule: The average duration of membership at the end of the first full legislative term (1983–7) was 3.19 years, and it rose to only 5.46 years at the end of the 1997–2001 term. This indicates that history alone cannot explain the current brevity of legislative careers

Current reelection rates are also quite low in comparative perspective. Table 3.4 shows reelection rates for a number of countries. Argentina presents the lowest reelection rate except for Mexico, where reelection is not allowed. Why are Argentine legislators not reelected? One possible reason is that the voters are throwing the rascals out. But a closer look at Table 3.4 shows that the low reelection rate is not always the voters' choice: Only a small percentage of legislators seek reelection. Of those who sought reelection in Argentina, 67 percent succeeded, a number that is not particularly low in international comparison. But only 26 percent actually sought reelection.[17]

---

16. The Venezuelan Congress became increasingly "experienced" during the post-1958 democratic period. In the term 1988–93, for example, only 38 percent of legislators were freshmen. Another 30 percent had served one previous term, and 32 percent had served two or more previous terms (see Carey 1996: 75). (There have been some recent changes due to the "Chavista Revolution"; see Monaldi et al. 2004.) Brazilian legislative careers show a somewhat similar pattern. The proportion of successful reelection-seeking legislators in Brazil has been increasing since 1986 (Pereira, Leoni, and Renno 2001).

17. Once a candidate is on the ballot, or party list, whether that candidate is reelected depends on the overall vote for the party as well as on the order in which they appear on the list. Between 1989 and 1999, two thirds of those incumbents who obtained a position on the party list were reelected.

Table 3.4. *Reelection Rates in Selected Countries*

Country	Percent Seeking Reelection	Percentage of Candidates Reelected	Total Percent Reelected
Argentina (1997)	26	67	17
Brazil (1995)	70	62	43
Chile (1993)	76	78	59
Mexico (1997)	0	0	0
United States (1996)	88	94	83
Italy (1953–72)	n.a.	n.a.	82
Great Britain (1950–74)	n.a.	n.a.	81
West Germany (1957–76)	n.a.	n.a.	70–5
Panama (1999)	n.a.	n.a.	49
Colombia (1990)	n.a.	n.a.	48
Japan (1963–90)	91	82	74
Turkey (1950–80)	n.a.	n.a.	56
Portugal (1991)	n.a.	n.a.	57.8

n.a. = not available.
Source: Morgenstern (1998), Archer and Shugart (1997), Molinelli, Palanza, and Sin (1999).

Having established that the high rotation of Argentine legislators is not due to voter choice, in the next couple of sections we study in more detail the nature of Argentine political careers, as well as how the decision is made whether or not legislators are renominated for Congress.

Political Careers: Professional Politicians, Amateur Legislators

Argentine members of Congress are amateur legislators but professional politicians (Jones et al. 2002). The position of national legislator is merely one station on a lengthy political career path that normally begins and ends in the legislator's home province. Virtually all deputies and senators occupy some type of government or party position prior to being elected to Congress. Most of these deputies and senators serve only one term in Congress. But following their tenure in Congress, most deputies and senators do not withdraw from politics; rather, they occupy a political position at the national, provincial, or municipal level.

Jones (2004) provides information on the positions held by deputies elected between 1991 and 1999 and senators elected between 1986 and 2001. Three prominent conclusions can be drawn from his analysis. First, virtually all deputies (97 percent) and all senators occupied either a governmental (82 percent of deputies and 93 percent of senators) or party

(15 percent of deputies and 7 percent of senators) position immediately prior to being elected. This fact underscores the presence of relatively stable career pathways in Argentine political parties. Second, prior to assuming office, the majority of national deputies (62 percent) and senators (54 percent) held governmental or party positions in their home province, with an additional 24 percent of deputies and 35 percent of senators representing their province in the Congress. In contrast, only 7 percent of deputies and 11 percent of senators held a position in the national executive branch immediately prior to assuming office. In sum, virtually all relevant candidates for the office of national deputy and national senator are chosen from a pool of governmental and partisan officeholders in the provinces.

Jones also provides information on the percentage of different elective and appointive positions occupied by national deputies and senators at any time during a democratic period prior to their being elected as national deputies and senators. Among national deputies, the most common past position was that of provincial legislator (35 percent had occupied that post prior to being elected as national deputies), followed by national deputy (28 percent had been national deputies prior to their reelection as deputy between 1991 and 1999), municipal councilor (23 percent), and member of the provincial executive branch (21 percent). Only 12 percent had held a position in the national executive branch.[18]

An adequate understanding of the nature of legislators' political career pathways requires knowing both what positions legislators held before their tenure in the legislature and what positions they held afterward. Jones (2004) carried out a study of the positions occupied by all national deputies elected between 1991 and 1999 in the three years following the end of their terms. Of those individuals for whom postcongressional career information was available, an absolute majority (51 percent) continued to represent their province in the national legislature (44 percent as national deputies and 7 percent as senators). Over a third of deputies returned to their province to occupy positions in the provincial executive branch (13 percent), in the provincial legislative branch (17 percent), or at the municipal level (5 percent). In sum, an average of 86 percent continued in a career that was directly linked to the province – that is, they

---

18. Among national senators, the most common shared position was that of national deputy (33 percent), followed by member of the provincial executive branch (31 percent) and national senator (21 percent). A total of 17 percent of the national senators had previously held a position in the national executive branch.

either continued to represent the province in the national congress or they returned to occupy an elective or appointive position in the province.

In contrast, only an average of 10 percent of the deputies went on to hold a position in the national executive branch following their tenure in Congress, positions that in some instances they obtained in "representation" of their province (that is, their provincial party boss obtained the positions for them). There was a PJ president in office in all but one of the five roster years examined by Jones, and hence it is unsurprising that a higher percentage of PJ members occupied posts in the national executive branch during this period. All the same, even for the PJ, the number of former deputies holding national executive branch posts (15 percent) pales in comparison to the number holding posts directly linked to their province.

The data just presented coincide with a more detailed prior analysis of the position held by major party (PJ and UCR) deputies of the 1991–5 class as of mid-1998 – that is, two and a half years following the end of their term in office (Jones et al. 2001). This analysis highlighted the high percentage (85 percent) of deputies who continued to occupy a partisan or governmental post following their tenure in office, with a large majority (69 percent) holding a post at the provincial level (44 percent) or representing their province in the national congress (25 percent).

This section has provided evidence of the provincial-based nature of Argentine political careers. Focusing on national legislators (with special attention placed on national deputies), it demonstrated that an overwhelming majority of political careers begin at the provincial level. Furthermore, most politicians continue these political careers at the provincial level, either by continuing to represent their province in Congress or by returning home to occupy a position at the provincial or municipal level. In the next section, we look at the provincial connection in more detail.

The Subnational Connection: The Role of Provincial Party Bosses

As the previous discussion suggests, the keys to career advancement are held by the provincial leaders of the parties to which legislators belong. Therefore, in this section,[19] we take a closer look at these leaders, whom we call "provincial party bosses." We do this by studying who they are, identifying their sources of power, and showing how they interact in

19. This section draws from Ardanaz, Leiras, and Tommasi (2005). We thank Martín Ardanaz and Marcelo Leiras for their input into this section.

national policy making, especially through Congress and in key policy events. The important role played by party bosses is suggestive of how subnational (provincial-level) politics influences national politics.

In Argentina, the twenty-four provinces of the federation (actually twenty-three provinces plus the City of Buenos Aires) serve as electoral constituencies for congressional elections. This makes the province the locus of party competition and the base of political support for politicians and parties.[20] As shown earlier, political careers are usually province-based, and even positions in the national government are often a consequence of provincial factors.

It is common for a single person or small group of politicians to dominate political parties at the provincial level. In provinces where the party controls the governorship, the governor is, with rare exceptions, the undisputed (or at least dominant) boss of the provincial-level party. In many other provinces where the governorship is not held by the party, the party is nonetheless dominated in a comparable manner by a single individual, but there is a greater amount of space for intraparty opponents. In the remaining provinces where the party does not control the governorship and there is not a single dominant leader, there is usually a small group of influential party leaders who predominate in party life.

Following the presidential office, the governorship is the most important institutional position in the Argentine political system. In fact, the governors – generally in a collective manner – have constituted a more relevant counterweight to the presidential authority than that represented by Congress or the judicial power (De Luca 2004).

Table 3.5 shows the list of governors by province since Argentina's return to democracy. Regarding the partisan control of governorships, the first thing to notice is the dominance exerted by the two major parties at the subnational level. The PJ controlled an average of 61.8 percent (ranging from 54.6 to 77.3 percent) of the governorships between 1983 and 2003, with the UCR placing second with an average of 23.3 percent (ranging from 9.1 to 33.3 percent). No other party ever possessed more than one governorship at any one time during this period, with the highest average for a third party being only 4.3 percent.

20. This fact has been highlighted by a spurt of recent literature, including Benton (2003), De Luca, Jones, and Tula (2002), Gibson and Calvo (2000), Jones et al. (2001; 2002), Jones and Hwang (2005), Levitsky (2003), Remmer and Wibbels (2000), De Luca (2004), Sawers (1996), Calvo and Abal Medina (2001), Tommasi and Spiller (2000), Spiller and Tommasi (2003), Tommasi (2002), and Wibbels (2003).

Table 3.5. *Governors by Province and Partisan Control of Governorships (1983–2003)*

Province	1983–1987	1987–1991	1991–1995	1995–1999	1999–2003
Federal Capital		F. De La Rua	A. Ibarra		
Buenos Aires	A. Armendáriz	A. Cafiero	E. Duhalde	E. Duhalde	C. Ruckauf
Catamarca	R. Saadi	V. Saadi	A. Castillo	A. Castillo	O. Castillo
Cordoba	E. Angeloz	E. Angeloz	E. Angeloz	R. Mestre	J. De la Sota
Corrientes	J. Romero Feris	R. Leconte	R. Romero Feris	R. Romero Feris	P. Poccard
Chaco	F. Tenev	D. Baroni	R. Tanguinas	A. Rozas	A. Rozas
Chubut	A. Viglione	N. Perl	C. Maestro	C. Maestro	J. Lizurume
Entre Rios	S. Montiel	J. Busti	M. Moine	J. Busti	S. Montiel
Formosa	F. Bogado	V. Joga	V. Joga	G. Insfrán	G. Insfrán
Jujuy	C. Snopek	R. De Aparici	R. Domínguez	G. Snopek	E. Fellner
La Pampa	R. Marín	N. Ahuad	R. Marín	R. Marín	R. Marín
La Rioja	C. Menem	C. Menem	B. Arnaudo	A. Maza	A. Maza
Mendoza	S. Llaver	J. Bordón	R. Gabrielli	A. Lafalla	R. Iglesias
Misiones	R. Barrios	J. Humada	R. Puerta	R. Puerta	C. Rovira
Neuquen	F. Sapag	P. Salvatori	J. Sobisch	F. Sapag	J. Sobisch
Rio Negro	O. Álvarez	H. Massaccessi	H. Massaccessi	P. Verani	P. Verani
Salta	R. Romero	H. Cornejo	R. Ulloa	J.C. Romero	J.C. Romero
San Juan	L. Bravo	C. Gómez Centurión	J. Escobar	J. Escobar	A. Avelín
San Luis	A. Rodríguez Saá	A. Rodríguez Saá	A. Rodríguez Saá	A. Rodríguez Saá	A. Rodríguez Saá
Santa Cruz	A. Puricelli	R. Del Val	N. Kirchner	N. Kirchner	N. Kirchner
Santa Fe	J. María Vernet	V. Reviglio	C. Reutemann	J. Obeid	C. Reutemann
Stgo del Estero	C. Juárez	C. Iturbe	C. Mujica	C. Juárez	C. Juárez
Tucuman	F. Riera	J. Domato	R. Ortega	A. Bussi	J. Miranda
T. del Fuego		José Estabillo	José Estabillo	C. Manfredotti	
Number of Provinces	22	22	23	24	24
PJ	54.6	77.3	60.9	58.3	58.3
UCR/Alianza	31.8	9.1	17.4	25	33.3
Provincial Party/Other	13.6	13.6	21.7	16.7	8.3

Note: The table does not show federal interventions. In the 1983–2003 period, there have been six federal interventions: Tucumán (1991), Catamarca (1991), Corrientes (1992 and 1993), Santiago del Estero (1993), and Corrientes (1999).

Another noticeable feature in Table 3.5 is the high degree of name repetition. This is an indication of the fact that many provinces are controlled by single individuals or families over extensive periods of time.[21] Finally, a review of this name list shows that some of the most salient national political figures have been long-time provincial governors. In fact, all presidential candidates from the major parties (the PJ and UCR) were governors before running in presidential races.[22]

The power of provincial party bosses has been reinforced over time since the return of democracy both by political reforms (induced by these very leaders) and by the process of market-oriented reforms of the 1990s that moved the redistributive game from national policies to territorial policies. Ardanaz et al. (2005) explore these dynamics in more detail.

Governors, as party bosses, have at their disposal a number of institutional and political resources that render them powerful actors within and outside their respective provinces. Among provincial party bosses' sources of power, one could include the following items:

Constitutional prerogatives. As shown in Figure 3.1, in 1983, no provincial constitution allowed governors to be reelected. By 2003, all but six of the twenty-four provinces had provided for the immediate reelection of the governor, four of them without imposing restrictions on the number of terms that a governor could serve (De Luca 2004; Calvo and Micozzi 2004).

Accordingly, governors' reelection rates are high: Of the thirty-three times since 1983 that an elected incumbent governor was eligible to seek immediate reelection, that governor ran in all but four instances. In twenty-five of these twenty-nine elections, the incumbent was victorious. Given this success rate, incumbent governors are likely to be

21. Gibson (2004) provides a vivid account of one of the strongest examples of what he terms "subnational authoritarianism" in the province of Santiago del Estero, which has been "owned" by the Peronist caudillo Carlos Juárez since he first assumed the governorship in 1949. Bill Chavez (2003) provides a somewhat similar depiction for the province of San Luis, which has been dominated for many years by Adolfo Rodríguez Saá (briefly Argentine president during the December 2001 crisis) and his family.
22. More generally, some of the most salient national political figures since the return to democracy have been long-time provincial governors or members of family-run provincial governments. These include the cases of Angeloz (UCR, Córdoba, 1983–95), Duhalde (PJ, Buenos Aires, 1991–9), Kirchner (PJ, Santa Cruz, 1991–2003), Massaccesi (UCR, Río Negro, 1987–95), Menem (PJ, La Rioja, 1983–9), Rodríguez Saá (PJ, San Luis, 1983–2001), and Ramón Saadi and Vicente Saadi (PJ, Catamarca, 1983–91).

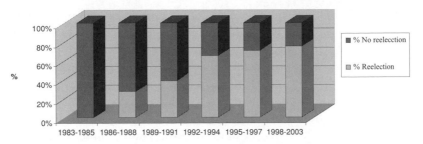

Figure 3.1. Percentage of provincial constitutions that allow for governors' immediate reelection

among the most influential actors in the province because not only do they control the provincial administration, but it is also extremely likely that they will continue to control it for the next four years (De Luca, Jones, and Tula 2002).

Local electoral rules. Partisan control of electoral reforms provided most governors with significant seat gains and allowed them to minimize the risk of electoral defeat, improve their control of local legislatures, and escape the negative externalities of more competitive national arenas (Calvo and Micozzi 2004). As an example, take the case of the electoral cycle, or the timing of elections. Electoral rules allow governors to choose local and national congressional electoral dates. This provides governors with the chance to choose electoral dates strategically, thus gaining independence from the national political arena. In fact, there has been a growing tendency of provinces to hold elections for provincial offices and national offices at separate intervals. All national and local elections were held simultaneously in 1983, but by 2003 only two provinces held gubernatorial elections concurrently with the presidential election (Ardanaz, Leiras, and Tommasi 2005).

Access to state resources. The governor heads the provincial public administration and thus has the ability to staff it. Jobs in the provincial public sector, known as "contracts" in party vernacular, are distributed on strict party-based criteria, going to party activists (or their relatives) and rank-and-file party members. These contracts often represent a family's only income source. The size of the provincial public sector is quite large in most provinces. In 2000, for example, the ratio of private to provincial employees was above 10 in only three provinces (Buenos Aires, Capital Federal, and Córdoba) and as low as 3 in four provinces (Catamarca, Formosa, La Rioja, and Santa Cruz), with a median value of 6. If one includes all public employees (national, provincial, and municipal), public employees account for over 25 percent of the work-force in six provinces, with a median percentage among the twenty-four provinces of 19. Finally, all but one province spends over 50 percent of its total revenue on provincial public employee salaries, and over half spend more than 67 percent (Jones 2004).

Execution of public policy. Governors exercise considerable influence over the execution of public policy not only through their direct control of the provincial budget but also through their discretionary control over the execution of national government–funded programs in the areas of education, health, public safety, public works, social welfare, and transportation. This influence allows a governor to obtain and maintain the loyalty of his machine through the granting of privileges in the distribution of material/economic subsidies, low-interest loans, scholarships, and so forth. It also allows him to construct a relationship with a wide variety of other organized groups (De Luca, Jones, and Tula 2002).

In sum, the dominance exercised by provincial party leaders over the political process in their respective provinces is based principally on patronage, pork barrel politics, and clientelism (Calvo and Murillo 2004). Campaigns, both primary and general election, are funded primarily through the use of resources gained from patronage, pork barrel, and clientelistic activities. Government financing of campaigns and party building also exists, although it represents only a very modest fraction of the resources used for campaign activity by the relevant parties (Jones 2004).

Patronage positions are particularly important for maintaining the support of second- and third-tier party leaders, who in turn possess the ability to mobilize voters, especially for party primaries. The ability to engage in pork barrel politics improves the party's reputation with key constituents and aids clientelistic practices through the provision of jobs to party supporters and the infusion of money into the party coffers, which in turn is employed to maintain clientelistic networks. Clientelism assists party leaders at all levels in maintaining a solid base of supporters.

Provincial Party Bosses and the National Policy-Making Process

The previous discussion suggests that provincial party bosses are able to dominate local politics by mobilizing a variety of resources. Their powers are not restricted, however, to the confines of their respective provinces. In fact, there are political and institutional variables that enable governors, through their control of legislative contingents in the national Congress, to enjoy national leverage – mainly the control of candidate selection methods and legislative malapportionment.

Candidate Selection. Political parties, not the government, run party primaries for both party leadership positions and candidacies for national, provincial, and municipal public office.[23] Primaries involve a considerable amount of voter-mobilization efforts on the part of the competing intraparty lists. The electorate for these contests consists of either party members alone (since elections for party leadership positions are restricted to party members) or party members and those unaffiliated with any party. When a primary is held, success thus depends almost entirely on candidates' financial or material resources. Whether or not a politician will faithfully represent (or has faithfully represented) the interests of his or her constituents normally has no significant impact on success in the primary contest.

It is in the best interest of the regional party boss to avoid internal regional conflict because conflict increases the influence of the national party and the independence of its legislators. Because governors are likely to bear a disproportionate share of the costs of any divisive primary, they have both the incentive and the means to arrange a negotiated list of candidates. Most governors are able to impose their candidates, co-opt potential opponents, or successfully negotiate an agreement with other party factions. Given the high reelection rate of governors who seek it, the power of the governor depends in part on whether the provincial constitution restricts reelection. In contrast, where the provincial-level party is in opposition at the provincial level, the resources at the disposal of its leader are minimal in comparison to those held by a governor; its leader is therefore much less likely to be undisputed. In such circumstances, national-level organizations have more influence on the provincial list composition, and the chance that a primary will be held is higher.

The decision within the PJ and UCR to hold a primary depends first and foremost on whether the party controls the governorship at the provincial level and secondarily on whether the incumbent governor is eligible to seek reelection. Regardless of which method is used, the provincial-level party leaders are the key players in the nomination process, with

---

23. This subsection draws from De Luca, Jones, and Tula (2002) and Jones (2004).

the national party leadership and rank-and-file members playing a decidedly secondary role. Furthermore, even when a direct primary election is held, the weight of the party leadership in the outcome of the contest is quite powerful, since unlike in current U.S. primaries, Argentine primary elections are clashes of party machines, with the victory going to the machine that is able to mobilize the largest number of voters to vote. As José Luis Lizurume, Chubut governor from 1999 to 2003, recently stated, "La interna es aparato puro" (The primary is pure machine) (*Diario El Chubut*, 07/18/03 in Jones 2004).

The importance of province-level political variables in explaining the method used to select candidates for the National Congress underscores the decentralized nature of the Argentine party system and highlights the prominent influence of provincial politics on national politics. We now explore yet another way in which subnational (and specific party bosses') interests are articulated in the national policy-making process: through legislative malapportionment.

Legislative Malapportionment. Argentina has a high degree of malapportionment; citizens living in small, peripheral provinces are overrepresented. According to Samuels and Snyder (2001), the Argentine Senate ranked highest on a scale of territorial overrepresentation among the world's upper chambers. Until 1995, the peripheral region, with 30 percent of the national population, held forty of forty-eight seats in the Senate – 83 percent of the total. This overrepresentation also extends to the lower chamber of the Congress, the Chamber of Deputies, where peripheral-region provinces, with 30 percent of the population, hold 52 percent of the seats (Sawers 1996; Gibson and Calvo 2000).

This institutional overrepresentation, together with the subnational drag on legislators' incentives provided by candidate selection mechanisms, has two main implications: First, it means that electoral accountability exists in Argentina, but it is accountability to provincial party bosses. To put it succinctly, Argentine legislators are the pawns of their provincial party leadership. In turn, party bosses mediate support of the legislators for the president. Second, it means that no national winning electoral or legislative coalition could be put together without the support of the regional structures of power in the periphery. This last point takes us into the next section, where we provide further evidence of the important role that provincial party bosses play in the national policy-making process. We do this by looking at a policy example: the market-oriented reforms introduced by the national government in the 1990s.

The Politics of Reform and the Subnational Connection

The market-oriented reforms introduced by the national government in the 1990s provide an example of the prominent role of provincial party bosses in the national policy-making process.[24] These reforms have been regarded in the literature (at least until recently) as a salient case of radical and "unconstrained" reform. Yet a closer scrutiny of the process and its outcomes reveals that the building and maintenance of political support for the reforms determined the pace, depth, and characteristics of the new policies and institutions. The idiosyncrasies of Argentina's political institutions and political configurations, including prominently the federal dimension, conditioned the coalition-building strategy and hence the outcomes.

The economic reforms were the product of a series of transactions between the executive and some key subnational actors (mostly within the governing coalition, and especially provincial governors) at every step of the process. The importance of provincial governors in the process was magnified by the fact the national executive had its own party contingent of around 50 percent throughout the period, increasing the marginal value of the block of votes under any given provincial party leadership. Consequently, during the economic reform of the 1990s, the peripheral coalition played an important role, and the burden of the costs of reform was shouldered predominantly by the metropolitan constituency.

The reforms were structured in a fashion that produced earlier and heavier hits on the central provinces as well as differential benefits in favor of the peripheral provinces. There was a redistributive component favoring the provinces, which are net recipients in the common pool of tax sharing (see the next chapter on fiscal federalism). This means that the central provinces of Buenos Aires, Córdoba, and Santa Fe and the capital city of Buenos Aires were net losers; that the province of Mendoza broke even; and that all the other provinces were net winners. The greatest increase in unemployment, for example – which was one of the undesired consequences of the reforms – was concentrated in the metropolitan provinces. Regarding the handouts that were granted in order to achieve

---

24. This discussion draws on Tommasi (2002) and Gibson and Calvo (2000). For a more general view of the politics of market-oriented reforms in Argentina, see Acuña, Galiani, and Tommasi (2005) and references there.

cooperation, the most salient were the subsistence and increase of industrial promotion schemes, the 1992 *Fondo de Desequilibrios Regionales* (Fund for Regional Imbalances), the asymmetric reduction of labor taxes, and the distribution of contributions from the national treasury. All of them benefited the smaller provinces.

THE ARGENTINE CONGRESS IN COMPARATIVE PERSPECTIVE

This section reinforces the general message of this chapter about the policy-making weaknesses of the Argentine Congress by providing two comparative glimpses. The first is a brief comparison of the Argentine and Brazilian senates. The second is a comparison of the policy-making roles and capabilities of eighteen Latin American congresses.

Argentine and Brazilian Senators: Evidence from a Survey

A survey of Argentine and Brazilian senators (see Llanos 2003) suggests that the Argentine Senate is a weaker policy making body with lower technical capabilities than its Brazilian counterpart. Committees in the Argentine Senate are perceived to be less important than in Brazil. Argentine senators seem to look for instructions from provincial governments to a much greater extent than do their Brazilian peers. They see their main job as obtaining resources for the province. When conflicts arise, they vote more according to the needs of their province and less according to the party line than do Brazilian senators. These are remarkable findings given the presumption in the specialized literature about the strong subnational drag to legislative careers and policy making in Brazil (see, for instance, Samuels 2000; 2003). We summarize next some of the evidence in Llanos's study.

The Subnational Connection. In Argentina, 85 percent of the surveyed senators expressed the view that the opinions of their provincial governments are very important in their decisions, compared to just 64 percent of the senators surveyed in Brazil. Two thirds of Argentine senators stated that obtaining resources for their respective provinces is a very important part of their legislative activity. Only 45 percent of the senators surveyed in Brazil shared this opinion. When asked whether they would side with their provincial interests or with their party in case there was a conflict of interest, 80 percent of Argentine senators said they would always favor their province's point of view, and only 6 percent said they would always vote with the party. In the case of Brazil, only 55 percent of the senators said they would always vote with their province, while 13 percent answered that they would always favor their party's point of view.

Role and Importance of Legislative Committees. Most of the Argentine senators who participated in the survey expressed a negative opinion about the workings of the committee system in the Argentine Senate. Nine out of ten respondents said that the functioning of the system was hindered by the existence of too many committees. In Brazil, only 21 percent of the senators offered a similar response. Also, more than half the respondents in Argentina said that committees are not an arena for the technical discussion of bills. Only 11 percent of the Brazilian senators expressed a similar response. Finally, 87 percent of the senators in Argentina said that the work of committees is severely underappreciated by their peers, who seldom participate in the meetings. Half of the senators in Brazil shared this opinion. In terms of legislative oversight, 70 percent of the Argentine senators expressed the opinion that investigative committees do not play an important role in making governmental activities more transparent. This opinion contrasts sharply with that of their Brazilian peers: 98 percent of them expressed the opposite opinion.

The Subnational Connection and Legislative Committees. With respect to committee membership, 96 percent of Argentine senators said that taking into account their districts' interests played a very important role in deciding which committees to join.[25] Partisan considerations were only viewed as very important by 33 percent of them. In the case of Brazil, the opposite is true. A large majority of the surveyed senators (83 percent) said that taking into account their party's interests played a very important role in deciding which committees to join, while district-based considerations were only viewed as very important by 56 percent of them.

Legislative Work. Floor debates seem to play a more important role in the voting decisions of Brazilian senators. Thirty-three percent of the Brazilian respondents, against only 9 percent of Argentine respondents, said that they took floor debates into consideration when deciding whether to

25. This result is at odds with our study of committee membership in the Chamber of Deputies, where, as we report earlier, we find that legislators' choice of committees is not driven by constituency or provincial interests. See Jones et al. (2002).

support a bill. In every single category, the views of Brazilian senators with regard to the technical inputs at their disposal were significantly more favorable than those of Argentine senators. The inputs in question included technical assistance, the information office, computer services, the library, and infrastructure and equipment.

The Argentine Congress in Latin American Comparison

A good part of this chapter has described and analyzed some characteristics of the Argentine Congress in an implicit comparison to the most studied legislature in the world, the U.S. Congress. This section draws on some recent work developed in the Inter-American Development Bank that attempts to assess some of the characteristics emphasized in this chapter in a comparison of several Latin American congresses. Following the logic about the policy-making capabilities of Congress developed in this chapter, Stein and Tommasi (2005), drawing from Saiegh (2005), have developed some comparative indicators about congressional organization, public image, and characteristics of legislators.

Table 3.6 compares Latin American legislatures according to several indicators that attempt to measure some dimensions of legislative capabilities. Five are quantitative – either objective measures or the result of opinion surveys external to the judgment of the authors. The first two assess the confidence of citizens and businesspeople in the performance of Congress. The third and fourth indicators – the average years of legislator experience and the percentage of legislators with university education – attempt to gauge the qualifications and experience of legislators. The average number of committee memberships per legislator attempts to measure the degree of specialization of legislative committees, and thus their effectiveness. The next three qualitative measures – strength of committees, whether the legislature is a good place to build a political career, and technical expertise – were constructed by Sebastián Saiegh, drawing from a variety of secondary sources, mainly from a legislator survey by the University of Salamanca. A composite index based only on the first five columns (objective measures) correlates well with one based on the last three (subjective measures), so that we utilize all the columns to build an index of Congress policy-making capabilities across Latin America, which is presented in the last column.

In terms of that aggregate index of strength, Argentina shares the lowest value of the index with Guatemala and the Dominican Republic. This confirms the weak role in policy making of the Argentine Congress

Table 3.6. *Policy-Making Capabilities of Latin American Congresses*

Country	Confidence in Congress, Average 1996–2004[a]	Effectiveness of Law-Making Bodies[b]	Average Experience of Legislators (Years)	Percentage of Legislators with University Education[c]	Average Number of Committee Memberships per Legislator	Strength of Committees	Place to Build Career	Technical Expertise	Congress Capability Index
Argentina	20,5	1,6	2,9	69,6	4,50	Medium	Low	Low	1,4
Bolivia	19,9	1,8	3,3	78,4	1,66	Medium	Medium	Medium	1,8
Brazil	24,9	3,1	5,5	54,0	0,92	Medium	High	High	2,4
Chile	36,0	3,7	8,0	79,4	1,95	High	High	High	2,7
Colombia	20,3	2,7	4,0	91,6	0,86	High	High	Medium	2,4
Costa Rica	29,9	2,2	2,6	80,4	2,09	High	Medium	Low	1,9
Dominican Republic	n.a.	2,0	3,1	49,6	3,54	Low	High	Low	1,4
Ecuador	13,3	1,7	3,5	83,1	1,26	High	Medium	Low	1,9
El Salvador	27,7	2,1	3,9	64,0	2,44	Medium	High	Low	1,9
Guatemala	19,9	1,8	3,2	68,4	3,24	Low	Medium	Low	1,4
Honduras	30,8	2,6	3,0	73,1	2,34	Low	Low	Low	1,6
Mexico	27,4	2,0	1,9	89,5	2,43	High	Medium	Medium	2,0
Nicaragua	23,1	1,6	3,5	85,6	1,96	Low	Medium	Medium	1,7
Panama	22,5	1,8	5,8	81,3	1,86	Medium	High	Low	2,0
Paraguay	25,0	2,2	5,5	75,4	3,15	Low	High	Low	1,7
Peru	22,1	1,7	5,2	92,9	2,44	Low	Low	Low	1,6
Uruguay	38,2	2,7	8,8	68,4	0,98	High	High	Low	2,5
Venezuela	27,8	1,4	4,9	74,6	0,97	Medium	Medium	Low	1,9

Source: Stein and Tommasi (2005).

not just when compared to its U.S. counterpart but also in a broader regional comparison.

CONCLUSION

This chapter applies the insight that legislative behavior and the organization of legislative institutions are affected by electoral rules to reveal some basic features of Argentina's national legislature. By making legislators more beholden to the provincial party boss than to the voters, Argentina's electoral rules, along with a constitutional system that places limited constraints on unilateral executive actions, have created an amateur Congress, one whose members have neither the expertise nor the incentives to initiate influential legislation, control public administration, or even invest in strengthening congressional institutions.

The evidence presented here shows, though, that these are not amateur politicians. Argentine legislators' progressive ambition causes them to leave Congress, but not politics. The center of political careers is in the provinces. In turn, provincial politics is heavily influenced by the objectives and resources of provincial governors. The next chapter focuses on the interactions of provincial governors and national political actors in the crucial domain of fiscal federalism.

4

Federalism, Argentine Style

WITH SEBASTIÁN SAIEGH

Federalism in general and fiscal federalism in particular are crucial axes of Argentina's history, of Argentina's present, and of Argentina's possible futures. This chapter provides a brief description of some basic characteristics of federalism in Argentina, with focus on many deficiencies of federal fiscal arrangements. Then it applies the analytical framework developed in Part I to explain those inefficiencies as the dynamic outcome of a game among the national government and provincial governments. This gaming around federal fiscal issues (the distribution of taxes, transfers, and spending responsibilities) permeates national and subnational policy making in crucial policy areas such as the social sectors.

The 2001 article from *Business Week* reproduced here provides some vivid examples of the importance of fiscal federalism and intergovernmental politics in Argentina:

To investors in emerging markets, 2001 could well be the year of Argentina. Fears that Latin America's third-largest economy might default on its $123 billion public debt have eased, thanks to a $39.7 billion Christmas gift from the International Monetary Fund. But it's now up to President Fernando de la Rúa to prove to the fund that Argentina can sort out its finances. If he fails, the consequences could be dire for bourses from Buenos Aires to Moscow.

Yet the key to Argentina's success in this grim struggle doesn't lie in the presidential palace. Instead, investors must pay close attention to what happens in Argentina's interior. It's the far-flung provinces, with their budget-busting spending, that have helped push the country to the brink. De la Rúa, as part of his bid for IMF aid, has extracted a hard-won pledge from Argentina's 23 governors to freeze expenditures for five years. It's the most concerted effort to bring the unruly provinces to heel since the bloody 19th century dictatorship of Juan Manuel de Rosas.

But will the pact with the provinces hold? Concluded in a flurry of backroom negotiations at the end of November, the agreement is one of the cornerstones of the de la Rúa administration's efforts to rein in a pernicious fiscal deficit now running at $6.7 billion, or 2.3% of gross domestic product. Yet with midterm elections in October and unemployment still hovering near 15%, it will take all of the political capital de la Rúa can muster to keep governors true to their word.

The problem is rooted partly in Argentina's constitution. This requires the federal government to share tax revenues with the provinces on the basis of a rigid formula. However, authorities in the capital have virtually no control over how the funds are spent. Such local autonomy has fueled patronage and, in some cases, outright corruption. Provincial operating expenditures have risen by more than 25% since 1995 even though inflation averaged −0.1% during the same period.

The backwater province of Formosa is a prime example. Located on the northern border, Formosa has only 450,000 inhabitants and contributes a pittance to overall GDP. Yet its 30 provincial legislators each collect a whopping $12,000 a month in salary. What's worse, the federal government bankrolls such excesses by financing up to 90% of Formosa's budget.

EXPENSIVE VOTES. While such flagrant abuses make for good headlines, the real damage caused by fiscal indiscipline originates in Argentina's larger provinces. Perhaps the biggest threat comes from Buenos Aires. The stand-alone province is home to one-third of Argentina's population of 36 million and boasts an annual GDP greater than that of Colombia. Yet its fiscal accounts have undergone a precipitous deterioration since former Governor Eduardo Duhalde launched his failed 1999 presidential bid. In the two years leading up to the elections, expenditures rose an alarming 22%, mostly in the form of patronage jobs doled out to secure voters' support.

If the provinces are going to break their agreement to freeze spending, it will likely start with Buenos Aires' current governor, Carlos Ruckauf. Like his predecessor, he hails from the opposition Peronist party and harbors his own presidential ambitions. Despite Ruckauf's campaign pledge to mend the province's finances, by October Buenos Aires had already run up a $983 million operating deficit, 10% greater than the original projection for the entire year.

FLOCK OF FLACKS. Buenos Aires Economy Minister Jorge Sarghini blames the poor performance on Argentina's ongoing recession, which he claims has been exacerbated by a federal tax increase in April. "We paid the price for their nearsightedness," says Sarghini. Yet it's hard to feel much sympathy for Buenos Aires when one reads in the papers, as Argentines did recently, that the province is adding 11,255 jobs to its payroll this year. Local authorities claim the cost of new hires will be offset by reductions in the provincial investment budget. More worrying is the fact that Buenos Aires is getting deeper into hock. A $200 million Eurobond issue, now in the works, will bring Buenos Aires' total debt to near $5 billion.

Unfortunately, there is not much de la Rúa can do to tame spendthrift governors like Ruckauf. That's not the case in Brazil, where local authorities that overshoot targets can be fined and even jailed. The 19th century dictator Rosas, whom critics dubbed the "Caligula of the River Plate," used the sword to keep Argentina's provinces in line. De la Rúa's pact may turn out to be a far blunter weapon. (Joshua Goodman, "Argentina's Provincial Profligates," *Business Week Online*, January 29, 2001)

Unfortunately, the article's last prediction was accurate.[1] The national government was not able to shore up the fiscal adjustment that might have prevented (or eased) the huge crisis and debt default that exploded in December of 2001, and federal fiscal and political gaming was a crucial factor in bringing on the crisis.[2]

Federalism is a crucial axis of Argentina's history, present, and possible future. Federalism in general, and fiscal federalism in particular, are vital components of the institutional structure that determines the characteristics of the Argentine policy-making process, even for policy areas that do not a have a direct connection to federal (that is, intergovernmental and provincial) issues. This chapter describes the federal political and fiscal system and intergovernmental relations. It also explains the evolution and recent state of the federal fiscal system, using and extending the theory developed in Part I of this book.

THE PROVINCES (AND THE GOVERNORS)

The first four decades after independence in 1810 were characterized by violent struggles over the constitution of a national government. That process of struggle resulted in the Constitution of 1853, which established a constitutional federal republic. This constitution suffered some modifications in 1860, with the province of Buenos Aires finally endorsing it. The provinces were granted autonomy in the administration of their territories. A set of federal government functions was established, the provinces were granted residual powers over any matters not specified as federal, and an internal economic union was promulgated with the elimination of internal customs controls. The Constitution gave the federal government the power to "intervene in the provinces' territory."[3] Despite some later

1. The article does contain some inaccuracies. For instance, the rigid tax-sharing formula it mentions was not engraved in the Constitution but was achieved through a fiscal pact, as we explain later in the chapter.
2. See "Argentina Says It Will Restructure Debt; Government Hopes to Avoid Defaulting on Loans as Economic Crisis Deepens," *Washington Post*, October 29, 2001, p. A14, and "Argentine Leader in Talks to Avoid Default on $132 Billion Debt," *New York Times*, November 1, 2001, p. 6.
3. This power was meant to be a safeguard against any threats to republican principles. The text is almost a translation of Federalist XLIII: The federal government has the power "to guarantee every State in the Union a republican form of government; to protect each of them against invasion; and on application of the legislature or the executive (when the legislature cannot be convened) against domestic violence." Over the years, however, national authorities have used the power mostly to favor

modifications, the essential federalist structure of the 1853–60 Constitution remains in force today.[4]

Argentina has twenty-three provinces plus the autonomous city of Buenos Aires. Each province has its own constitution and a directly elected governor and legislature. There were fourteen provinces at the time the original Constitution was signed in the middle of the nineteenth century. Eight additional provinces were created out of formerly national territories during the presidency of Juan Domingo Perón from 1951 to 1955.[5] Perón's opportunistic creation of provinces was part of a plan to build bastions of political support and to bias national representation.[6] This practice has been continued by outgoing military governments. In 1972, for example, the outgoing government put in place an electoral reform that increased the overrepresentation of the less-populated provinces in the Chamber of Deputies (Botana and Mustapic 1991).[7]

The provinces have diverse geographic and demographic characteristics (see Table 4.1). The province of Buenos Aires is by far the largest, with almost 14 million people. Three jurisdictions have approximately 3 million people each (Córdoba, Santa Fe, and the City of Buenos Aires). Mendoza has 1.6 million inhabitants, followed by seven provinces with populations in the 0.8–1.3 million range. Another twelve jurisdictions have populations of 200,000 to 620,000. The smallest is Tierra del Fuego at the tip of the continent, with about 100,000 inhabitants (see map in Figure 4.1). The provinces' level of economic development varies substantially as well. The high-population provinces are at the top of the scale; others are blessed with strong natural resource bases (prime land in the humid pampas; oil in the south). There is a concentration of less-developed provinces in the north. Even in the more developed regions, migration has

those groups within the provinces that supported the national government (Botana 1993).
4. The national Constitution was sanctioned in 1853 and reformed in 1860, 1866, 1898, 1949, 1956, 1957, 1972, and 1994. Since 1930, democracy in Argentina has been interrupted by military dictatorships in the periods 1930–2, 1943–6, 1955–8, 1962–3, 1966–73, and 1976–83.
5. In 1990, the former national territory of Tierra del Fuego became the twenty-third province. The 1994 Constitution granted autonomy to the capital city of Buenos Aires.
6. The connection between Peronism and the backward provinces is well developed by Sawers (1996).
7. That outgoing military government also produced a tax-sharing agreement strengthening the fiscal rights and bargaining power of several provinces in the hope that those more conservative political forces would counterbalance the power of future national governments.

Table 4.1. *Basic Characteristics of the Argentine Provinces*

Province	Population (1,000s) (2001 Census)	GDP per Capita ($1999)	Percentage of Population with NBI[a]	Population with NBI[a] (1000s)	Geographic Area (square km)	Vertical Fiscal Imbalance (% of National Resources/Total Provincial Resources)
Buenos Aires City	2,729	15,634	8	221	200	8
Buenos Aires	13,756	8,325	17	2,352	307,571	47
Catamarca	331	4,887	28	93	102,602	87
Córdoba	3,053	6,132	15	461	165,321	57
Corrientes	927	5,569	31	291	88,199	81
Chaco	979	5,967	40	387	99,633	84
Chubut	408	6,303	22	89	224,686	58
Entre Ríos	1,152	6,447	21	237	78,781	71
Formosa	489	4,520	39	191	72,066	95
Jujuy	609	3,812	36	216	53,219	81
La Pampa	299	7,633	14	40	143,440	63
La Rioja	288	5,836	27	78	89,680	90
Mendoza	1,574	6,511	18	277	148,827	54
Misiones	961	4,721	34	323	29,801	81
Neuquén	472	6,464	21	101	94,078	32
Río Negro	549	6,083	23	127	203,013	67
Salta	1,065	3,836	37	395	155,488	76
San Juan	617	6,341	20	122	89,651	83
San Luis	367	6,367	2	9	76,748	68
Santa Cruz	197	6,278	15	29	243,943	49
Santa Fe	2,976	7,061	18	524	133,007	58
Santiago del Estero	796	4,269	38	304	136,651	85
Tucumán	1,332	4,925	28	369	21,571	75
Tierra del Fuego	100	7,682	22	22	22,524	61
Total	36,027	7,722	20	7,169,381	2,780,440	56

[a] NBI stands for *Necesidades Básicas Insatisfechas* (unsatisfied basic needs), a commonly used measure of poverty.

Source: World Bank, INDEC, and authors' computations.

Figure 4.1. Map of Argentina

created pockets of poverty. In the province of Buenos Aires, for example, there are densely populated slums outside the federal capital.[8]

Besides political power, subnational and local governments have ample constitutional independence in fiscal and spending functions. Furthermore, as discussed in Chapter 3, electoral rules and party statutes and practices make provincial governors (as regional party leaders) individually and collectively very powerful actors in national politics. The question, then, is: What are the objectives of these provincial governors? That question takes us into the realm of fiscal federalism. Governors need money, both to provide public goods in their provinces and to provide particularistic goods and run their political machinery.[9] Most of that money comes through the common pool of taxes collected by the national government from joint and delegated tax sources.

FEDERAL FISCAL ARRANGEMENTS

Revenue and Spending

Although the Argentine Constitution establishes substantial room for subnational taxation, in practice the provinces have delegated to the national government large amounts of revenue-raising responsibility (including the collection of income, sales, excise, and fuel taxes), leading to the situation depicted in Table 4.2.[10]

The resulting revenue concentration took place in concert with a spending decentralization process, whereby the responsibility for key social functions is in provincial hands. The only activities over which the national authorities have exclusive authority are those associated with defense and foreign affairs. In the areas of economic and social infrastructure,

---

8. Migration toward the slums around the city of Buenos Aires is an indication that although the federal fiscal system redistributes resources to the poorest provinces, those resources do not have much impact on the quality of life of some poor citizens.

9. Governors' dominion over their political fiefdoms (as well as their weight in national politics) is crucially tied to their capacity to finance their sources of support: A Governor's dominion, De Luca argues, "derives from an important group of political and institutional resources, such as the governor's control over jobs in the provincial public sector, the provincial budget and the provincial party organization."

10. Such delegation was the outcome of a process that had its high point around the 1930s crisis, when the reduction in foreign trade tax revenues forced a substitution of other tax sources. This evolution is analyzed by Saiegh and Tommasi (1998).

Table 4.2. *Government Revenues, 2000 (percentage of total)*

	Level of Government			
	Federal	Provincial	Municipal	Total
Income tax (personal and corporate) and capital gains tax	19			19
Social security contributions	21			21
Taxes on goods, services, and transactions	38	10	0.1	47
Wealth tax	2	4	0.3	6
Trade taxes	3			3
Other	1	3		5
Total	83	17	0.4	100

Source: Tommasi (2002).

the national government shares responsibility with the provinces, while the latter have exclusive responsibility for primary and secondary education and local (municipal) organization and services. The Constitution defines a broad area of public services for which both national and provincial authorities can participate in legislation and public service provision, though the tendency in the 1980s and 1990s was for the national government to decentralize direct operation in these areas to the provinces.[11] Thus, the provinces are currently in charge of most social expenditures (including basic education, health services, poverty programs, and housing) and the economic infrastructure. The national government maintains some regulatory power in many of these areas and directly manages several programs. Still, subnational governments are responsible for almost 50 percent of total consolidated public sector expenditures (see Table 4.3). This figure is even higher if we exclude the most rigid part of the budget, the pension system.

The Transfer System

A high degree of vertical fiscal imbalance has resulted from expenditure decentralization and tax centralization. In 2000, for example, 56 percent of total resources received by the provinces came from the common pool of

11. Even though not explicitly analyzed here, the very process of decentralization of several social services was fraught with the opportunistic behavior and transactional difficulties emphasized throughout this book. See Section IV of Tommasi (2002) on the decentralization of education.

Table 4.3. *Expenditure by Level of Government, 2000 (percentages)*

	National Government	Provincial Governments	Municipalities
Total expenditure	52	40	8
Administration	39	46	15
1 Services	31	52	17
2 Debt service	84	15	1
Social expenditure	51	41	7
Education	20	78	3
Health	50	44	6
Water	15	85	0
Housing	1	99	0
Social assistance	25	53	23
Pensions	80	20	0
Employment	91	9	0
Other services	65	12	23

Source: Tommasi (2002)

national taxes, while only 44 percent was financed directly by provincial revenues. The vertical fiscal imbalance is not only large but also asymmetric among provinces. Fifteen of the twenty-four provinces finance less than 30 percent of their spending with their own resources (see last column of Table 4.1).

Argentina addresses this fiscal imbalance through a complex system of intergovernmental transfers. Its most important component is the tax-sharing agreement, called *coparticipación*, the process by which some of the taxes collected by the central government are reallocated to the provinces. Over time, the system has tended to redistribute resources to the most backward and low-density provinces, in large part because they are overrepresented in the national Congress. Even though the pattern of redistribution is "in the right direction," it is very far from being objective and transparent.

The last *coparticipación* Law of 1988 established a fixed set of taxes that would be shared by the national government and the provinces, explicating in detail the share that would go to the national government and to each province. Several other laws further regulated the distribution of specific taxes to finance predetermined activities. In the early 1990s, "fiscal pacts" introduced important changes. In 1992–3, the amount to be shared with the provinces was reduced to finance the growing deficit of the pension system resulting from social security reform. In addition, special channels link some fraction of specific taxes to specific, often economically unrelated spending purposes. This has led to a convoluted system that has been labeled by local experts as the "federal fiscal labyrinth" (see Figure 4.2).

The 1994 constitutional reform stipulated that a new tax revenue–sharing agreement had to be decided and put in place by the end of 1996. At this writing in 2006, the constitutional mandate remains unfulfilled. In the 1999 and 2000 fiscal pacts, the (then new) national government promised the provinces some fixed-sum transfers and some minimum revenue guarantees, assuming the role of residual claimant. But the national government was forced by financial circumstances to violate those clauses during the 2001 crisis, and the grievances over those obligations were a compounding factor in the political stalemate that led to the demise of President de la Rúa and to Argentina defaulting on its debt in late December 2001.

Major Deficiencies of the Federal Fiscal System

The federal fiscal system in Argentina has been under attack for many years by scholars, analysts, international organizations, participants (governors as well as national and provincial finance ministers), and the public. In ten letters of intent signed between the International Monetary Fund (IMF) and Argentine authorities between January 1999 and September 2003, the Argentine government promised some reform of the federal fiscal system. A list of the system's major deficiencies follows:[12]

- *High deficits, increasing indebtedness, and procyclical finances of provincial governments.* Budget deficits in the Argentine provinces throughout the 1990s constituted a key element of the convertibility regime's fiscal vulnerability. Furthermore, provincial public spending has been highly procyclical.
- *Bailouts.* In several instances and through several different channels, the federal government undertook financial rescue operations in some provinces.

12. The list is taken from a consensus developed at a forum in Argentina convened by the think tank Fundación Gobierno y Sociedad with the participation of political and academic specialists from throughout Argentina (summarized in the document CEDI 1999). Most international specialists agree with this diagnosis. See, for example, Tanzi (1996), Bird (1996), and Shah (1994). See also Cuevas (2003), Schwartz and Liuksila (1997), and World Bank (1996; 1998). For statements by the actors themselves, see Ardanaz (2004), who provides an account of statements about the federal fiscal system during the constitutional convention of 1994.

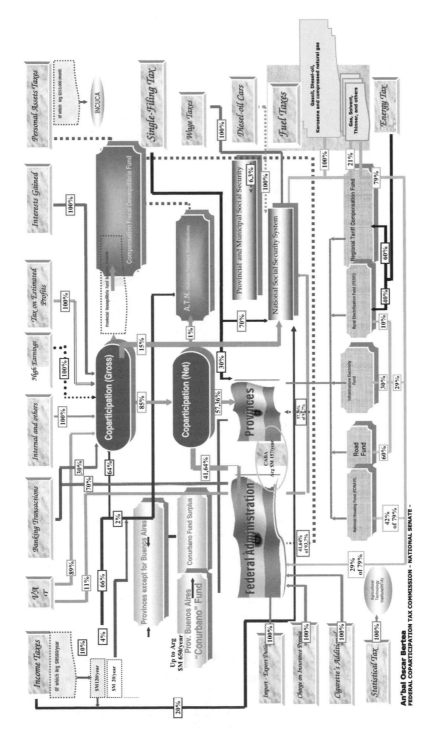

Figure 4.2. Argentina: *Coparticipación's* labyrinth – March 2002

- *Poor provincial and national tax collection.* Tax compliance at the provincial and national levels is quite low by international standards. Provincial authorities have few incentives to raise local taxes or to assist in the enforcement of national taxes.
- *Distortive national taxation.* The fact that some taxes are shared and others are not creates a bias in national tax policies toward nonshared taxes, which end up being inefficiently high. In the past, these taxes included trade taxes and the inflation tax. After the reforms of the 1990s, tariffs and the inflation tax were reduced, but the national government opportunistically manipulated payroll taxes and taxes on financial transactions.
- *Very distortive provincial taxation.* Most provincial revenues come from the gross receipts tax, a complex sales tax applicable at all stages of production. It leads to very high final effective rates for particular goods, and it fosters potentially large differences in effective rates for different types of final goods and even for producers of the same good (Cuevas 2003: 14).
- *Inefficiencies in the fiscal mix and difficulties for national fiscal adjustment.* During periods of fiscal stress, the national government is forced to adjust too much national spending, given that any effort to increase tax collection automatically funnels 50 percent to the provinces, which tend to spend it.
- *Inefficiencies in the provision of local public goods.* The federal system does not provide stable financing for critical goods provided by the provinces, such as education.
- *Insufficient capital spending by the provinces.* Provincial programs are increasingly financed by earmarked transfers from the center. The *Business Week* article at the beginning of this chapter refers to the tendency of provincial governments to substitute current spending for capital spending.

The Sources of Argentina's Fiscal Inefficiencies: Entering the Labyrinth

Following the approach of Part I, we can interpret the evolution and performance of the federal fiscal system as the outcome of a noncooperative game involving national and subnational authorities.[13] Argentina's fiscal

13. For this first approximation, we are ignoring agency problems between citizens and their representatives. As a matter of fact, there are important reinforcement

inefficiencies can be interpreted as the results of opportunistic actions in a noncooperative equilibrium, and rigidities that the players impose in order to protect themselves from the opportunistic actions of the others.

One typical example of opportunism is when subnational governments adopt a lax fiscal stance in the expectation that they will be bailed out in the event of a fiscal crisis. Such behavior is mirrored in the opportunism of the federal government, whose generosity at bailout time depends on the political alignment of the subnational government in question or on the exchange of bailouts for favorable votes in the national Congress.

Noncooperative behavior also affects the quality of the tax system. Intergovernmental agreements tend to create a systemic incentive for the national government to increase nonshared taxes, which are often less efficient ones. Rigidities such as minimum revenue guarantees were gradually introduced in intergovernmental negotiations as a way of ensuring some property rights in a weak institutional environment.

The features of policies pertaining to fiscal federalism, then, can be explained applying the logic of Proposition 1 in Chapter 2. The federal fiscal game is a game nested within the broader Argentine political game this book is about. This important nested game has noncooperation as an equilibrium for reasons that relate to the general incapacity of the Argentine political system to strike intertemporal political agreements that lead to efficient policies as well as to path-dependent features of the federal fiscal game itself. At each step, inefficient rules, clauses, and temporary provisions establish a reality that is extremely difficult to change in subsequent negotiations. These problems, as well as the unfulfillment of promises made in "fiscal pacts" are illustrations of transaction cost politics at work in a poor institutional environment. We devote the rest of the chapter to developing an analytic narrative of some of the key events in the recent evolution of the federal fiscal system.

THE EVOLUTION OF FEDERAL FISCAL ARRANGEMENTS IN ARGENTINA: TRANSACTION COST POLITICS AT WORK

Background: Historical Evolution of Argentine Fiscal Federalism

The 1853 Constitution established a division of tax sources. It gave the federal government exclusive rights to fix import and export duties and

effects between the transaction cost politics across governmental units that we emphasize here and the quality of democracy in Argentina. We come back to this important point later.

to levy taxes for a specified time "whenever the defense, common safety, or general welfare of the State so require." Provincial governments were explicitly forbidden to impose export and import taxes, and only the national Congress could require "special contributions."

Even though the scope of action reserved for the central government was originally limited, as soon as national unification was achieved, the national government started to intervene extensively.[14] In spite of this expansion of the federal government's regulatory authority, until 1890 the balance of power among the two levels of government was maintained, mostly as a result of the restrictive electoral participation of the time. The presidential selection process relied on a system of local party bosses, and seats in the national Congress were held by the provincial elites who ruled their communities (Rock 1987). Federal intervention was mainly used to maintain the balance of power among factions.

Financially, both the federal government and the provinces had their own sources of revenue, the former using taxes on foreign trade and the latter relying on internal taxes. Because there were almost no transfers between levels of government, each had to adjust its spending to meet its own budget constraints. Over time, however, this balance started to unravel. During the mid-1880s, many provincial leaders discovered that they could circumvent budget constraints by taking on public debt. The provincial banks soon became the chief source of new paper money issues, trebling the amount of paper money in circulation. Benefiting from the country's reputation, the provinces turned into heavy gold borrowers abroad. By 1890, the provincial banks and provincial governments held some 35 percent of Argentina's foreign debt.

In 1890, a crisis of confidence hit the Argentine economy. New British investment ceased abruptly, and the prices of Argentina's goods declined. As a result of this, export earnings fell by some 25 percent. This crisis brought about the first important change in the effective distribution of tax powers. The ordinary resources of the federal government were affected by the balance-of-payments crisis (customs taxes represented four fifths of the national government's revenue) at the same time that the availability of foreign credit was interrupted. In this context, the national government

---

14. The most salient actions of the national government in the second half of the nineteenth century included the consolidation and refinancing of all public debts and the establishment of a national currency, a banking system, a national legal system, an integrated judicial system, a professional army, a taxation system, a national treasury, a national customs office, a national voting law, a system of public schooling, an academy of science, and other technical institutions.

assumed many of the debts the provinces had contracted during the previous decade. In return, the provinces were obliged to surrender control of certain local revenues and taxes. Consumption taxes were imposed as an emergency one-year measure. This "temporary" law was renewed year after year until 1935.

Thus, contrary to the U.S. experience of the 1840s, in exchange for being allowed to collect domestic taxes, the Argentine federal government bailed out the provinces from financial difficulties caused by aggressive spending funded by borrowing.[15] This was an important change in the rules of the game, as the tax bases were no longer separated. The gray area that was created acquired a life of its own. It set the stage, moreover, for the evolution of intergovernmental relations in the future. In the following years, additional arrangements further centralized taxation and added to the redistributive nature of the federal fiscal system.

The 1890 crisis also had political consequences, including the eventual formation of an important opposition party to the conservative regime, the Unión Cívica Radical. In 1912, the expansion of the electorate strengthened the UCR, which captured the control of some provinces, increased its representation in Congress, and eventually attained the presidency in 1916. The system of decentralized authority that had characterized Argentine politics became unglued, and the country entered a period of increasing centralization of power. In order to carry out his program, President Hipólito Yrigoyen needed control over Congress, so he turned to the device of federal intervention to supplant the conservatives and their party machines in the provinces.[16]

In 1930, in the midst of the international economic crisis, a military coup inaugurated a period of deep political instability. Unstable semidemocratic and military regimes dominated the political scene for the next fifty-three years. These political fluctuations also had an impact on the federal fiscal system, as policies that were adopted by civilian governments were subsequently reversed by military regimes and vice versa. During the first military government (1930–2), new national taxes were created to reduce the government's dependence on revenue from import duties. Under the subsequent administration, the then-restored Congress passed a series of laws restructuring the tax system. In particular, Law

15. See Wibbels (2003) for an explanation of the "no bailout" outcome of the U.S. state debt crisis of the 1840s.
16. During his term, there were an unprecedented twenty interventions, fifteen of them by executive decree (Rock 1987: 199).

12.139, Unification of Internal Taxes, initiated the tax-sharing, or *coparticipación,* era. The law placed tax collection under the national government and established the sharing of its proceeds by the provinces. As a result of this new scheme, each province traded the right to collect taxes in its own territory for a share of the total taxes collected throughout the country.

In later years, when power was more concentrated in the national government (mostly during military regimes), changes tended to shift the distribution of shared taxes in its favor. This was achieved by different means, such as explicitly decreasing the proportion of tax revenues the national government had to share with the provinces, or (more subtly) by introducing new taxes not to be shared or increasing the rates of existing but unshared ones. Some military governments also weighted the federal fiscal system and electoral laws in favor of backward provinces, which they thought might become their future political strongholds. Conversely, under more democratic regimes, the once-again elected provincial governors and legislators fought to reverse the changes that the previous regime had instituted.

The long night of recurring military interruptions to democracy ended in December of 1983, when the violent 1976–83 military dictatorship surrendered the government to President Raúl Alfonsín of the UCR. The extant tax-sharing law, dating from 1973, expired in 1983. During the first several years of democratic government, there were intense negotiations for a new law, but it was impossible to reach a rational agreement. For most of that time, the revenue from shared taxes was distributed in an ad hoc manner on the basis of spot bargaining power. In 1987, the government lost the midterm congressional election to the Peronists and was under IMF pressure to reform its tax system. In that context, a 1988 law reduced the primary share going to the national government and froze some secondary sharing coefficients that were the (path-dependent) product of bargaining power at that time. The province of Buenos Aires, for instance, in the hands of the same party as the national government, was forced to surrender part of its share in order to get the small, overrepresented Peronist provinces to approve the tax reform package requested by the IMF.

The story briefly narrated here (see Saiegh and Tommasi 1998 for more details) is full of opportunistic behavior and the use of economically inefficient instruments to obtain political advantages, given an inability to bargain more efficiently. In the rest of the section, we provide a slightly more detailed analytic narrative of the evolution of the federal fiscal system throughout the 1990s, using the logic of the theory developed in Chapter 1 in order to understand that evolution.

An Analytical Framework for Looking at the Recent Dynamics of Federal Fiscal Arrangements

We begin by casting the Argentine federal fiscal process in the language of a dynamic political transactions game, characterized by (1) contracting moments in which rules are set and (2) regular play given those rules. After synthesizing the theory applied to this game, we describe the main contracting moments and the actions actually undertaken in the last several years in the federal fiscal game. The players in this game are the twenty-four subnational governments plus a national actor. For simplicity, we treat provincial governments (but not the national government) as unitary actors.[17] We use the term *national actor* instead of *national government* because we treat the national government as a whole (including Congress) as one of the decision arenas in which this game is played. National interest, then, refers to those interests represented in the national government that are purely "national." We can think of the executive as representing the national actor. This national actor has, on the one hand, a more encompassing interest in national public goods (such as macroeconomic stability and economic growth) than do provincial governments, but it also has some private political interests (for example, it enjoys political benefits from national spending but dislikes the political costs of national taxation).

Inherited features of the fiscal and political environment would map onto key parameters of the game. Vertical fiscal imbalances, the discretion of the executive to allocate the national budget, and the possibility of creating special channels through Congress all constitute part of the description of the stage-game. Other aspects of the Argentine political system in general and of intergovernmental arenas in particular correspond to the intertemporal patterns of play and to possible enforcement technologies.

The stage-game, then, is characterized by the following:

1. Governance rules, including the effective workings of the institutions of the federal government, as well as inherited features of the federal fiscal system. Some of these rules, such as fiscal assignments, can be

---

17. In the next section, we consider problems of agency between provincial citizens and provincial governments.

changed at contracting moments. Others are exogenous, such as the role of the Supreme Court in mediating conflicts between the national government and provincial governments.

2. Economic shocks (θ, in the language of Part I), such as changes in tax technologies, fiscal needs, or the fiscal capacities of the different jurisdictions. If the national government gets an important fraction of its revenue from taxing international trade, for example, its revenue-raising possibilities could be severely affected by factors such as the international prices of the country's main exports.

3. Political shocks (μ, in the language of Part I), which describe the relative power of different actors at different points in time. Presidents, for example, have a tendency to favor their regions of origin, and partisan configurations of the national Congress make different sets of provinces pivotal in the governmental coalition.

4. Economic state variables that are affected by economic shocks as well as by the actors' previous choices.[18] The level of debt or debt-servicing capacity, for instance, will be affected by exogenous factors such as international interest rates or terms of trade, as well as by past choices regarding taxation and spending.

Note that the game we are describing is a little bit more complicated than the one we analyzed in Chapter 2. The introduction of state variables makes this a truly dynamic game as opposed to just a repeated game. For the sake of simplicity, we will assume that a repeated game like the one analyzed in Chapter 2 is played between contracting moments and that contracting moments are convened depending upon the value of state variables and of economic and political shocks.

The regular actions that each player could take include (a) participating in collective choices under the extant governance rules; (b) making individual policy choices, such as how much to spend on particular goods or how much revenue to raise from different tax sources; and (c) participating in political deals, such as when a province sells its votes in Congress in exchange for a fiscal favor from the national government or when the national government delivers such a favor.[19]

---

18. In dynamic decision problems, state variables are variables that are taken as given at any particular decision moment but that are affected by previous actions. Games that include state variables are called dynamic games.

19. Such opportunistic political deals would not be undertaken in a globally cooperative equilibrium of the game.

Contracting moments (pacts) will be convened under some circumstances. The decision whether to convene a contracting moment will depend on whether the costs of convening them are low and whether the expected future payoffs from continuing to play the game as before are low enough for actors with sufficient political power. The 1994 constitutional change is one such example. In 1994, the president needed a constitutional change to be allowed to seek reelection, and that opened a window of opportunity for a contracting moment (a constitutional convention) in the federal fiscal game.[20]

At those contracting moments, actors attempt to do several things, including adjust to economic shocks or to the evolution of economic state variables, coordinate changes in actions, improve relative positions, fix rigid sharing rules, and modify procedures to avoid opportunism (change governance rules). Some of these things are efficiency enhancing, some are opportunistically redistributive, and many have elements of both efficiency and redistribution.

Enforcement of those contracts may be problematic; some things will be easier to enforce than others. Instantaneous actions with instantaneous payoffs are more likely to be undertaken than those that require high up-front costs or continuous action. (In the language of Chapter 2, the Z characteristics of the different policies will matter.) Fulfilling or not fulfilling the promises contained in the pacts will also be individual decisions later on during regular play of the game.

Using this language, we now provide a brief overview of some of the main contracting moments during the 1990s.

The Fiscal Pacts of 1992 and 1993

Two of the salient moments in the recent history of fiscal federalism in Argentina are the so-called fiscal pacts of 1992 and 1993. For brevity, and given their closeness in time, we treat them jointly.

Background. The 1992–3 pacts and some related measures were the result of President Menem's successful core economic policies in the early 1990s. The main effect of those market-oriented reforms on intergovernmental relations was to shift the net fiscal position of the national and provincial governments in a way that increased provincial total revenues, decreased

---

20. The value of μ in our federal fiscal game is in part related to events in other connected games such as national politics.

Table 4.4. *National Tax Revenues, 1988–1994 (millions of year 2000 pesos)*

Year	Social Security	External Trade	VAT	Fuel and Internal Taxes	Income Tax	Other Taxes	Total Legislated Taxes	Inflation Tax
1988	10,901	3,651	6,333	7,898	3,093	7,083	38,962	11,758
1989	8,574	5,836	4,574	6,268	2,343	809	35,718	26,421
1990	9,308	4,537	5,796	5,130	1,380	6,077	32,231	13,052
1991	12,114	1,750	8,805	6,062	1,444	6,997	37,175	2,536
1992	9,926	2,219	15,376	5,268	2,892	4,083	39,768	
1993	11,203	2,537	17,000	4,352	4,389	2,540	42,086	
1994	11,558	2,735	17,432	4,231	5,846	2,133	43,934	

Source: Tommasi (2002).

national total revenues, and increased national spending responsibilities. (These changes constitute an "economic shock" from the point of view of the federal fiscal game.)

The increase in provincial total revenues came mostly from an increase in shared taxes and a sympathetic increase in provincial tax revenues. The increase in shared taxes was due to a reverse Olivera–Tanzi effect after stabilization (that is, a reduction in inflation that increased real tax collection), as well as to changes in the structure of taxes. The new structure of taxes was characterized by a large increase in the value-added tax due to increased rates and base and in income taxes and by a decrease in trade taxes due to economic liberalization. The drop in relative national revenues was due to this decrease in exclusive trade taxes as well as to the loss of seigniorage from reduced inflation. Table 4.4 gives a sense of the quantitative significance of these changes.

On the side of spending responsibilities, the main change was induced by the reform of the pension system. The pension reform included a series of measures, most of which increased the short-term fiscal burden of the national government. Its main component gave people the option of staying in the public pay-as-you-go system or moving to one of private accounts. Given the nature of the transition, most senior workers stayed in the public system, while most younger workers moved to the private one, increasing the short-term fiscal burden of servicing pension obligations. This factor was a crucial component of the fiscal pact negotiations.

As mentioned earlier, in 1992 the national executive changed the distribution of federal taxes by means of a series of laws and decrees aimed at providing funds to increase pension payments. Because it was a unilateral move by the executive, the provinces initiated legal actions in the Supreme Court. Indeed, a clause in the first fiscal pact stated that those provinces that had initiated legal action against the national government in reference to those decrees had to cancel them. (The events described in this paragraph reflect some of the transactional difficulties of the case.)

Objectives. The federal fiscal pacts of 1992 and 1993 were a manifestation of rather complex political exchanges that included efficiency-enhancing reforms, attempts to deal with economic emergencies, attempts to adjust some allocations to changing circumstances, and some clever (and at times opportunistic) political maneuvering. (In the language of our framework, the previous sentence combines economic shocks, political shocks, and opportunistic behavior.) Among the worthy objectives pursued by the federal government, we might include an attempt to push for fiscal retrenchment at the provincial level, an attempt to reform some very inefficient provincial taxes, and the privatization of some provincial public utilities and public provincial banks.

Content and Political Exchanges. The 1992 pact diverted 15 percent of *coparticipación* funds to help pay for reform of the national pension system. In return, the government established a guaranteed floor on *coparticipación* payments. To reach this pact, the president used other transfers, as well as the reform itself, to put together a coalition that spanned both houses: He allied with Buenos Aires province for its weight in the Chamber of Deputies and with the low-population provinces for their weight in the Senate. A new special fund, *Fondo del Conurbano,* helped secure the support of legislators from Buenos Aires. For the small provinces, the new arrangement promised *coparticipación* revenues plus discretionary transfers that, in a few cases, were very high (for details, see Tommasi 2002). In the second fiscal pact, in exchange for being granted the requests listed earlier, the federal government agreed to increase minimum *coparticipación* transfers, to postpone and possibly forgo certain provincial debt obligations, and to take over responsibility for funding provincial pension systems. (Several of these clauses, especially the *coparticipación* floors, represent the type of rigidities identified in our theoretical framework.)

The Pacts and Their Fulfillment. The fulfillment of these pacts was partial. Promises that were easier to implement were fulfilled. Some promises by

Table 4.5. *Some Features of the 1992 Fiscal Pact*

Agreement	Degree of Fulfillment
a. 15% of the total *coparticipación* (prior to all distribution) was assigned to finance the pension system.	Total
b. The federal government guaranteed a monthly transfer of 725 million pesos to the provinces.	Total
c. A monthly fund of 43.8 million pesos (Fondo de Desequilibrios Regionales) was established, in order to finance regional imbalances. This fund was distributed among the provinces without regard for the secondary distribution stated in Law 23.548.	Total
d. The federal government would automatically transfer resources from the National Housing Fund (FONAVI), Federal Electricity Development Fund (FEDEI), and the Federal Roads Fund (Fondo Vial Federal).	Total
e. Provinces would ask their legislatures to sanction balanced budgets.	None
f. Both the federal government and the provinces agreed not to increase their expenditures more than 10% above the 1992 current expenditure.	5 provinces

Source: Tommasi (2002)

the national government, such as the *coparticipación* floors, were easy to comply with given the good macroeconomic situation, but many of the fundamental reforms at the provincial level did not take place. Table 4.5 lists some components of the pacts and the degree to which they have been fulfilled. Table 4.6 provides a more detailed description of the fulfillment of different reforms by different provinces.

Table 4.6 shows that the degree of fulfillment was uneven across provinces and across reforms, with some key reforms, such as the replacement of the turnover tax, failing altogether. The following description is particularly telling:

Tax reform was clearly the centerpiece of the second fiscal pact. Provinces adhering to the pact committed themselves to eliminating stamp taxes on checking accounts, taxes on the transfer of fuel, gas and electricity and, most important, phasing out the provincial turnover tax. . . .

   Other alternatives for improving provincial revenue would be beneficial in the long run, but would not yield short-term results. . . . Similarly, improving real estate taxation would require substantial initial efforts, including, for example,

Table 4.6. *Degree of Fulfillment of 1992 and 1993 Fiscal Pacts*

Legend: Total fulfillment · Partial · no fulfillment · no · municipal

improving property mapping and property registries; providing better and more consistent application of valuation techniques; improving the exchange of information between local tax offices, property registries. . . .

The announcement in December 1993 that federal payroll taxes levied on employers would be reduced, depending on region and sector, in those provinces participating in the second pact, increased pressure on provincial governments to join. By May 1994, all but one provincial legislature had ratified the second fiscal pact, and most had taken at least some initial steps toward implementation. Also the provinces were given a minimum revenue guarantee and some other guaranteed fixed payments that provided a floor of federal transfers equivalent to about 4.5% of GDP annually.

The second fiscal pact clearly shows the "horse-trading" that is involved in implementing structural reforms of the system of fiscal federalism, . . . but came at the expense of making payroll taxes an explicit instrument of regional and sectoral policies, and contributed to the growing social security deficit. (Schwartz and Liuksila 1997: 408–12)

The 1992–3 pacts illustrate the Argentine government's inability to make intertemporal trades that have the nature of investments (that is, up-front costs and a later stream of benefits). It shows that the extant federal governance structure of Argentina cannot support such trades. All in all, the 1992–3 pacts left a mixed landscape, including some successes, like the privatization of some provincial banks, and some failures, such as the nonreform of provincial tax systems. Clearly, the basic incentives and fundamental governance of the underlying federal fiscal game were not altered. That is reflected in the need for later reform attempts, such as the one in the 1994 Constitutional reform, to which we now turn.

The Tax-Sharing Regime in the 1994 Constitution

Toward the end of his first term, President Menem promoted a constitutional reform that would allow him to run for election to a second term in office.[21] He made a pact with the leader of the opposition party (UCR) in which they proposed some changes to the Constitution. Several provincial leaders saw an opportunity to add some clauses to the tax-sharing regime specified in the Constitution and made their support in Congress (and later at the constitutional convention) conditional on that. (This opportunity to engrave some principles of tax sharing in the Constitution constitutes a political shock lowering the cost of convening a contractual moment over federal issues.)

---

21. This section draws from Ardanaz (2004).

The final constitutional text regarding federal fiscal arrangements was the outcome of complex negotiations among the federal government (the president and national ministers) and the provinces (provincial governors and provincial party leaders). The alliances among these actors changed throughout the process according to the issues at stake and the positions adopted by their districts.

The provinces initially tried to get actual sharing coefficients written into the Constitution, but the national executive was able to convince them to settle for procedural mechanisms regarding the future sharing agreement. The provinces were able to establish procedures that would in principle protect them from the federal government's unilateral influence. The negotiations at the constitutional convention as well as the final text are very clear illustrations of transaction cost politics at work. We present now a summary of the final text (National Constitution, 1994, art. 75, para. 2), with our transaction cost–politics interpretation of the clauses:[22]

A Ley Convenio *based on understandings between the nation and the provinces will establish systems of* Coparticipación *in taxes.*

A *Ley Convenio* is a special procedure that requires a law, after being approved by Congress, to be authorized by each provincial legislature before taking effect. This clause results from actors' distrust of each other based on past failures to honor agreements and open attempts to violate them. The conditions are so demanding that it would be rare to see such an agreement come to life; no such law had been passed by the time of this writing.

The automatic delivery of funds is guaranteed.

This relates to the fact that sometimes in the past the federal government delayed payments.

All taxes collected by the national government (other than foreign trade taxes) should be shared.

22. Even the morphology (in particular, the length) of this paragraph is an anomaly within the Constitution, reflecting the political saliency and transactional complexity of this issue. Ardanaz (2004) presents multiple statements by members of the constitutional convention, such as provincial governors, explaining the rationale of each of the clauses by reference to previous opportunistic behavior by other actors, especially the national government.

This clause is intended to prevent the opportunistic creation of nonshared taxes, a very common practice that was even repeated *after* this version of the Constitution was approved.

The distribution between the nation and the rest of the districts – and among these districts – shall be carried out in direct conformity with the capacities, services, and functions performed by the jurisdiction, in compliance with objective distribution criteria.

This clause calls for the application of the criteria of "fiscal capacity" and "fiscal needs," which are standard principles of tax assignments in federal systems (Ter-Minassian 1997).

This distribution must be based on principles of equity and solidarity, giving priority to the achievement of similar levels of development, living standards, and equal opportunities throughout the national territory.

This is a typical constitutional declaration of a very "incomplete contract" nature, providing the foundation for interjurisdictional redistribution.

The Ley Convenio *is to be originated in the Senate and shall be enacted with the absolute majority of all the members of each house.*

This procedure is a warranty, mainly for small provinces, that actors such as Buenos Aires (because of its numerical superiority in the Chamber of Deputies) or the federal government (an actor with sufficient resources to buy support) would not be able to pass a reform of the federal fiscal regime without support from most of the provinces. The selection of the Senate as the chamber where the bill should originate favors the small provinces. The requirement of an absolute majority of all members of each house also protects against opportunism and increases the procedural hurdles to be overcome by a new law.

It may not be unilaterally amended nor regulated, and must be approved by the provinces.

The explicit mention of unilateral actions is a clear demonstration of the concerns of the provinces. The ability of the national executive to act unilaterally has been behind the nation's inability to enforce the political transactions necessary to build a more efficient system.

No transfer of jurisdiction, services, or functions can be done without the corresponding reallocation of funds approved by a law from Congress and by the relevant province or the city of Buenos Aires, as required in each case.

This clause, which also intends to protect the provinces against opportunistic actions by the national government, is a response to previous experiences with the decentralization of public services in which the national government did not always transfer adequate funding to carry out assigned responsibilities. (See the discussion of education decentralization in Tommasi 2002.)

A federal fiscal entity [Organismo Fiscal Federal] *shall be in charge of controlling the implementation and execution of this article, in accordance with the abovementioned law. The representation of all provinces and of the city of Buenos Aires in the composition of this institution is guaranteed.*

The requirement that a federal fiscal institution be created to control the implementation of decisions is a clear sign that the provinces do not trust the federal government – the default actor in charge of the implementation. Along with all the other mechanisms set forth to ensure that they would not be tricked into accepting losses when designing the regime, the provinces believed that during the implementation phase the federal government could misinterpret – or ignore – agreements reached earlier. To prevent that from happening, the implementation was to be supervised by an organ that represents all the districts. This is a clear illustration of the importance of governance in a context of incomplete contracting.

All the highlighted points reflect the transaction cost politics nature of the problem. The very constitutional status of the issue is a reflection of its importance and of the fear of opportunism by some actors. Furthermore, all the important clauses represent the actors' attempts to protect themselves from opportunistic behavior (by procedural means, by forbidding certain actions, and by adding veto gates). These procedures, while giving some assurances to the parties involved, have at the same time decreased the likelihood of a comprehensive reform of the system.

The Saga Continued

The Constitution required that the *Ley Convenio* establishing the new tax-sharing agreement be sanctioned by the end of 1996. That constitutional mandate was not fulfilled then, and it has not been fulfilled yet. No proposal has yet mustered enough support (even within the executive branch) to get serious political attention. Argentina has signed several agreements with the IMF promising to pass a *Coparticipación* law but has failed to do so. On the one hand, the complex procedural constraints imposed by the Constitution do not facilitate the passage of a new law, and this adds to the intrinsic transaction cost politics complexity of passing a definitive regime. Furthermore, the usual agenda setter in these matters is the national executive branch, which is reluctant to adopt a regime that would constrain some of its own unilateral moves.

In hindsight, it is clear that the fiscal path Argentina chose was far from the best one to prevent a terrible crisis like that of 2001–2.[23] Both a more relaxed fiscal stance in the second Menem administration and the dynamics of provincial finances put the country on a risky path that, combined with several negative shocks and wild fluctuations in international market conditions and sentiment, precipitated the crisis. During the 1993–8 period, when the Argentine economy was generally performing well and the Argentine government was receiving substantial nonrecurring revenues from privatization and enjoying other temporary fiscal benefits, the public sector debt nevertheless rose by 12 percentage points over Gross Domestic Product (GDP). Spending rose substantially (especially at the provincial level) during the good years after Mexico's 1994 crisis, and the adjustment to the difficult times starting in 1999 was too late. From 1996 to 1999, primary expenditures increased almost 20 percent at the provincial level and 14 percent at the national level.

The inadequate fiscal discipline displayed by national and provincial authorities was the consequence of politics as usual, in spite of the fact that some loopholes had been closed by the convertibility regime and some additional measures.[24] The behavior of public finances was in large measure linked to the 1999 presidential campaign. Early in the game, when President Menem attempted to run for a third term despite its unconstitutionality, he eased the national fiscal stance in order to gain support. The other contender for the Peronist candidacy was the governor of Buenos Aires, Eduardo Duhalde. First in fighting Menem's reelection bid and then in fighting the interparty presidential competition as the Peronist candidate, Duhalde made generous use of the largest budget in the country, that of the province of Buenos Aires. Given the importance of the province and

---

23. Galiani, Heymann, and Tommasi (2003) provide a nuanced analysis of the determinants of the 2001–2 crisis.
24. These measures led to an overly enthusiastic assessment of the fiscal sustainability of Argentina by international organizations such as the World Bank and the International Monetary Fund, who were bullish about some accomplishments such as the privatization of several provincial banks and the approval of a fiscal responsibility law in 1999. Braun and Tommasi (2004) provide a more detailed critique of some of those assessments.

its strong federal fiscal linkages, those actions had dire consequences for Argentina.

In spite of all these efforts, Duhalde lost the 1999 presidential election to Fernando de la Rúa, the candidate of an alliance between the traditional UCR and the Frepaso (a newly formed federation of center-left parties). Right after the presidential election and shortly after the incoming administration took office, two new fiscal pacts (1999 and 2000) were signed. These pacts turned out to be a crucial link between fiscal federalism and the Argentine disaster of 2001–2.

The turn of the century found Argentina trying to overcome the harsh recession that began in the middle of 1998, which was mainly a result of the Brazilian and Russian crises of the latter part of the decade and was intensified by the Brazilian devaluation of 1999. As soon as the results of the presidential election were known, the future economics minister announced that the budget for 2000 would need to be scaled back because the Menem administration's predictions of growth had been too high. But the opposition Peronist governors, who controlled a large chunk of the congressional vote, withheld their support for this plan. In order to comply with the deficit limits allowed by previous agreements with the IMF, the incoming administration decided to negotiate a new fiscal pact – economic and political shocks pressuring for a contractual moment. This agreement was reached in December 1999, four days before the de la Rúa administration came into office.

The central government committed to transfer a fixed amount to the provinces independently of the revenues collected – a new rigidity. The new administration envisioned that by raising income and sales taxes (the so-called *impuestazo*) it could collect enough to neutralize the fiscal deficit. The central government also committed to implement a plan of financial assistance and financial reform to support the provinces in 2000 called the Fondo Fiduciario para el Desarrollo Provincial (FFDP). The provinces agreed to pass solvency and fiscal responsibility laws and to fulfill the terms of the FFDP. The (partial) degree of fulfillment is summarized in Table 4.7. Note that the pact calls for the fulfillment of clauses in the 1992 and 1993 pacts, clauses that remain unfulfilled today.

After taking office, the de la Rúa administration weakened rather quickly. The government needed yet another fiscal pact in order to pass a budget for 2001. The circumstances and bargaining dynamics did not change much: They included an executive under foreign pressure for consistency, opportunism by some provinces, negotiations over topical issues as well as quasi-structural reforms, and some efficiency-enhancing

Table 4.7. *Some Features of the 1999 Fiscal Pact*

Agreement	Degree of Fulfillment
a. The federal government fixed a monthly transfer of 1,350 million pesos to the provinces.	Total until the 2001 disaster
b. Both the federal and the provincial governments commit to sanction the new *coparticipación* law (required by the 1994 constitution) during the year 2000.	None
c. The provincial governments commit to pass both solvency and fiscal responsibility laws in their provinces along the lines of the federal Fiscal Responsibility Law (FRL).	14 provinces passed this kind of law, but few fulfilled its requirements
d. Implementation of the FFDP program.	Mixed
e. Tax harmonization at all levels of government.	None
f. The federal government commits to finance provincial pension system deficits gradually if the province allows a federal audit.	Some assistance as provided to the provinces of Córdoba and Santa Fé

Source: Tommasi (2002).

paragraphs affecting budgeting practices and fiscal transparency that were added here and there. Governors complained loudly that the previous pact remained unfulfilled; some provinces blamed other provinces. They once again agreed to pass a *Coparticipación* law. Provincial governments gained some more room to administer the few remaining national social programs, a gain that was of limited use in solving the deep social problems of the country but of high political leverage given the clientelistic use of targeting. Once again, the degree of fulfillment was quite partial (Tommasi 2002).

The most important clause in practice was the establishment of a fixed amount to be transferred to the provinces. The following depiction of both pacts explains:

One major component of the Federal Agreement was that during the year 2000, the provinces would receive a fixed amount in automatic transfers. This provided the provinces with predictability in income, but the amount was also designed to allow the federal government to keep a larger share of incremental revenues expected both from an economic recovery and an increase in federal tax pressure. The calculation of the monthly fixed amount of $1.350 billion during 2000 was roughly based on the average of the previous two years.

The Agreement also established that during 2001 the provinces would begin to receive an average of the three most recent years' legal amounts. [. . .] in addition, the provinces were offered a minimum guaranty for 2001 that was set at a level 1 percent higher than the fixed amounts of 2000. . . .

One year later, this agreement was followed by a more comprehensive *Compromiso Federal por El Crecimiento y la Disciplina Fiscal*, signed in November 2000 by all provincial Governors, except the Governor of Santa Cruz, a small province in the south. This agreement included a number of clauses for provincial reforms in the area of state modernization, budgeting and the transparency of fiscal accounts. In terms of stabilizing transfers, this new agreement established a timetable for switching permanently to the moving average concept. However, as described below, there would still be guaranteed minimum amounts over the transition period.

For 2001 and 2002, the provinces would receive a fixed monthly amount equal to $1.364 billion. This figure was the guaranteed minimum for 2001 that had been stated in the previous 1999 *Compromiso* (where the actual amount was to be an average of the three most recent years). Now it would be *both* a floor and ceiling for *both* 2001 and 2002. The amount itself implies an increase of $14 million, or about 1 percent, over the amount received during 2000.

Note that it is not clear what the federal government would do with the expected savings from the lower transfers. A fiscal stabilization fund that would lock up the savings so that they could be used later during recessions is not explicitly established by this *Compromiso*, although there is general language stating that this fund would be established in due course. Depending upon what growth rates one assumes, over the five year period, the provinces would lose anywhere from $1.5 to $7 billion in transfers that they would have otherwise received.

Any major recessions over the period would have implied that the provinces could break even or come out ahead. As it turned out, the floor did not strongly favor the provinces during the first half of 2001. In addition, the federal government created a new financial transactions tax with the revenues proceeding exclusively to the federal treasury. However, during the second half of the year, the fixed transfers would have implied significantly more resources than otherwise would have been the case. For 2001, as a whole, the provinces were to receive about $2.8 billion (about 1.1 percent of GDP) in transfers beyond what they would have received without the guarantee. This contributed to substantial fiscal, political and social stress during the latter part of the year. Ultimately, the federal government was not able to transfer the full guarantee and arrears accumulated. (González, Rosenblatt, and Webb 2002: 6–8)

The bickering over this clause was an important factor in the demise of the de la Rúa government and the ensuing Argentine default. The delay by provincial governments in signing a new agreement and their issuing of low-denomination provincial debt to cover wages were key factors in demolishing Argentine credibility in the eyes of international markets (see "Back from the Brink," *The Economist*, November 16, 2001).

Political Institutions, Policy Making, and Policies

SOME NOTES ON FEDERALISM AND DEMOCRACY IN ARGENTINA

Before concluding the chapter, we want to highlight one dimension of crucial importance that, even though not the direct focus of our analysis, is deeply intertwined with Argentine-style federalism. That is what economists might refer to as the "agency problem" between citizens and politicians and what political scientists might refer to as the issue of "democratic accountability."

Several features of Argentine federalism and its impact on the Argentine political process not only lead to inefficient policies but also weaken the democratic accountability links between citizens and their representatives. Let us highlight here three channels by which the federal connection affects the quality of democracy in Argentina. First, national senators and deputies tend to represent provincial political powers, not citizens in general or specific groups of citizens. These powers, in turn, want to do little more than ensure that the center does not hold them accountable for fiscal transfers that allow them to maintain their political-economic machines.

Second, provincial citizens, especially in the majority of small, backward provinces, tend to overwhelmingly elect and reelect as governors the bosses of those clientelistic machines. Given the nature of the political and policy-making game, it is rational for voters to elect those politicians (or political machines) who are best at the game of extracting rents from the common central pool, even if they are not the most honest or competent administrators. Jones, Sanguinetti, and Tommasi (2002) and Remmer and Gelineau (2003) present evidence suggesting that the way in which voters respond to the policy performance of subnational governments attenuates rather than strengthens the nexus between policy responsibility and electoral accountability. Incumbent governors are not punished at the ballot box for inefficient fiscal policies or for poor economic performance, but they are rewarded for receiving more fiscal benefits from the center. These politicians clearly understand the system. Upon taking office in 2003, the incoming governor of Tucumán, José Alperovich, stated that the main objective of his administration would be to "obtain as much as we can from the central government" (Granado 2003: 4).

A third channel between Argentine federalism and the quality of democratic representation operates through its effects on the party system. Electoral rules combined with federal fiscal arrangements create a majoritarian bias in the political system, favoring dominant provincial parties in the small provinces that in turn are overrepresented in the national political arena. Furthermore, these biases interact with the differential capacity of different parties to translate fiscal resources into electoral support via clientelistic networks (see Calvo and Murillo 2004; 2006). These arrangements strengthen the political power of local party bosses in backward areas. At the same time, this system underrepresents the most modern segments of the population, the urban middle and upper classes, which are the potential base of support for more programmatic center-left or center-right parties, and so reinforces the weaknesses of the national policy-making arena.

CONCLUDING REMARKS

In this chapter, we have explored the intricate links between national and subnational policies and politics, with special focus on federal fiscal arrangements. We showed how the evolution of these arrangements and the poor political and fiscal incentives they generate could be traced to the logic of transaction cost politics. The incentives generated by the federal fiscal game, in turn, reinforce the institutional weaknesses of the national policy-making arena emphasized in this book.

In the next two chapters we look into the workings of two possible "technologies" for the enforcement/implementation of political and policy agreements: the judiciary and the bureaucracy.

5

The Supreme Court

WITH MATÍAS IARYCZOWER

In previous chapters, we discussed some of the features of the Argentine polity that limit the ability of politicians to enter into complex intertemporal transactions. In Chapter 3, for example, we showed that legislators lack basic incentives to develop professional careers, to invest in legislative capabilities, and to develop expertise that would allow them to control the bureaucracy. We claim that one of the features that limits legislators' incentives is the lack of judicial enforcement of policy agreements. In this chapter, we analyze the incentives and constraints facing Argentine justices that make it so that in equilibrium and on average the Court has not been a binding constraint on the workings of the Argentine executive.[1]

The common wisdom on the Argentine judiciary is that the Court is too obliging, too connected to the other political powers to serve as an independent source of political enforcement (Ekmekdjian 1999). Nevertheless, the lonely voices of those who question whether the Court really lacks independence have found support in the results of two studies, which show that in the second half of the twentieth century the Argentine government lost cases in a proportion similar to that of the U.S. government.[2]

---

1. This chapter draws from Iaryczower, Spiller, and Tommasi (2002).
2. Among them, Molinelli (1999) is perhaps the most outspoken. He has argued that there are several indications that since the 1930 coup the Court has increased its autonomy. After that, the court started to name its president, and justices started to come from within. In the 1950s, the Court introduced injunctions, which were only later introduced by law. The same happened with the concept of arbitrariness. In 1950, the Court began reducing the discretion of the presidents during de facto regimes. During the 1960s and 1970s, the Court increased the ability of litigants to sue the state, and it reduced the scope of the "political issues" doctrine. Thus, a more systematic approach to the study of Argentina's Supreme Court decisions is needed. See also Helmke (2002).

Hence, it is not obvious that the government's appointment powers are so overpowering as to void the implications of the division of power theory: that is, that an "aligned" Court will indulge the president and be unresponsive to changes in the political environment.

In this chapter, we explore these contrasting views of the Argentine courts using the analytical lens of positive political theory. A fundamental insight of the last fifteen years of PPT research is that in environments where political fragmentation is the norm, the judiciary is able, over time, to create a doctrine of judicial independence without fear of political reprisal. Similar attempts in more unified political environments, however, generate political clashes, eventually limiting the judiciary's power. The evolution of the doctrine of judicial review in the United States seems to fit this theory.[3] Yet the power, will, and ability of the U.S. Supreme Court to limit administrative discretion are less evident in other latitudes. Some very interesting research has shown that the power of the judiciary is limited in parliamentary systems like those in Japan and Europe, where the cabinet's control over the legislature limits the ability of the court to innovate.[4]

In this chapter, we present a study of judicial decision making in Argentina over the past sixty years. According to the division of power theory, the constitutional political fragmentation of Argentina should have produced a relatively independent judiciary. In fact, legal scholars have argued that this was the case until the first coup d'état in 1930. According to these studies, a doctrine of judicial independence was developing that was similar to the one developed in the United States.[5] Political instability, however, seems to have brought about a fundamental change in the relation of the polity to the Argentine Court.[6] Since the 1930s, civilian and military regimes have alternated regularly, the federal government has taken over various provincial administrations during civilian and military regimes alike, and economic policies have systematically generated low and volatile rates of economic growth. Such political instability generates the potential for judicial manipulation. Indeed, the Argentine Supreme Court has had its share of political manipulation. Justices have been removed via impeachment procedures and by force, the size of the Court

---

3. See Gely and Spiller (1992), Epstein and Knight (2000), and Helmke (2000). But see also Segal (1997) and references therein.
4. See, in particular, Cooter and Ginsburg (1996), Ramseyer and Rasmusen (1997), and Salzberger and Fenn (1999).
5. See, for instance, Miller (1997) and references therein.
6. See also Alston and Gallo (2005).

has grown and shrank, and in general, presidents from the mid-1940s until 1999 and from 2003 on have been able to govern with relatively sympathetic Supreme Courts. Contrast this scenario to the United States, where judges serve so long that they may die from natural causes on the bench or soon after leaving it, where more often than not presidents have to deal with antagonistic Court majorities, and where attempts to manipulate the size of the Court receive widespread press and public criticism.[7]

Hence, in contrast to the predictions of the division of power theory, political fragmentation seems to have created Argentine Supreme Court justices who, as the common wisdom suggests, would tend to treat successive federal governments with velvet gloves.[8] However, as we discussed earlier, recent scholarship challenges the notion that the government's appointment powers are so overpowering; instead, in the face of adverse political circumstances, the Argentine Supreme Court still presents as much a level of defiance to the executive as that of the United States.

Judicial independence is, though, an elusive concept. We refer to judicial independence as the extent to which justices can reflect their own judgments in their decisions without fearing retaliation from Congress or the president. From this, it follows rather directly that judicial independence cannot be measured simply by considering judicial reversals of governmental acts. The probability of a justice voting to reverse a governmental act is related to whether the justice *can* challenge the president but also to whether the justice *wants* to challenge the president. That is, it depends not only on the political constraints faced by the Court (on how fragmented its policy competitors are) and the possible political repercussions of reversal (such as legislative re-reversal of the Court's decision, expansion of the Court, or impeachment of a justice) but also on the justices' political alignment. Political alignment, in turn, depends on both the nomination process, which to some extent will reflect the political preferences of the time – at least as represented by elected officials – and on turnover on the Court. Courts whose justices' formal tenure is very short will naturally tend to be aligned with the appointing powers,

---

7. See Gely and Spiller (1992).
8. This is in fact the common wisdom, reflected both in public opinion polls and in most analysts' writings. See "Grandes Temas Pendientes de Argentina: Justicia," *La Nación*, Colección Especial, November 1999; and J. Miller (2000).

limiting the potential for conflict between the Court and the other political institutions. Courts whose tenure is indefinite or very long may alternate between political alignment and political opposition to the sitting government. Indeed, in the limit case, justices with policy preferences identical to those of the executive would face no political constraints, and their behavior would be, as a consequence, unaffected by the degree of political fragmentation.[9]

In this chapter, we test these two contrasting views of Argentine judicial decision making. On the one hand, the common wisdom is that the appointment powers of the president are so overwhelming that the justices' main political reference is simply the president. We test the common wisdom against the hypothesis that justices are strategic, and that their extent of defiance of the president will depend on the extent of political fragmentation. Thus, we develop a test of the independence hypothesis by empirically examining the political incentives of Argentine individual justices in their decision making. Our results show a complex story of often-defiant justices subject to constraints. Our measure of defiance is the probability of a justice who is not aligned with the government voting against it. We find that, in the middle of so much chaos and political upheaval, the Argentine Supreme Court has not been a simple rubber stamp. The probability of a justice's voting against the government depends on the political alignment of the justice, but the appointment power is bounded and does not by itself lead to complete political control of the Court. As Molinelli (1999) and Helmke (2000) have shown for the later period of our sample, over time the Court has reversed the government in a surprisingly large number of reasonably important cases, and the Court has more often reversed decisions made by de facto governments than those made by civilian governments.[10] We also find support for the division of power theory of Courts: Judicial decision making has been strategic. The probability of voting against the government falls as the control of the president over the legislature grows stronger and in particular with the president's ability to increase the Court's size or to successfully start impeachment procedures against justices.

---

9. See Spiller (1996). This is not true, however, when the executive loses its ability to veto legislation, as it would if the opposition dominated the legislature.
10. We cannot, however, discard the hypothesis that there is a selection bias in the types of cases brought under consideration during military governments.

Politics matter, then, in understanding Argentina's Supreme Court decisions. Argentine political history has tended to generate unified rather than divided governments, and there has been a path-dependent tendency of presidents to tinker with the composition of the Court. Thus, we find that the dependence of the Argentine Court is more the result of politics than of any lack of doctrine or of a pliable Supreme Court. A major result from this chapter, which we develop further in the last chapter of this book, is that the way to generate judicial independence in Argentina does not pass via judicial reform. Judicial independence, instead, will rise with the lengthening of Argentina's political actors' horizons.

The structure of this chapter is as follows. We provide next a historical background on the Court, showing the historical evolution of the Court and the remarkable instability in its composition. We then develop a model of judicial decision making under constraints, which serves as the framework for our empirical analysis, described together with the empirical results in the subsequent two sections. The chapter ends with concluding remarks.

ARGENTINA'S JUDICIARY: HISTORICAL BACKGROUND

Argentina embraced the U.S. system of constitutional control, in which justices, because of their formal independence,[11] have the authority to challenge norms that emanate from the political powers.[12] As in the United States, the Court's power to review the constitutionality of norms enacted by Congress or the executive was not granted explicitly in the Constitution but instead rose through Supreme Court decisions. As in the

---

11. Article 110 of the Constitution establishes that "The Supreme Court Justices and the lower courts of the Nation will keep their employment as long as in good standing, and will receive for their services a compensation determined by law, which will not be reduced in any way as long as they remain in their functions."

12. By norms, we mean laws, presidential decrees, administrative decisions, and resolutions. In Argentina, the Supreme Court may only forbid the application of a given norm to the particular case at hand. *Stare decisis* is the concept underlying the doctrine of precedent: An issue decided in a prior case should apply to a similar case that arises later on. Although in Argentina the *stare decisis* doctrine does not formally exist, the situation is practically the same as in the United States, for if lower courts do not apply the Supreme Court's jurisprudence, the affected party can always appeal to the Supreme Court, which will subsequently revoke the sentence. This may require the Court to see a large number of cases. See Molinelli (1999) and Bidart Campos (1982).

United States, the Argentine Supreme Court interpreted the Constitution to grant itself such authority, and it has continuously established doctrines defining the boundaries of this authority.[13] Even though the Court asserted its power of judicial review, it did so with restraint, just as the U.S. Supreme Court did (Nino 1992). In Argentina, though, self-restraint emerged in the midst of political instability and military interruptions of the democratic order.

Argentina's constitutional structure is similar to that of the United States, but its political history is extremely different. Between the first coup d'état in 1930 and the resumption of the democratic period in 1982, Argentina suffered six interruptions of democratic government. This instability had direct effects on the rotation of incumbent politicians, leading to extremely short tenure among presidents (on average, 2.6 years), national legislators (2.9 years), and provincial governors (1.9 years). The Supreme Court did not escape this instability. Although Supreme Court justices are appointed for life, from 1930 to 1990 their average tenure has been only 4.4 years, shorter than in most other countries (see Table 5.1).

Although the United States and Argentina had similar institutional beginnings, political instability has reduced Argentine justices' tenure dramatically (see Figure 5.1), and only at the end of the 1990s, after three consecutive democratic periods and despite President Menem's enlargement of the Court in 1990, did the tenure of justices start to return to a more normal level. The removal of justices during the Kirchner administration, however, again lowered the average tenure of the Court from a peak of 12.74 years to less than 8 years with the successful impeachment of Justice Boggiano in late 2005.[14]

13. See Arts. 31 and 116 of the Constitution. See also Ziulu (1998). As in the *Marbury v. Madison* decision, in the 1887 *Sojo* decision the Argentine Supreme Court declared the power of Courts to impose constitutional control over federal legislation (see Corte Suprema de Justicia de la Nación, *Fallos* 32:120). The following year, in *Municipalidad de la Capital c/Elortondo*, the Court expressly declared the unconstitutionality of a congressional law (see CSJN, *Fallos* 33:162). It had already considered the constitutionality of a presidential decree (see, for example, its 1863 *Ríos* decision in CSJN, *Fallos* 1:36).

14. The Senate impeached Justice Boggiano in September 2005. On August 2006, his removal was confirmed by an appeal panel at Federal Justices, acting in place of the Supreme. See "El Senado destituyó a Boggiano y lo inhabilitó para cargos públicos," *Clarín*, September 29, 2005; and "Boggiano, ratifican la remoción," *La Nación*, August 17, 2006.

Table 5.1. *Supreme Court Justices' Average Tenure in Selected Countries,*
1960–1990

Country	Judicial Tenure (number of years)	Country	Judicial Tenure (number of years)
USA	18.8	United Kingdom	6.4
Norway	16.2	Sri Lanka	5.8
New Zealand	15.3	Chile	5.7
Malaysia	14.7	Zambia	5.6
Ireland	14.7	Ghana	5.5
Australia	14.6	India	5.4
Singapore	14.5	Botswana	5.2
Canada	14.2	Philippines	4.9
Belgium	13.2	Zimbabwe	4.6
Guyana	12.7	Kenya	4.6
Germany, FR	12.2	Malawi	4.6
Netherlands	12.1	Pakistan	4.4
Italy	11.1	ARGENTINA	4.4
Jamaica	10.9	Peru	4.0
Trinidad & Tobago	10.6	Dominican Rep.	3.6
Nigeria	10.1	Cameroon	3.3
South Africa	8.3	Mexico	3.3
Bangladesh	8.1	Honduras	2.8
Brazil	7.2	Colombia	1.9
Nicaragua	7.1	Ecuador	1.9
Sudan	6.8	Guatemala	1.8
France	6.6	Paraguay	1.1
Israel	6.5	Total Average	8.0

Source: Henisz (2000).

After the impeachment of four of the five sitting justices during the
first Perón administration, the norm of judicial independence was lost.[15]
Molinelli describes the progression of the problem:

> The Argentine experience since 1948 does not look good: [we saw the] impeach-
> ment of four of its five members in that year; a constitutional requirement in
> 1949 that all sitting judges obtain legislative renewal at that time; the removal
> of all Supreme Court justices and of some judges of first and second instance by
> the military regimes of 1955, and the same in 1966 and 1976; an increase in the
> number of justices of the Supreme Court in 1960, attempts to do the same by Pres-
> idents Illia and Alfonsín, and a successful attempt by President Menem in 1990.
> (1999: 4)

---

15. For discussions on the break in the independence norm, see Miller (1997), Molinelli
   (1999), Helmke (2000), and Alston and Gallo (2005).

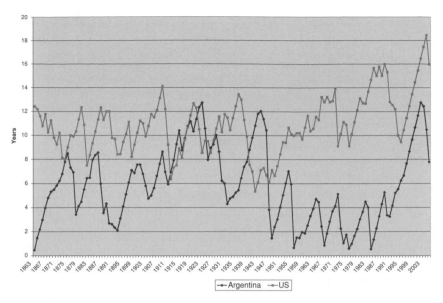

Figure 5.1. Supreme Court justices' tenure in Argentina and the United States, 1863–2005.
Note: The tenure of Argentine justices increased in the 1990s because of President Menem's long tenure in office (and despite his enlargement of the Court). As of the writing of this book, five judges have since been replaced.

To this list, we would add the successful complete renovation of the Supreme Court by President Kirchner.[16]

The change in the norm is clearly seen in numbers. Until Perón's presidency, 82 percent of Supreme Court justices left the Court because of (natural) death or retirement; between then and 1999, only 9 percent of the justices did so, while the other 91 percent resigned, were impeached, or were removed for other reasons (Molinelli, Palanza, and Sin 1999).

16. The renovation started in late 2002 when President Duhalde named Justice Maqueda after the resignation of Justice Bossert, who resigned after his failed impeachment. Chief Justice Nazareno resigned in June 2003 after a peculiar public condemnation by President Kirchner; Justice López resigned in October 2003 (dying a few months later); the Senate impeached Justice Moliné O'Connor in December 2003; and, upon the initiation of impeachment proceedings against him, Justice Vázquez resigned in September 2004. The renovation was completed with the impeachment of Justice Boggiano in September 2005. Overall, the new Peronist administration that replaced President De la Rúa left only two justices named from previous administrations, Justices Fayt and Petracchi, both named by former Radical President Alfonsín. As of the writing of this book, President Kirchner still has to appoint the impending vacancy of Justice Boggiano. See "El Senado destituyó a Boggiano y lo inhabilitó para cargos públicos." *Clarín*, September 29, 2005.

To these striking figures we should add the effect of Court enlargements, which at the very least have the potential to produce the same results as justices' removal, changing the Court's median voting position and potentially its final decisions.

These changes in Court composition constitute our first direct concern. In an environment of alternating governments, the appointment and dismissal procedure for justices that arises from Argentina's Constitution should naturally generate a balanced Court, with policy preferences being relatively independent of those of the sitting executive. Gradual replacement of departing justices by governments of different parties would rarely allow abrupt changes in the median justice's preference. Furthermore, in a divided government scenario, a balanced Court would lessen the power of the president to sway the composition of the Court through the nominating process. Instead, the maneuvering room enjoyed by each appointing president to name some or all Court members and the corresponding extremely short tenure of Argentine justices breaks this natural balance. The result is that since the first Perón administration only occasionally has a sitting president faced a Court whose majority was appointed by presidents from opposing political parties (see Figure 5.2).[17]

But irregular removals and appointments, the strategic alteration of the Court's size, and forced resignations are not the whole story. In addition, judicial behavior tends to be lenient toward the executive regardless of the Court's political alignment whenever the executive has the ability to punish the Court, whether by impeachment or by altering its size. First military interruptions and later the administration of President Perón generated a fundamental transformation in the relation between the Supreme Court and the Argentine polity. Whereas the 1930 coup d'état forced the Court to create the so-called emergency doctrine,[18] the impeachment by the administration of President Perón of four of the five sitting justices in the late 1940s seems to have broken the norm of judicial independence, making such a move a tolerable political action. The higher is society's

---

17. Analysts argue that this politicized appointment process and its implications for judicial independence is behind the low public esteem of the judiciary in Argentina. See Nino (1992), Ekmekdjian (1999), Morello (1996), and Masnatta (1997).
18. See also Cayuso and Gelli (1988), who claim that the military regime that arose from the coup of 1930 attempted to generate legitimacy by not removing the members of the Supreme Court, who, in turn, seem to have reciprocated by recognizing the provisional government. They did so by considering the need to impose a limit on the power of the provisional government. By considering the need to impose a limit, the court de facto recognized the military government.

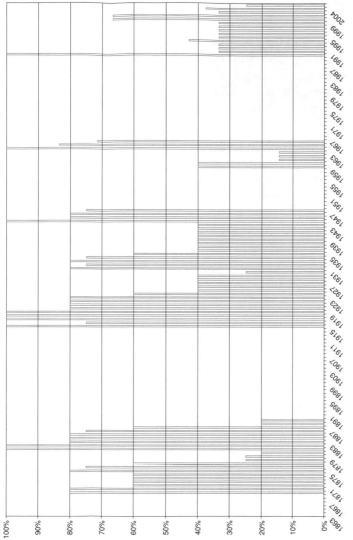

Figure 5.2. Percentage of Supreme Court appointed by presidents with opposing political leanings.

tolerance of these maneuvers, the higher is the credibility of the implicit threats and hence of justices' fear of retaliation. The result is erratic judicial processes and the development of a more permissive doctrine. Nino puts it this way: "The constant in the Argentine Supreme Court, with a few exceptional periods like the one of 1983–1989, was not a restrictive doctrinal approach to the judicial control of constitutionality, but an attitude of deference to the political power, that generally implied, although not always, a modest exercise of that control" (1992: 670).

Hence, while political fragmentation should have produced an independent judiciary, institutional instability and the weakening of the norm of judicial independence led analysts to argue that the Argentine Supreme Court did not constitute an effective check on the executive's wishes. Court independence has been questioned, sometimes severely, by legal opinion, and public opinion of the Argentine Court has been systematically low.[19] Figure 5.3 shows public confidence in the judiciary in seventeen Latin American countries. Only in Nicaragua do a higher fraction of respondents indicate no confidence in their judiciary.

A MODEL OF JUDICIAL DECISION MAKING UNDER CONSTRAINTS

In this section, we develop a simple model, which we implement empirically in the next section. The simplicity of the model is driven by the lack of roll calls in the Argentine Congress, which makes it almost impossible to develop independent measures of legislators' preferences and hence of justices' ideology (see Bergara, Richman, and Spiller 1999). Thus, we do not present a spatial model based on the standard liberal/conservative dimension, because it is not implementable for Argentina.

The model consists of three building blocks: players, preferences, and sequencing. There are three players: justices, the president, and Congress. We assume that justices are both strategically and politically motivated (Gely and Spiller 1990). They look ahead and vote strategically to maximize their policy benefits from their decisions. The president and members of Congress also have policy-oriented preferences. Their policy objectives, however, may not be similar. The president may or not have full control over the Congress. The formal sequence of events is as follows: Nature draws a particular piece of legislation. The Court reviews its

---

19. For some of this criticism, see Garay (1995), Nino (1992), Carrió (1996), Veronica Alter, "Es de Difícil Cumplimiento la Ley de Acceso a la Información," *La Nación*, July 11, 2000; and Petracchi (1987: 709).

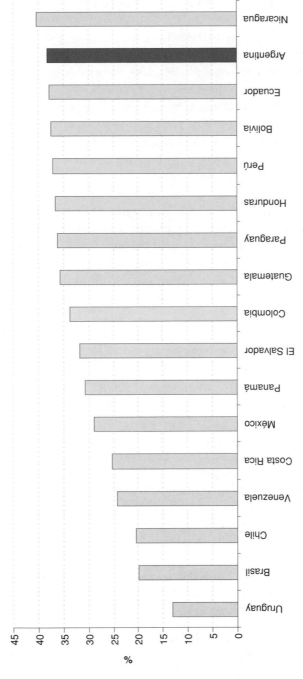

Figure 5.3. Public confidence in the judiciary – percentage of survey respondents expressing "No Confidence." *Source:* Latinobarómetro.

constitutionality and may uphold it or declare it unconstitutional. If it upholds it, the game ends. If the Court declares it unconstitutional, the president may punish the Court, either by expanding the Court or by replacing justices via impeachment. To punish the Court, the president needs strong support in Congress. If the president punishes the Court, the piece of legislation the Court reversed takes effect.

We solve the model backwards by looking at how a justice decides how to vote. Assume the justice to be pivotal so that on, say, a three-member Court, two justices have voted, one to uphold and one to reverse. Assume that the third justice agrees with the president. In that case, the decision is simple: uphold. Assume now that the third justice disagrees with the president. When the president has strong control over Congress, if the justice votes to reverse, the justice knows that the president can indeed punish the Court and also implement the contested law. Thus, the justice's dominant strategy would be to uphold the law. But if the president does not have strong control over Congress, then the dominant strategy for the third justice would be to vote against the constitutionality of the norm because the Court's reversal will go unpunished, and the norm will remain unconstitutional.[20]

This model has strong empirical implications: It says that, holding all else constant, the probability of a pivotal justice voting to uphold the constitutionality of a challenged norm increases with the strength of presidential control over Congress and the political alignment of the justice with the president. We test this model next.

AN EMPIRICAL INVESTIGATION OF STRATEGIC SELF-RESTRAINT

The strong conclusions of qualified analysts do not seem to leave much room for further argument: Throughout the twentieth century, Argentina's Supreme Court did not constitute a reliable check on political power. Still, a quantitative, systematic assessment of the issue is lacking. Only two authors, Helmke (2002) and Molinelli (1999), have provided initial steps in this direction. Focusing on the reversal ratio in "important" Court decisions about the constitutionality of norms between 1983 and 1997, Molinelli reports that Argentina's Supreme Court found

---

20. Observe that if the justice is not pivotal, his or her vote has no direct policy implication. Thus, the justice will be indifferent between upholding and reversing. Such would be the case if two justices had already voted to uphold or two justices had voted to reverse. Because the third justice's vote would be of no consequence, he or she will be indifferent about his or her vote.

unconstitutional 26 percent of 195 challenged national norms.[21] Using a different sampling procedure and focusing on the period 1976–95, Helmke finds a slightly higher level of reversals. She states that under both the military government of 1976–83 and the Alfonsín presidency (1983–9), the average percentage of cases decided against the government was forty-one; under the first Menem administration (1989–95), the average percentage of cases decided against the government was thirty.[22] This reversal ratio is not too distinct from that of the U.S. Supreme Court. It may be due to multiple underlying factors. Helmke addresses this issue in part by studying the effect on justices' decisions of an "expected" change in the political orientation of the government.[23] Here, we attempt to perform a fuller test of the strategic approach to the Supreme Court's constitutional control using data from 1935 to 1998, which enables us to reflect the changing political environment more systematically.

Data, Models, and Variables

Argentina's Supreme Court decides several thousand cases a year.[24] The circumstances of many of these cases are identical, although with different plaintiffs, and the political significance of the cases brought before the Court is extremely diverse. Thus, the first issue to address is the scope of the sample. Both Helmke and Molinelli limit the pool of cases considered.

21. While these results provide a first approximation of the degree to which the Court checked political power, it is difficult to reach clear conclusions without further analysis. As Molinelli says: "Looking at the facts, we have found – at least – an interesting number of national norms considered unconstitutional by the Court since 1983, and in particular since 1990. The most prudent thing to do is to consider this as an indication of some degree of independence. To determine whether this degree is adequate, much more work needs to be done" (18).
22. Helmke uses a variety of cases in which either the government was a litigant or an executive decree handed down by the sitting government was named in a case.
23. Helmke uses an analytic narrative to construct these expectations for President Alfonsín's democratic succession of the military regime in 1983, President Menem's election in 1989, and his reelection in 1995.
24. Because the Argentine Supreme Court does not have the ability to issue *certiorari* decisions and the *stare decisis* doctrine does not formally exist, the Argentine Supreme Court considers a very large number of cases per year (Bidart Campos 1982). Since 1991, the Court has handled between 5,000 and 8,000 cases annually (Molinelli 1999). But the thousands of cases mask the fact that many are repetitive. Until very recently, the Court did not have the ability to declare a law unconstitutional per se but rather had to deal with the unconstitutionality of its application to a particular case (person); therefore, the Court has ruled on multiple cases but essentially implemented a single decision multiple times.

Molinelli considers only the cases published in extenso in *La Ley*, the main judicial publication in Argentina. Helmke does not limit the sample to these cases but does introduce a dummy variable indicating whether a case was fully published or not. Here, we follow Molinelli. Using Molinelli's methodology and under his supervision, we commissioned an extension of his sample to include cases originating as far back as 1935.[25] Thus, our data set encompasses cases from 1935 to 1997 and includes Molinelli's original data set as well as the extension.

In order to distinguish between important and unimportant cases, following Molinelli, we determined that a case had to meet three conditions to be included in our data set: It had to involve the constitutionality of government norms,[26] the Court had to have actually decided for or against the constitutionality of the challenged norm,[27] and the case had to have been published *in extenso* in *La Ley*.[28] This leaves us with 1,646 cases, 1,052 of which consider national norms.

25. We are thankful to Fundación Gobierno y Sociedad and the United Nations Development Program for funding this extension, and to Prof. Jorge Bercholc from the Law School of Universidad de Buenos Aires for undertaking the study. We thank the late Guillermo Molinelli for his intellectual guidance.
26. We exclude cases in which the constitutionality of a lower court decision was questioned (*arbitrariedad*) and cases in which the constitutionality of the interpretation of a norm by a lower court but not the norm in itself was questioned.
27. Cases in which the Supreme Court decided not to pronounce on the constitutionality of the challenged norm, alleging formal or technical reasons, were excluded. This is in fact a very disparate category, including multiple types of issues: lack of foundation, improper presentation, political question, and others (see Molinelli 1999). For this condition to substantially bias the sample, the Court must be faced with a government decision it dislikes but one that it cannot oppose for fear of reprisal and so declines to review on the basis of technical reasons. To explore this potential bias, we divided the sample into democratic and dictatorship periods. We find that the probability of the Court rejecting a case for technical reasons is the same (around 22 percent) in both democratic and dictatorship periods. Thus, we do not believe that this sample selection biases our results.
28. Even though these criteria may neglect some relevant information, since we are focusing on the interaction of the Court with federal political institutions, this risk is relatively small. The loss of information is limited primarily to cases that consider provincial norms and low-level administrative resolutions, instead of laws or presidential decrees, both instances where the potential for political conflict is reduced. There might also be some loss of data in cases where the Court decided the constitutionality of the challenged norm but for political reasons the cases were considered less relevant by *La Ley*. Such could be the case with highly politically charged cases decided under military regimes, although the data set includes several highly charged cases, like that of Jacobo Timmerman, a famous journalist and newspaper owner jailed for opposing the military regime. Helmke finds that, on average, cases that are reported at length in *La Ley* tend to reverse the government more often than those that are not reported at length.

Our purpose is to determine the behavioral factors that contribute to the probability of a Supreme Court justice voting for or against the constitutionality of national norms. We model that decision using a logit model, where the dependent variable is a justice's decision for or against the constitutionality of the challenged norm. The independent variables are indicators of the president's political strength, justices' preferences, and some case-specific variables, including the solicitor general's opinion, which is described later.

We test strategic behavior in two ways. In the first approach, we look at the Court as a whole. Assuming that the Median Voter Theorem holds, we use the Court's final decision as the dependent variable and the imputed preference of the median justice as an explanatory variable. This approach raises the problem of multidimensionality inherent in the voting environment.[29] Thus, our second approach is to explore justices' individual decisions rather than the decision of the Court as a whole. In the first model, the dependent variable, CONSTITUTIONAL, takes the value 1 when the Court considers a law, decree, or resolution to be constitutional and 0 when it considers it to be unconstitutional.[30] In the second model, the dependent variable, CONSTITUTIONAL$_j$, is built in exactly the same way as CONSTITUTIONAL, but for each case it is applied to each individual judge j.

We now turn to describing the independent variables, which are intended to measure the political strength of the president, justices' preferences, the solicitor general's opinion, and some of the specific characteristics of each case.

Political Environment. The theory presented earlier suggests that justices' votes adjust partially to reflect the president's ideal policy whenever he has the political strength to retaliate. Given an institutional structure like that of Argentina, this will in turn depend on the president's degree of control over Congress. The two dangers faced by justices in Argentina over our period of analysis, apart from constitutional reform, were Court enlargement, which until the reform of 1994 could be achieved with a simple law, and impeachment, which requires a supermajority in both chambers.

29. Ideology is not the only determinant of voting; politics plays a role as well. And without a proper model of ideology in Congress (see more later), it becomes difficult to move the model to a single dimension.
30. Whenever two or more norms were involved in the same case, CONSTITUTIONAL takes the value 1 when all of them were considered by the Court to be in agreement with the Constitution.

To capture presidential control over Congress, we created a set of categorical variables that allow us to distinguish the various political scenarios. Democratic governments are classified at the time of each Supreme Court's decision as "unified" or "divided," generating two variables for democratic periods, UNIFGOV and DIVGOV. By "unified government," we mean a situation in which the presidential party has an absolute (more than 50 percent) or relative (plurality) majority in both chambers of Congress. Governments that are not unified are divided.

To reflect the difference between potential Court enlargement and impeachment (a tougher measure), we distinguished two cases within the unified government case. UNIFIEDSIMPLE indicates that the government can be classified as a unified government, but the president does not have the majority required to impeach Supreme Court justices. UNIFIED-SUPER indicates that the president not only controls a unified government but also has the supermajority required to successfully impeach Supreme Court justices. The complement to these three scenarios (DIVGOV, UNI-FIEDSIMPLE, and UNIFIEDSUPER) is DICTATORSHIP, which takes the value 1 whenever the presidency is occupied by a military officer and 0 when the president has been democratically elected.

We also want to capture the fact that the political strength of the government depends on the length of time it is expected to remain in office. For this reason, we introduce the variable TIMETOPOLCH, which measure – at each point in time – is the expected time remaining until a president is replaced by a different president with opposing political views. In building TIMETOPOLCH, we assume perfect foresight, so that the expected amount of time until a change in the presidency occurs is indeed the actual amount of time it takes such a change to occur.[31]

Justices' Preferences. An important part of the empirical exercise is to account for justices' policy preferences and thereby to measure the importance of appointing friendly justices. Measuring preferences is obviously not an easy task. A first approximation could be achieved by creating an absolute index over time reflecting more or less liberal positions of judges and Congress derived from voting behavior.[32] Nevertheless, the

---

31. Helmke uses a different methodology; she coded the time for a transition as a dummy variable taking the value 1 whenever the time remaining until change was less than twenty-four months.
32. See Bergara, Richman, and Spiller (1999) and Segal (1997).

absence of ideological national political parties with fairly stable positions in the policy spectrum and the lack of roll call data make this a very difficult task for Argentina. Here, instead, we compute the extent of political alignment between the justice and the sitting president by examining the appointment process. The basic idea is to look at whether the justice was appointed by the sitting president, a friendly past president, or a past president from an opposition party and then to combine this measure with a measure of the appointing president's control over the Senate.

To compute our political opposition variable (POLOPOS), assume initially that Congress does not participate in appointing the justices. That is, the president can appoint anyone he wants. In this case, the president would appoint a justice with preferences identical to his own. During this president's tenure, the justice has 100 percent political alignment. Thus, our political opposition variable, POLOPOS, will take a value of 0 for that particular justice, reflecting the fact that the president and the justice have the same political leanings. Assume now that a new president is elected and that the justice is still on the Court. Since we are assuming that the justice is a perfect clone of the nominating president, the value of POLOPOS assigned to the justice will depend on a comparison of the two presidents' political leanings. If the new president has the same political leanings as the former president, the value of POLOPOS will still be 0. If the new president has opposing political leanings, POLOPOS will take the value 1.[33]

Before it was reformed in 1994, the Argentine Constitution required Supreme Court candidates to be nominated by the president and approved by the Senate by a simple majority. Since 1994, a two-thirds majority in the Senate has been required. To get a more accurate description of the Argentine appointment process, we modify the POLOPOS variable as follows: Whenever the president has the required majority in the Senate, we assume that the president can appoint his preferred judicial type. When the president does not have the required majority in the Senate, however,

---

33. This method allows us to classify justices' and presidents' preferences for the complete sample (1935–98) without having to use a common measure for long-ago presidents in very different political environments. This would be a daunting task given the absence of national political parties with fairly stable ideological positions. Instead, we only need to compare presidents who "share" justices, which, given the volatility of the Court, substantially simplifies the task. A similar method is what gives continuity to the "Nominate" approach to estimate congressional preferences; see Poole and Rosenthal (1991).

the equilibrium nomination will reflect a bargaining process between the president and the opposition in the upper house. We assume this bargaining takes the following form: We assign a value of 0 to the position of the president on the policy opposition spectrum. An opposed Senate, then, has a value of 1 on the policy opposition spectrum.[34] Whenever a vacancy occurs, the president must nominate someone to fill it. If the Senate does not accept the nominated candidate, the position remains vacant. In this case, the position of the median voter on the incomplete Court (call this MVI) becomes the status quo, and the payoff that this situation provides to the players becomes each player's outside value in the bargaining game. The president would like, as in the previous exercise, to nominate a clone but anticipates that such a candidate would not be accepted by an opposing Senate, which would not accept a justice of a type located further away from its policy ideal than the MVI. Since the president, in turn, will not nominate a justice of a type that is more distant than the MVI, in this simple game an equilibrium appointment is a person of a type identical to the MVI.[35]

This procedure is used to calculate our political opposition variable for the entire sample, POLOPOS. Figure 5.4 shows the value of POLOPOS for the median justice across the entire sample period (1935–98). Only seldom did a president have to deal with a median justice named by the opposition.[36]

Not all justices' votes, however, will matter in determining a case. A justice who cannot influence the outcome may vote nonstrategically because

34. Because the president lacks a sufficient majority, he must bargain with the opposition. As mentioned before, without roll call records, it is almost impossible to quantify the degree of political opposition of the opposition. Thus, we assign a value of 1 to the political opposition.

35. Our method may be inaccurate when multiple appointments are considered at the same time. In this case, appointments away from the MVI are feasible as long as they are balanced (that is, one to each side of the MVI). Snyder and Weingast (2000) develop a similar model for the appointment of commissioners to the U.S. National Labor Relations Board.

36. The short administration of President De la Rúa (1999–2001) faced a Court named by the political opposition. Since a justice with prior political experience may be more politically attuned, we also collected from Molinelli, Palanza, and Sin (1999) the complete employment history of the sixty-nine justices in our sample. In particular, we are interested in whether justices held political positions before and/or after their tenure on the Court. We define two variables: PREVCARP takes the value 1 if the judge held a political position (chief executive, minister, or legislator either in the national or provincial government) before his or her tenure on the Court; POSCARP takes the value 1 if the judge held a political position after being on the Court.

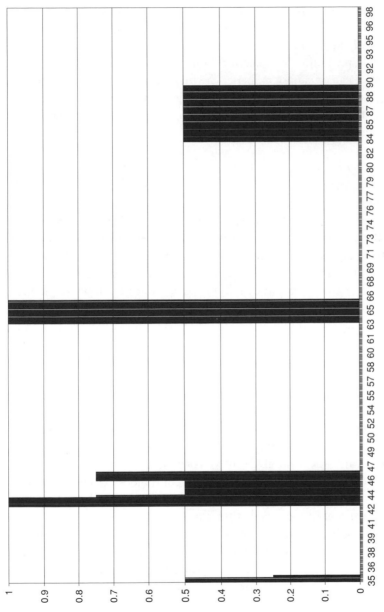

Figure 5.4. Median degree of political opposition among Supreme Court justices: 1935–1998. *Source:* Authors' own computations based on data in Molinelli, Palanza, and Sin (1999).

his or her vote will bring no credible political response, whereas such behavior by a pivotal justice could be politically costly. Since the final decision of the Court is the aggregation of these decisions by majority rule, we expect different behavior from a justice depending on whether that justice can or cannot influence the final outcome. Thus, we introduce a categorical variable (PIVOTAL) indicating whether, for a given decision, a given justice is or is not – individually, and taking all the other justices' votes as given – a pivotal voter.[37]

Information for Each Case. Each case raises specific issues. We attempt to partially capture these by considering variables that describe, in different dimensions, some basic characteristics of the norms that are being challenged. The first of these variables is LAW, which takes the value 1 when the challenge is to a federal law and 0 when the case challenges executive decrees or resolutions. We expect the coefficient of this variable to be positive. The enactment of a law requires the agreement of a larger number of actors with (potentially) diverse preferences, which makes it more likely that these norms will be in a less extreme location on the policy preference spectrum than presidential decrees. In addition, retaliating against a challenge to a presidential decree requires the president to garner support in Congress, support that must already exist if the challenge is to a law.

So far we have assumed that the president's coalition is interested in maintaining all existing norms, but it is quite possible that the president is less interested in maintaining norms that were enacted by previous governments. To explore this possibility, we introduce, for a subset of the sample, a categorical variable (CURRENTNORM) that indicates whether the norm is contemporary to the sitting president (CURRENTNORM = 1) or not (CURRENTNORM = 0). Unfortunately, the database has this information for only a subset of the sample (862 cases).

Moreover, because it could be argued that democratic administrations might want to repeal norms introduced by military governments (and vice versa), we classified norms according to the nature of the government that made the original norm and of the ruling government when the

---

37. We construct PIVOTAL as follows: For each decision, we look at whether each justice changing his or her vote would change the decision. Thus, for decisions that are not narrow – for example, 7 to 2 on a nine-member court, no justice is PIVOTAL. For narrow decisions (say, 5 to 4), all justices in the majority are PIVOTAL and none in the minority are PIVOTAL. (We assume away the forming of stable logrolling coalitions within the Court.)

Court ruled on the norm's constitutionality. This creates six categorical variables reflecting these combinations.[38] We were also able to classify, for a different subset of the sample, the challenged norms according to their subject (administrative, constitutional, labor, Social Security, fiscal, civil, commercial, contraventional, or penal).

The Solicitor General. The solicitor general (*Procurador General de la Nación*, SG) is the head of the Public Ministry, which houses all the prosecutors who perform in front of national courts, including the Supreme Court. In spite of the importance of this body, its role and institutional characterization were not clear until the 1994 reform, which established it as an independent body with both functional and financial autonomy. Several authors highlight the division in the doctrine among those who regarded the Public Ministry (and the SG) as part of the judiciary and those who considered it to be a simple administrative body within the executive branch.[39] This division is found both in Court jurisprudence and in the legal system regulating the Public Ministry.[40] In fact, even the prosecutors' appointment procedure was unclear.[41]

This discussion might have important implications for the interpretation of our analysis. Were the SG responsible to the executive, the SG's opinion could be taken to represent a mixture of the executive's will and the abstract quality of the case. The SG would in this case act as a noisy signal of the president's interest. If the SG were independent, however, his opinion could be taken to represent a good signal of the specific legal quality of the case. In this case, the residual (and not the direct) effects would represent "politics."[42]

38. These include laws passed during democracy being reviewed during a democratic administration; the equivalent for a presidential decree, laws issued during democratic periods but reviewed during de facto administrations, the equivalent for a presidential decree, decree laws passed during de facto administrations and reviewed under democratic administrations, and decree laws passed during de facto administrations and reviewed under de facto administrations. (Dictatorships issue only one type of norm, the "decree law.")
39. See Ekmekdjian (1999), Ziulu (1998), and Molinelli, Palanza, and Sin (1999).
40. See Ziulu (1998) and Ekmekdjian (1999) for examples of contradictory jurisprudence.
41. Molinelli, Palanza, and Sin (1999) report that although the solicitor general is appointed with the agreement of the Senate, such appointment is unconstitutional.
42. It could be argued that our measures of unified government are a proxy for legislative quality. It could also be argued that, facing no checks and balances, dictatorships produce legislation of the lowest quality, while divided governments, because of the need to produce consensus among competing political parties,

We introduce two variables that indicate the opinion of the solicitor general. SGCONST equals 1 if the SG supports the constitutionality of the norm and 0 otherwise, and SGFORMAL equals 1 when the SG supports dismissal for purely formal reasons (*Defecto Formal*).[43] We have information on the solicitor general only for the earlier period (1935–82) because Molinelli did not collect that information in his original study. Thus, for the 1,052 national cases, we have SG information only for 576 of them. Table 5.2 provides sample statistics and variable definitions.

Empirical Results

Like Molinelli and Helmke, we find that in roughly 30 percent of the important cases considered between 1935 and 1997 the Supreme Court ruled challenged norms to be unconstitutional (see Table 5.2). Whether this percentage is small or large, we cannot tell. Some nontrivial constitutional control is being practiced, though. Before presenting the results of our econometric analysis, it is interesting to compare Court rulings in relation to federal and local norms. Since local governments' capacity to retaliate against the Court is nil or very small, we do not expect justices to feel constrained in these cases. Even though the Court ruled favorably on national norms 71 percent of the time, it did so only in 47 percent of the cases that considered local norms. This result provides initial support for our strategic theory of judicial behavior. But we are not just concerned with reversals. We explore next the behavioral determinants of these events.

The Court's Vote as the Unit of Analysis. Table 5.3 shows the results obtained from the estimation of five logit equations. The dependent

produce norms of the highest quality. It could then be predicted that dictatorships will be reversed more often than unified governments and unified governments more often than divided governments. This latter prediction is the opposite of that predicted by strategic considerations. The opposite argument can be made, though. The bargaining process surrounding the drafting of laws takes place in an iterative manner, where in later rounds single sentences and individual words are bargained over, often leading to pieces of legislation of dubious logical integrity, and this event is more likely the more divided the government. (This is reminiscent of the "monstrosities" of bureaucratic agency design referred to by Moe 1990 and 1997.)

43. Although we do not include the cases in which the Supreme Court decides based on the *Defecto Formal* reason, we do include cases considered by the Court in which the SG recommended *Defecto Formal*. It must also be noted that introducing the SG's opinion entails losing a large amount of data, since information on the SG's opinion is available for only a fraction of the 1935–82 sample.

Table 5.2. *Sample Information and Variable Definition*

Variable	Definition	Observations	Mean	Std. Dev.	Min.	Max.
Aggregate Court						
CONSTITUTIONAL	1 if norm is found constitutional	1,051	0.71	0.46	0	1
UNIFIEDSUPER	1 if government holds sufficient majorities to impeach a justice	1,052	0.14	0.34	0	1
UNIFIEDSIMPLE	1 if government controls both houses but not enough to impeach a justice	1,053	0.31	0.46	0	1
DIVGOV	1 if government does not control Congress	1,053	0.15	0.35	0	1
POLOPOS – Median	Median judge value of political opposition	1,048	0.15	0.29	0	1
LAW	1 if norm is a law	1,053	0.56	0.50	0	1
PERCENTPOLOP	Percentage of justices appointed by politically opposed presidents	1,048	0.20	0.29	0	1
DICTATORSHIP	1 if government was not elected	1,052	0.41	0.49	0	1
CURRENTNORM	1 if norm issued during current government	862	0.24	0.43	0	1
SGCONST	1 if solicitor general opines Court should find norm to be constitutional	576	0.63	0.48	0	1
SGFORMAL	1 if solicitor general opines Court should not take case because of a formal defect	576	0.15	0.35	0	1

(continued)

Table 5.2 (continued)

Variable	Definition	Observations	Mean	Std. Dev.	Min.	Max.
Individual Justices						
CONSTITUTIONAL	1 if justice voted norm to be constitutional	5,318	0.640	0.480	0	1
UNIFIEDSUPER	1 if government holds sufficient majorities to impeach a justice	5,781	0.123	0.328	0	1
UNIFIEDSIMPLE	1 if government controls both houses but not enough to impeach a justice	5,786	0.382	0.486	0	1
DIVGOV	1 if government does not control Congress	5,786	0.134	0.340	0	1
POLOPOS	Justice's value of political opposition	5,781	0.198	0.333	0	1
POLPIV	POLOPOS times PIVOTAL	5,513	0.054	0.205	0	1
LAW	1 if norm is a law	5,786	0.568	0.495	0	1
TIMETOPOLCH	Months to change in political tendency of president	5,781	48.683	33.974	1	146
PREVCARP	1 if justice held a political position prior to appointment	5,781	0.270	0.444	0	1
POSCARP	1 if justice held a political position after tenure at the Court	5,781	0.028	0.166	0	1
SGCONST	1 if solicitor general opines Court should find norm to be constitutional	2,984	0.624	0.484	0	1
SGFORMAL	1 if solicitor general opines Court should not take case because of a formal defect	2,984	0.149	0.357	0	1
CURRENTNORM	1 if norm issued during current government	4,756	0.256	0.437	0	1
DICTATORSHIP	1 if government was not elected	5,781	0.361	0.480	0	1

Table 5.3. *Determinants of Pro-Constitutional Supreme Court Decisions: Court Level*

		Eq. 1a	Eq. 2a	Eq. 3a	Eq. 4a	Eq. 5a
Political environment	CONSTANT	0.20	0.28	0.14	−2.17	−2.11
		1.57	2.09	0.92	−6.68	−6.43
	UNIFIEDSUPER	1.29	1.31	1.40	2.13	2.27
		(5.01)	*(5.08)*	*(4.81)*	*(4.59)*	*(4.82)*
		22.8%	23.3%	24.4%	26.9%	29.1%
	UNIFIEDSIMPLE	0.62	0.72	0.63	1.01	1.17
		(3.70)	*(4.18)*	*(3.43)*	*(3.22)*	*(3.64)*
		12.9%	14.8%	13.3%	17.5%	20.3%
	DIVGOV	0.06	0.02	0.22	−0.53	−0.04
		(0.31)	*(0.12)*	*(0.95)*	−*(1.52)*	−*(0.11)*
		1.4%	0.5%	5.1%	−12.5%	−0.9%
	POLOP – Median	−0.33	−0.25	−0.98		
		−*(1.38)*	−*(0.91)*	−*(2.30)*		
		−2.0%	−1.5%	−5.1%		
Justices' preferences	PERCENTPOLOP		−0.72			−1.53
			−*(3.05)*			−*(3.67)*
			−4.5%			−8.6%
	Discrete Change	−7.0%	−15.7%	−5.3%	−20.2%	−31.6%
	SGCONST				3.50	3.55
					(11.55)	*(11.55)*
					68.8%	69.3%
SG	SGFORMAL				2.55	2.55
					(7.09)	*(7.02)*
					56.3%	56.2%
	LAW	0.71	0.70	0.56	0.82	0.85
		(4.99)	*(4.94)*	*(3.50)*	*(3.35)*	*(3.44)*
		14.5%	14.4%	11.4%	14.5%	14.9%
Case	CURRENTNORM			0.34		
				(1.83)		
				6.7%		
Sample	Sample			C-NORM	SG	SG
	N obs.	1047	1047	858	571	571
	Prob > LR $\chi 2$	0.000	0.000	0.000	0.000	0.000
	Prob > Pear. Chi^2	0.340	0.015	0.000	0.000	0.000
	Area u/ROC curve	64%	65%	65%	85%	87%
Goodness of fit	Sensitivity	61%	72%	51%	85%	85%
	Specificity	57%	50%	71%	75%	75%
	Pos. pred. value	77%	77%	81%	89%	89%
	Neg. pred. value	38%	42%	37%	68%	67%
	Correctly classified	60%	65%	57%	82%	82%

variable is CONSTITUTIONAL, and the independent variables are measures of the political environment, justices' preferences, the opinion of the solicitor general, and case-specific variables.

The table contains two different types of information. The first part of the table shows for each independent variable the estimated raw coefficient, the value of the Z-statistic, and the differential effect over the probability of a proconstitutional outcome of a discrete change in the independent variable. This discrete change is computed for categorical variables as having that characteristic (as opposed to not having it) and as one standard deviation increase for the continuous variables (POLOPOS – Median, the degree of political opposition of the median justice, and PERCENTPOLOP, the percentage of justices appointed by presidents of opposing political tendency). For these latter-type variables, we also show the effect of changing them from the lowest to the highest possible value. The second part of the table shows sample information, the LR test, and different measures of the goodness of fit.

In Equation 1a (as in all the other equations), the political environment is captured through UNIFIEDSUPER, UNIFIEDSIMPLE, and DIVGOV. (DICTATORSHIP is the default.) In addition, justices' collective preferences are approximated by POLOPOS – Median. The value of the coefficient for the political environment variables has to be interpreted as the impact on the probability of a challenge under the given political environment over a military government. The first result to be noted, then, is that the Court treats military governments with as much deference as it treats democratic divided governments. The Court, however, gave much more deference to unified governments. Indeed, and according to the theory's prediction, the coefficients of UNIFIEDSIMPLE and UNIFIEDSUPER are highly significant and meaningful: The president having a sufficient majority to change Court size produces a 13 percent increase in the probability of a favorable outcome; the president having a majority sufficient to impeach justices produces a 23 percent increase in the probability of a favorable outcome. Hence, both cases differ substantially from the divided government case, whose impact is not statistically significantly different from that of military governments. The coefficient of LAW is also, as expected, significant and positive. When the challenged norm is a law as opposed to a presidential decree or resolution, the probability of a pro-constitutional decision rises by more than 14 percent.[44]

---

44. The results presented in Tables 5.3 and 5.4 use the standard maximum-likelihood variance estimator. The robust variance estimator would be an adequate choice for

Finally, as predicted by the theory, the degree of political opposition of the median justice, POLOPOS – Median, is negative, but neither its significance nor its magnitude is high. An increase of one standard deviation in POLOPS – Median reduces the estimated probability by only 2 percent and a change in its value from 0 to 1 (clone to totally opposed) by only 7 percent.[45] Since this result could be caused in part by the (possibly inadequate) use of the Median Voter Theorem assumption, we estimate the same equation using PERCENTPOLOP (the percentage of Court justices appointed by presidents with opposing political leanings) as a measure of judicial preference. While the other variables' coefficients remained practically unchanged, PERCENTPOLOP's coefficient is negative and statistically significant.

Equation 3a explores the sensitivity of these results to the difference between contemporary and old norms. Because we only have information about the origin of the norm for the earlier sample, the results are not directly comparable. Nevertheless, all other variables remain roughly unchanged from the results in Equation 1a. The coefficient of CURRENT-NORM is, as expected, positive and important. The probability of approving the constitutionality of a norm enacted during the current administration is higher by almost 7 percent than that of a norm enacted under a previous administration, further suggesting strategic thinking by the Court.[46]

We introduce the solicitor general in Equations 4a and 5a. Again, information on the SG is available only for the earlier period, thus limiting the sample size. The coefficients of SGCONST and SGFORMAL are positive and highly significant, and they have a large impact on the probability of a proconstitutional outcome. When the SG supports not considering the case, alleging *Defecto Formal*, the probability of a proconstitutional outcome rises by 56 percent, and when the SG supports the constitutionality directly, it rises by 69 percent (in both cases, as opposed to the situation in

---

a misspecified model; however, if this is not the case, the ML variance estimator is theoretically more efficient. See, for example, Sribney (1998). In any case, the results remain essentially unchanged using the robust variance estimator.

45. It should be noted that these results do not change when we consider only democratic periods. UNIFIEDSUPER, UNIFIEDSIMPLE, and LAW remain strongly statistically significant and meaningful in terms of magnitude: In comparison with a "divided government" situation, UNIFIEDSIMPLE increases the probability of a favorable outcome by 12.1 percent and UNIFIEDSUPER by 22.3 percent. In addition, changing POLOPOS – Median from 0 to 1 produces a 1.2 percent decrease in the probability of a favorable outcome, while LAW increases it by 13.9 percent.

46. This specification also includes a richer set of controls (not reported).

which the SC supports the unconstitutionality of the norm). In addition, the effect of the political environment variables remains unchanged, and (unlike in Equation 1a) the Court's preferences, measured by POLOPOS – Median, are also significant and relatively relevant (−5.1 and −20.2 percent). Equation 5a repeats this exercise but introduces PERCENTPOLOP. Again, the SG's variables are highly significant and relevant, and the power of the other variables rises.

The second part of the table shows the global significance of the variables in the equations and their predictive potential. Even though the global significance (see the LR-χ^2 test) of the variables used is always good, the predictive potential of the specified models is mediocre[47] with the exception of equations 4 and 5, which use the opinion of the solicitor general. The results are robust to the inclusion of additional controls, such as repeated norms in different cases, litigants in each case, and case subject area.

Individual Justices as the Unit of Analysis. Table 5.4 shows the results using the individual justice as the unit of analysis. In the four equations presented in this table, we use a fixed-effects logit model – grouped by individual justices – in which the dependent variable is CONSTITUTIONAL$_j$.[48]

Notwithstanding this basic difference, Equation 1b is similar to Equation 1a in Table 5.3, with two differences. First, on the preferences side of the equation, Equation 1b introduces POLOPOS$_j$ (the extent of political opposition of justice j) and POLPIV, where POLOPOS$_j$ interacts with the PIVOTAL indicator. As the table shows, POLOPOS$_j$'s coefficient is not statistically significant, which might be expected, since this reflects the

47. The following measures of fit are presented: sensitivity, specificity, positive predictive value, and negative predictive value. These are, respectively, the percentage of hits when the dependent variable is 1, the percentage of hits when the dependent variable is 0, the number correctly classified as 1 as a proportion of the number of cases classified as 1, and the number correctly classified as 0 as a proportion of the number of cases classified as 0. The table also shows the total percentage of cases correctly classified. The percentage of correctly classified cases is heavily dependent upon the choice of cutoff point. Although there is not a unique criterion for choosing this cutoff point, here we use the mean of the dependent variable. We also compute the area under the ROC curve, which overcomes the indeterminacy of the cutoff problem. In a ROC curve, the sensitivity and specificity (1-specificity) are plotted for the various cutoff points. An area under the curve close to 1 (which is the maximum value this area can attain) indicates a good prediction, while an area close to .5 indicates a poor prediction. See Afifi and Clark (1996).

48. Comparable results are obtained using the random effects logit model. See Iaryczower, Spiller, and Tommasi (2002).

Table 5.4. *Determinants of Pro-Constitutional Supreme Court Decisions:
Individual Justice Level Fixed-Effects (Individual Justices) Logit Model*

		Eq. 1b	Eq. 2b	Eq. 3b	Eq. 4b
Political environment	UNIFIEDSUPER	0.60	0.86	2.17	0.72
		(3.35)	*(3.45)*	*(6.15)*	*(3.40)*
		13.5%	**18.4%**	**34.3%**	**16.2%**
	UNIFIEDSIMPLE	0.48	0.49	1.36	0.51
		(2.71)	*(1.98)*	*(4.27)*	*(2.24)*
		11.0%	**11.3%**	**26.3%**	**12.0%**
	DIVGOV	0.45	0.07	1.45	0.39
		(2.22)	*(0.25)*	*(3.58)*	*(1.45)*
		10.3%	**1.6%**	**27.5%**	**9.1%**
	TIMETOPOLCH	0.004	0.002	0.001	0.003
		(2.84)	*(0.32)*	*(0.34)*	*(1.32)*
		3.1%	**1.3%**	**0.6%**	**2.1%**
Justices' preferences	POLOPOS	0.02	0.06	0.00	0.10
		(0.11)	*(0.74)*	*(0.02)*	*(0.57)*
		0.1%	**0.5%**	**0.0%**	**0.8%**
	POLPIV	−0.71	−0.39	−0.36	−0.66
		−*(4.33)*	−*(1.62)*	−*(1.53)*	−*(3.22)*
		−3.3%	**−1.9%**	**−1.8%**	**−3.3%**
	DISCRETE	**−16.7%**	**−7.7%**	**−8.5%**	**−13.6%**
	SGCONST		1.94	2.65	
			(18.17)	*(15.52)*	
			44.9%	**55.7%**	
SG	SGFORM		1.57	2.39	
			(11.25)	*(10.85)*	
			37.4%	**52.2%**	
SG & political environment (Interactions)	UNIFIEDSUPER & SGCONST			−1.70	
				−*(4.93)*	
	Interaction only		—	**−12.4%**	
	Combined effect		**−63.3%**	**65.1%**	
	UNIFIEDSIMPLE & SGCONST			−1.12	
				−*(4.38)*	
	Interaction only		—	**−10.0%**	
	Combined effect		**−56.2%**	**61.2%**	
	DIVGOV & SGCONST			−1.55	
	Interaction only			−*(4.19)*	
				−11.9%	
	Combined effect		**−46.5%**	**54.8%**	

(continued)

Table 5.4 *(continued)*

		Eq. 1b	Eq. 2b	Eq. 3b	Eq. 4b
	UNIFIEDSUPER &			−2.05	
	SGFORM			*−(4.25)*	
	Interaction only		—	−13.4%	
	Combined effect		−55.8%	54.0%	
	UNIFIEDSIMPLE &			−0.87	
	SGFORM			*−(2.62)*	
	Interaction only		—	−8.5%	
	Combined effect		48.7%	61.0%	
	DIVGOV &			−2.50	
	SGFORM			*−(5.41)*	
	Interaction only		—	−14.2%	
	Combined Effect		−39.1%	25.9%	
Case	LAW	0.51	0.29	0.22	0.20
		(8.06)	*(3.17)*	*(2.35)*	*(2.28)*
		11.6%	**6.6%**	**5.1%**	**4.5%**
	CURRENTNORM				0.28
					(2.77)
					6.4%
Control	Sample	Area	SG	SG	NORM & AREA
Sample	N obs.	5,307	2,924	2,924	3,344
	Prob > Pear. Chi²	0.000	0.000	0.000	0.000
Goodness	Area u/ROC curve	67%	77%	78%	67%
of fit	Sensitivity	62%	77%	79%	57%
	Specificity	63%	66%	65%	68%
	Pos. pred. value	75%	9%	79%	75%
	Neg. pred. value	48%	64%	65%	48%
	Correctly classified	63%	73%	74%	61%

preferences of nonpivotal justices. POLPIV's coefficient, however, is significant and quantitatively important. Globally, these two variables combine to produce a 16.7 percent decrease in the probability of a favorable outcome when a pivotal justice is not friendly.[49] Second, we continue using UNIFIEDSUPER, UNIFIEDSIMPLE, and GOVDIV as measures of the political environment, but we now add TIMETOPOLCH, the time remaining before a change in the political tendency of the president. TIMETOPOLCH's coefficient is positive, indicating that the longer the time remaining for a change in the political tendency of the president, the higher the probability of a proconstitutional decision. As before, the different behavior toward

49. The results, again, do not change when we only consider democratic periods.

unified and divided governments is reflected in the estimates, and the coefficient of LAW is positive and statistically significant.

Equation 2b introduces the SG. Again, the effect of the SG's opinion is strong (although not as quantitatively important as in Table 5.3), and the characteristics of both preferences and reaction to the political environment remain largely unchanged. The connection between the behavior of the SG and the political environment is further explored in Equation 3b. To test the "signaling device" hypothesis about the role of the SG, we introduce a series of interaction terms between the opinion of the solicitor general and the political environment. If the SG's views reflect the opinion of the president, then the Court should pay more attention to the SG when the president has a stronger hold on the legislature. But we find that, if anything, the signaling power of the SG seems to be negatively associated with the extent of political control of the president over Congress. In comparison with Equation 2b, the combined effect of a proconstitutional decision of the SG and a divided government is 8.3 percent higher than under a military government (54.8 percent versus 46.5 percent) but only 5.1 percent higher with a barely unified regime and 1.8 percent higher with a strongly unified regime, thus leading us to reject the signaling hypothesis.[50] Finally, Equation 4b introduces, as in Table 5.3, the difference between contemporary and previous norms with CURRENTNORM, together with an additional control, by considering the issue area of the legislation challenged.[51] The results remain unchanged.

In sum, the empirical results presented here comport remarkably well with the theoretical framework presented earlier. First, justices vote based

50. We performed a strong test of the hypothesis that the Court treats the SG the same regardless of presidential control over Congress during democracies. This hypothesis was tested by estimating the model assuming that the coefficients of the interaction terms were equal (for SGCONST and SGFORMAL). The likelihood ratio test shows a value of 16.40 (log L [restricted model] $= -1614.18$, log L [unrestricted model] $= -1605.98$), which exceeds the critical value of $\kappa 2(4, .01) = 13.277$. Although we reject this strong test, the pattern of coefficients does not conform to what would be expected if the SG were perceived as reflecting the view of the administration. For views of the SG in the United States, see, among others, Meinhold and Shull (1998), Segal (1989), and Waxman (1998).

51. We also explored the role of the political career of the justices. We find that the voting behavior of justices who in prior work were politicians was not significantly different from the behavior of those who were not. Justices who after leaving the Court become politicians, however, were more likely to vote in favor of the constitutionality of norms. This last result should not imply causality, though, because causality is likely to go the other way. ("Politically attuned" justices get rewarded with ex post political employment.)

on their preferences and the constraints they face. In particular, we find that the degree of political opposition of a pivotal justice to the president affects the probability of the justice voting against the government. Indeed, a nonfriendly pivotal justice, as compared to a friendly one, has almost a 20 percent reduction in the probability of voting in favor of the government. But politics, not just preferences, also matter. We find that the probability of voting against the government uniformly falls with the control the government has over the legislature.

CONCLUSION

The story of the Argentine Supreme Court is, then, more complex and nuanced than it has traditionally been told. Even with the repeated abuse of appointment powers, the Court did not lack judicial doctrines or will. Given the tendency of the Argentine polity to generate unified governments and the tendency of the executive to replace justices by threat or by impeachment, it is not surprising that the Court has been perceived as not independent. Courts, however, have behaved strategically, and when political conditions were right, politically opposed justices have shown their independence. Although the Argentine public does not have a positive view of the Argentine judiciary, that may say less about the Supreme Court itself than about the environment in which the Court operates. Indeed, should that environment change, our analysis suggests that a more independent Court could easily arise. In other words, the reason the Court has failed to serve as an independent check on the executive is not its lack of doctrine but rather that the political environment throughout most of the postwar period would not tolerate too much judicial review. This provided the various executives the ability to name friendly justices, and the potential for political retaliation gave the justices less of an incentive to limit executive discretion.

Our research, then, raises important modifications to the concept of judicial independence. We show that judicial independence cannot be measured by the percentage of government decisions reversed. There is no absolute level that classifies a Court as independent. Instead, judicial independence is a subtle concept. It relates to the extent to which a justice votes on the basis of the potential for political retaliation. We derive measures of potential political retaliation related to the extent of control of the executive over the legislature. We show that high degrees of political cohesiveness increase the degree of self-restraint among Argentine Supreme Court justices.

In the context of this book, we find that the political configurations of Argentine history and the progressive tendency of presidents to manipulate the composition of the Court produced a Supreme Court that did not challenge the executive as much as it could have under different political circumstances.

6

The Bureaucracy

WITH JULIANA BAMBACI

A strong and capable bureaucracy is likely to lead to better public poli-cies.[1] On the one hand, there is the obvious direct effect of the quality of the bureaucracy on the quality of policy implementation. On the other, our analytical framework emphasizes that political agreements leading to effective public policies are more likely to obtain in environments in which it is more feasible to delegate policy implementation to a quality bureaucracy. (The quality of the bureaucracy is an important component of the quality of the environment for political transactions.)

A high-quality bureaucracy does not descend from heaven, but it is itself the product of conscious political decisions over time. The building of a bureaucracy, "civil service policy," is a policy in itself. In the language of our framework, it is a policy with special investment-like transaction characteristics, and such policies place large demands on the implemen-tation capacity of political systems.

Thus, a poor bureaucracy worsens the policy-making environment, and a poor policy-making environment is unlikely to create a quality bureaucracy. We argue in this chapter that Argentina has suffered from this vicious circle. Political actors do not have a quality bureaucracy onto which to delegate policy implementation, and the weaknesses of the bureaucracy are themselves the result of the poor quality of the overall policy-making environment in Argentina.

In this chapter, we expose some problems of the Argentine bureau-cracy, and we argue that those problems are due to the lack of any rele-vant principal interested in providing long-term incentives to bureaucratic

---

1. This chapter draws extensively from Bambaci, Spiller, and Tommasi (2002) and from Iacoviello, Tommasi, and Zuvanic (2002). We thank Mercedes Iacoviello and Laura Zuvanic for their contributions to this work.

actors. Congress, being a marginal policy-making actor, lacks the incentives and ability to incentivize and monitor the bureaucratic apparatus. Executives, transient by nature, do not have long-term incentives to build a quality permanent bureaucracy either. Unable to motivate the permanent bureaucracy, they have tended to fill the main bureaucratic positions with transient loyalists, giving rise to the so-called parallel bureaucracy. This practice has had several deleterious effects on the incentives of bureaucrats and on the consistency and coherence of policies.

The next section of this chapter presents evidence on the current characteristics of the Argentine bureaucracy. The section after that provides a succinct argument and evidence that these characteristics are due to the lack of any long-term principal. The following sections explore in more detail some of the main effects of the lack of intertemporal attention to building a high-quality bureaucracy. The first describes the parallel bureaucracy, cohorts that come to office with each minister as a response to the lack of responsiveness of permanent civil servants. The second presents the dynamics of the Argentine civil service and the recurrent attempts at reforming it in the recent democratic period.

CHARACTERIZATION OF THE ARGENTINE BUREAUCRACY

In a comparison of three South American bureaucracies, Argentina was once characterized as "one of the clearest instances on record of an institutionalized, non-performance-oriented bureaucracy in a society with ample numbers of skilled human resources in which the primary interest within the state apparatus is survival, through securing one's future through a limited but sufficient salary to live on" (Graham 1998: 221–2). That statement, made shortly after the restoration of democracy in Argentina, is still accurate today.

Bureaucratic quality is not easy to measure precisely. In one of the best-known studies of bureaucracies in developing countries, Rauch and Evans (1999) collected survey data and constructed an indicator of bureaucratic coherence and competence in thirty-five countries. This index attempts to capture the degree to which some ideal "Weberian" criteria of effective state bureaucracies, including competitive salaries, the prevalence of meritocratic criteria in the selection and promotion of employees, and the existence of a civil service career, are present in each country. The quality of the Argentine bureaucracy according to this indicator ranks near the bottom (see Figure 6.1). This comparison is even more striking when we account for the level of human development in the thirty-five countries

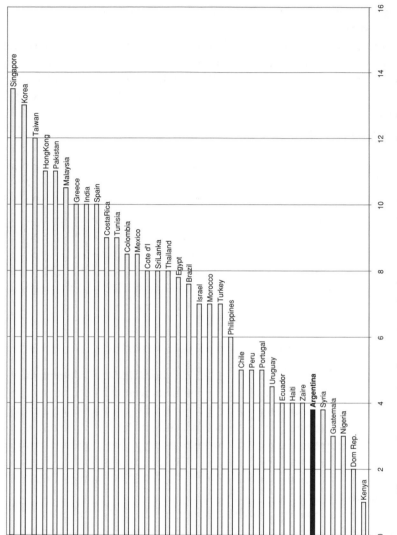

Figure 6.1. Bureaucratic coherence in 35 developing countries. *Source:* Rauch and Evans (1999).

Table 6.1. *Central Government Wages*
Divided by GDP per Capita, 1999

Country	Relative Wage
Argentina	1.65
Brazil	3.70
Chile	3.05
Colombia	3.25
Mexico	1.99
Uruguay	0.99

Source: Carlsson and Payne (2002).

in the sample. Plotting the index of "Weberianness" against an index of human development from the United Nations, we find that Argentina is even more of an outlier: It is a relatively developed country with a very poor bureaucracy (see Figure 6.2).[2]

For various reasons, the Argentine public bureaucracy does not attract the most talented people in the country. One probable reason is its salaries, which are among the lowest in the region (see Table 6.1). The relative wage in Argentina is about half that of Chile or Colombia and an even smaller fraction of Brazil's.[3]

Looking at other indicators, Argentine citizens have a low opinion of the quality of the country's public administration even in comparison to other Latin American citizens' perception of their own bureaucracies (see Figure 6.3). The country also lacks a well-structured civil service career track – it ranks twenty-third out of thirty-five developing countries in Rauch and Evans's (1999) index of adherence to bureaucratic civil service procedures. Although there have been attempts to build up the civil service, none of these attempts was sustained over time or had any broad impact on the system. Because the civil service was constantly being modified and altered by executive action, a civil service career has never been firmly established in Argentina (Oszlak 1999).

2. In that sample, there are only seven countries with an indicator of human development better than that of Argentina, while there are only four countries with a lower value of Weberianness. It is worth pointing out that if one takes a longer historical perspective, Argentina is slowly reducing its relative index of human development to match the quality of its public sector (consistent with Rauch and Evans's theory).
3. Brazil's GDP per capita is much lower than Argentina's. Nonetheless, Brazil is considered to have a relatively strong public bureaucracy. See Sikkink (1993), Graham (1998), and Schneider (1993).

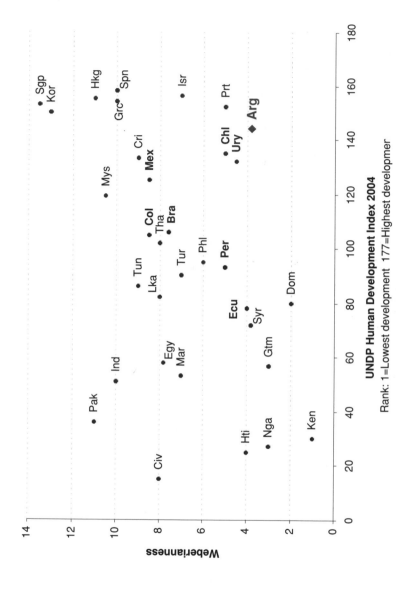

Figure 6.2. Weberianness of the bureaucracy in relation to human development in thirty-five developing countries.
Source: Rauch and Evans (1999) and United Nations Development Program (UNDP).

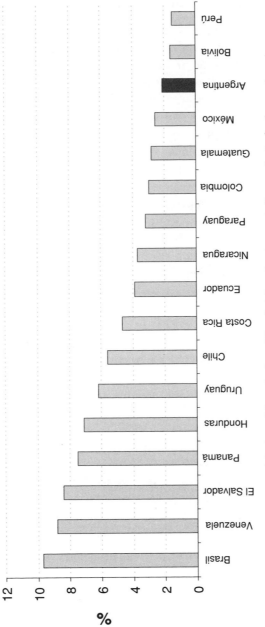

Figure 6.3. Citizens with high confidence in the public administration (percent). *Source:* Latinobarómetro (2001).

A BUREAUCRACY WITHOUT LONG-TERM PRINCIPALS

Some authors have argued that a professionalized bureaucracy requires at least one of its principals (the legislature or the executive) to have long time horizons.[4] We argue in this section that the Argentine bureaucracy is an agent with no long-term principal.

As discussed in Chapter 3, Argentine legislators are transient visitors of Congress with little to no incentives in policy, let alone in building strong bureaucratic institutions. In this scenario, Congress does not provide permanent bureaucrats with long-term incentives, such as a well-structured and well-remunerated bureaucratic career, or with close supervision of their actions. Instead, it gives the administration wide-ranging discretion in dealing with the bureaucracy, limited only by the constitutional protection of civil service jobs.

Since the 1930s and increasingly over time, the norms defining the structure, rules, and procedures of the bureaucracy have been defined in the executive branch by either civilian or military presidents. Up to 1940, norms were predominantly laws. After 1940, most norms, such as civil service regulation, administrative procedures, and the organization of the executive office, were produced as executive decrees. (See Figure 6.4.) Some of the most important recent reform attempts were introduced as executive decrees with limited congressional involvement.[5]

As also discussed in Chapter 3, the power of the purse does not work in Argentina either. Throughout the twentieth century, budgets presented by the president have either not been approved in time or approved with minimal modifications, in either case leaving the executive with substantial discretion.[6] In Argentina there is no such thing as Congress making the funding of a given governmental agency conditional on any performance indicator. Even at the aggregate level, Congress has not verified budget implementation in spite of its formal prerogatives (see Chapter 3). The delay in approving the *Cuenta de Inversión* (the ex post budget verification) has been such that it has never been approved while the president executing the budget was still in office (Tommasi and Spiller 2000; Uña et al. 2005).

---

4. See, for example, Spiller and Urbiztondo (1994) and references therein.
5. Contrast this situation to Chile, where extensive congressional debate preceded the recent civil service reform (*Ley de Nuevo Trato*). See Iacoviello and Zuvanic (2004).
6. Congress approved the budget on time in less than half the fiscal years in the 1864–2000 period (Molinelli, Palanza, and Sin 1999).

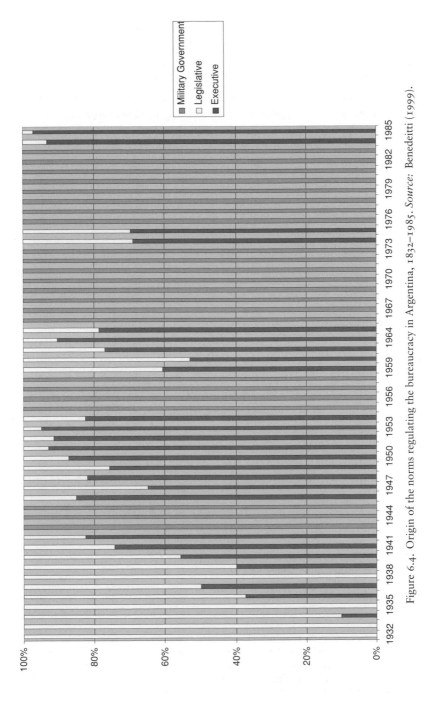

Figure 6.4. Origin of the norms regulating the bureaucracy in Argentina, 1832–1985. *Source:* Benedeitti (1999).

Congress has not exercised strong legislative oversight of the bureaucracy either. Palanza (2005) shows that although Argentina's Constitution and congressional rules grant the legislature substantial oversight powers over the bureaucracy,[7] the effectiveness of congressional oversight is in fact less than minimal. Indeed, as Palanza argues, "overall, mechanisms of oversight have not been prominent in holding the executive accountable" (2005: 9).[8] Palanza shows that the executive does not feel threatened by congressional oversight and that, in those instances when oversight could present a danger, the executive deflects the oversight, moving the negotiation to other arenas.

Having established that Congress is not a long-term principal for the bureaucracy, let's look now at the executive. Executives are transient in almost every democracy. They have been even more transient in Argentina. From the first military coup in 1930 until December of 1999, there has been no orderly constitutional transfer from one president to the next. The average tenure of Argentine presidents has been two years and four months in office.

High presidential turnover has generated even higher turnover at the ministerial level (see Table 6.2). Finance ministers in Argentina have an average tenure of just one year, half as long as the average tenure of finance ministers in developing nations, which itself is lower than the average reported for finance ministers in developed nations (2.4 years). Only Bolivian finance ministers serve for a shorter period of time than Argentine finance ministers.

The effects of turnover are magnified in the lower echelons of the Argentine ministries. That is, undersecretaries' tenure is shorter than secretaries' and consequently shorter yet than ministers'. (Very few secretaries outlast their ministers.) Although there are no cross-national statistics about the stability of secretaries, their attendance record at the annual meetings

---

7. The Argentine Constitution grants Congress the following rights: It can request written inquiries, interpellate cabinet members and remove the chief of cabinet, receive a monthly visit from the chief of cabinet, impeach cabinet members and the president, and exercise ex post review powers over the budget. On top of these powers, congressional rules allow Congress to summon officials to congressional meetings.
8. For instance, delay in responding to written inquiries is so substantial (an average of 1,361 days, with longer delays for more threatening issues) that it is equivalent to simply not answering, as legislators, on average, do not last 2,000 days in the lower chamber. Palanza argues that written inquiries are just position-taking strategies to signal the price of votes, rather than serious requests of information.

Table 6.2. *Average Turnover and Tenure of Finance Ministers in Developing and Developed Countries, 1950–1989*

Country	Average Turnover Rate	Average Tenure (years)
Developed countries	0.42	2.40
Developing countries	0.49	2.00
Kenya	0.13	8.00
South Africa	0.13	8.00
Malaysia	0.15	6.70
Singapore	0.15	6.70
Ethiopia	0.20	5.00
Philippines	0.23	4.40
Mexico	0.25	4.00
Hungary	0.25	4.00
Romania	0.25	4.00
Israel	0.28	3.60
Indonesia	0.30	3.30
Ghana	0.35	2.90
Pakistan	0.43	2.40
Costa Rica	0.45	2.20
Morocco	0.46	2.20
Venezuela	0.48	2.10
Brazil	0.55	1.80
Thailand	0.55	1.80
Uruguay	0.57	1.80
India	0.58	1.70
Egypt	0.58	1.70
Turkey	0.68	1.50
Colombia	0.68	1.50
Chile	0.83	1.20
Ecuador	0.83	1.20
Peru	0.85	1.20
South Korea	0.90	1.10
Argentina	1.05	1.00
Bolivia	1.18	0.90

Source: Castilla (2002).

of the Network for Poverty Reduction and Social Protection of the Inter-American Development Bank is illustrative (see Table 6.3). The record of attendance shows some stability in the attendance for most Latin American countries. The average country had only one personnel change during the four consecutive meetings, held every half year, while Argentina had four. Although the evidence on lower-level rotation is not

Table 6.3. *Number of Different Representatives*
to the IDB Biannual Meetings of the Poverty
Reduction and Social Protection Network,
2000–2002

Country	Number
Argentina	4
Bahamas	3
Paraguay	3
Peru	3
Barbados	2
Brazil	2
Chile	2
Costa Rica	2
Ecuador	2
El Salvador	2
Guatemala	2
Haití	2
Honduras	2
Mexico	2
Trinidad and Tobago	2
Uruguay	2
Bolivia	1
Colombia	1
Guyana	1
Jamaica	1
Nicaragua	1
Panama	1
Dominican Republic	1
Surinam	1
Venezuela	1
Average	**1.84**

Source: Elaboration by the authors from Inter-American
Development Bank, *Diálogo Regional de Políticas.*

conclusive, it is consistent with a very high rate of rotation at the top of
the administration.

CONSEQUENCES OF THE LACK OF LONG-TERM PRINCIPALS

The short-sighted characteristics of the principals are mirrored in the institutional features and operation of the Argentine bureaucracy and public
administration. The top echelons of the bureaucracy are populated by figures who serve short terms in office and who have short-term incentives

and mostly personal ties to their bosses. This has consequences for their behavior in office, for their relations among themselves, for their relations with the permanent staff, and even for the dynamics of the organizational chart of the national public administration. All of this feeds back into the low quality of the bureaucracy and of bureaucratic output.

Congress and the president turn over with high frequency. The Argentine Constitution, on the other hand, protects civil servants' job stability. Hence, working against these short-lived principals, there is a permanent, hard-to-motivate, and relatively unresponsive agent.

The president cannot abdicate his role as a principal of the bureaucracy. His own success depends to a large extent on the workings of the bureaucracy. Yet the tools with which he can motivate the permanent bureaucracy are weak, especially given the constitutional protection of civil servants' jobs. Short-term executives cannot make credible threats of punishment. To accomplish his goals, the executive needs to bring in political appointees to carry out the bureaucracy's day-to-day work. Politicization of the Argentine bureaucracy comes, then, in the form of a parallel bureaucracy whose life span is as short as that of the appointing minister. Since each new executive cannot be expected to uphold the commitments of his predecessor, the dominant strategy for parallel bureaucrats is to have as short a planning horizon as their political masters.

Although this parallel bureaucracy is responsive to the political needs and policy interests of the moment, it has important negative side effects. It further reduces incentives for the permanent bureaucracy to develop internal capabilities because the parallel bureaucracy fills the most important positions and enjoys more visibility and prestige. Since the parallel bureaucracy is transient by definition, its presence conspires against the long-term buildup of administrative capabilities. Furthermore, short-term top public servants do not cooperate much across jurisdictions because their loyalties are with the individual minister, secretary, or undersecretary who brought them to the post.[9] This creates coordination problems within the executive office and prevents the evolution of norms like interministerial cooperation, standardization, and quality control procedures, all crucial for producing high-quality policies.

Another consequence of having a short-term principal is that both the organizational structure of the bureaucracy and the policies regulating

9. Contrast that with the tradition of "Cabinet responsibility" that leads to the bureaucracy being accountable to the cabinet as a whole in the Westminster system. See Palmer (1995).

it are extremely volatile. Each new administration creates an organizational structure to match its own agenda and the political, coalitional, and electoral considerations of the moment. The result is further instability.

The combination of the short-term horizons of the principals in the executive branch with the (in principle) undefined horizon for permanent bureaucrats whose jobs are constitutionally protected makes it close to impossible for politicians to work productively with the permanent bureaucrats. At the outset of a minister's tenure, his or her relationship with permanent bureaucrats is tainted with distrust. Furthermore, it is very hard to convey any information on capacities at this point.[10] With an average tenure of less than two years, ministers have few tools to motivate bureaucrats, who then have no incentive to excel. Furthermore, too much cooperation with the current minister might become a liability for a permanent bureaucrat in the next period (under the next minister), and it is very likely that efforts in one direction will have to be reversed in the near future.

The organizational chart of the Argentine public administration is constantly changing. In 1999, some nongovernmental organizations began producing an annual "Map of the Argentine State" (*Mapa del Estado Argentino*), an organizational chart of the Argentine national administration. When maps from several consecutive years are viewed, they reveal a continuous process of merging, creating, and displacing divisions, especially around changes of government. Even though new laws are required to add or eliminate ministries, most lesser changes (in the number of undersecretaries, *direcciones nacionales*) occur by executive decree.

Often, the organizational chart is changed for micropolitical reasons, such as providing more or less power to a political faction or an individual. Even crucial policy areas are subject to turf battles between ministries. The location of international trade negotiations, for example, has switched back and forth between the Ministry of the Economy and the Foreign Ministry as the political fortunes of different key individuals have ebbed

---

10. Often, permanent civil servants are both willing and able to carry out some of the required tasks. Yet the equilibrium (with incomplete information) is such that newly appointed top bureaucrats are naturally suspicious of the loyalties and capabilities of the personnel under their jurisdictions. They usually invest valuable time and resources just attempting to sort out who the loyal and competent ones are. As one former undersecretary put it, "While the newcomer loses time trying to find out who is who, the permanent bureaucrat loses time trying to demonstrate how good and trustworthy a person he or she is" (Oszlak 1999: 295).

and flowed. Similarly, the responsibility for public utilities has been the subject of turf battles, going from the Ministry of Public Works to the Ministry of Economics and Public Works and Services to the Ministry of Federal Planning, Public Investment and Public Services.

The high sensitivity of the bureaucratic structure to political change is one more indication of the discretion with which the executive manages the bureaucracy in Argentina as well as of the lack of involvement of Congress in these matters. Important reorganizations take place even in the course of a single governmental term (see Oszlak 1999; Iacoviello, Tommasi, and Zuvanic 2002).

Even legal provisions that cap the number of ministries have been ingeniously circumvented by the creation of *secretarías con rango ministerial* (secretaries with ministerial rank) – that is, ministries with a different name. Originally, the Alfonsín government created about 32 secretariats and 65 undersecretariats, and the number grew during his presidency. In 1991, under the Menem administration, the total number of these units was reduced to fewer than 70; in the following years, their number grew again, reaching 192 units. Another restructuring measure, enacted in 1996, fixed the number at 125.

All that constant manipulation of the organizational chart of the public administration is both a manifestation and a cause of the patchwork and stop-and-go nature of Argentine public policies. Periodic streamlining initiatives reduce the number of secretaries and undersecretaries, only to be followed by a gradual recovery in the number of agencies (see Figure 6.5).

The next section looks in more detail at one of the main consequences of the lack of long-term principals, the parallel bureaucracy, in more detail.

THE PARALLEL BUREAUCRACY

The coupling of constitutional protections of civil servants' jobs with high levels of turnover in the executive branch and Congress's abdication of its role as a principal in the bureaucracy has produced unresponsive bureaucrats with little incentive to invest in their own capacities. Politicians' reaction to this lack of responsiveness is to bring with them into office a substantial number of people to replicate the structure of the permanent civil service.

Even though the phenomenon of the parallel bureaucracy is highlighted in every study of the Argentine government's human resources, information about its exact size is hard to come by. The budget does not specify the number of parallel bureaucrats that a particular national jurisdiction

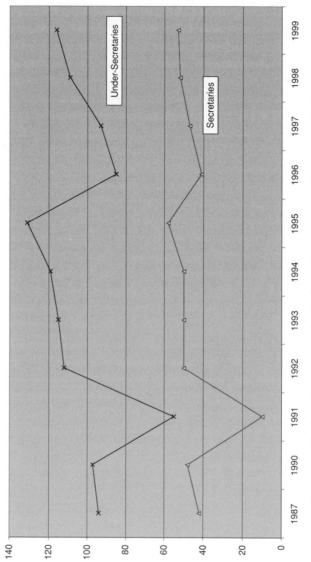

Figure 6.5. Number of secretaries and undersecretaries, 1987–1999. *Source:* Benedetti (1999).

Table 6.4. *Number of Official and Parallel Bureaucratic Positions in the Executive Branch*

Group	Offices in April 2002[a]
National System of the Administrative Profession (SINAPA)	25,211
Civil Personnel of the Armed Forces (PECIFA)	21,274
Personnel subject to collective bargaining (Law 14.250)	36,816
Scientific and technical agencies	12,367
Regulatory agencies	1,810
Special corps	627
Nonranked offices	524
Temporary *contratados*	16,509
Total[b]	116,729

[a] Does not include vacant offices.
[b] Does not include 152,876 offices of military, security, education, and health personnel.
Source: Iacoviello, Tommasi, and Zuvanic (2002).

(ministry, secretariat, or decentralized administrative unit) may have. As a consequence, estimates of the number of parallel bureaucrat employees vary drastically.[11] Some sources place the number of *contratados* (non–civil service employees under special contracts) in the national public administration at around 22,000 – a considerable figure in comparison with the 53,000 permanent employees under the *convenio colectivo* (collective bargaining agreement) (see Bonifacio and Falivene 2002). The Office of Public Sector Employment and Wages (Dirección de Ocupación y Salarios del Sector Público) estimated for 2002 that there were 16,509 *contratados* (see Table 6.4), while the National Office of Public Employment (Oficina Nacional de Empleo Público) puts the number of contract employees at 11,233.[12] Indeed, some agencies would not be able to function without these parallel bureaucrats. The Ministry of Social

11. Since 2001 there is a requirement that each governmental institution publish on its website information concerning contract employees. The fulfillment of that requirement has been uneven. See *http://www.sgp.gov.ar/sitio/empleo/regimenes/contratados/listadocontratados/index_main_rcpc.html.*
12. Part of the problem in obtaining a uniform number of contract employees is that the average length of contract employment seems to be less than one year. As a consequence, the average number of contracts held by each contract employee is 1.6. This may mean either that a given contract employee is hired by two separate offices or that the employee's contract is renewed during the period under analysis. Indeed, the Oficina Nacional de Empleo Público counts 18,029 parallel bureaucrat contracts during 2002. See Oficina Nacional de Empleo Público (2003).

Table 6.5. *Estimated Composition of Personnel in the
National Administration*

Ministry	SINAPA (%)	Parallel Bureaucracy (%)
Foreign Affairs	12	88
Social Development	44	56
Education	50	50
Justice	27	63
Presidency	83	17

Source: Oficina Anticorrupción, Ministerio de Justicia (2000).

Development, for example, has approximately 1,700 employees, 500 of whom are permanent and 1,200 of whom are *contratados*. But as Table 6.5 shows, this is not an extreme case, but rather the norm among Argentine ministries.[13]

Parallel bureaucrats, even when occupying high positions, do not have the same legal authority as permanent bureaucrats – they are not allowed to sign official papers. A "parallel" National Director's acts must be endorsed by the signature of the secretary or the minister who appointed them. This contributes to the politicization of bureaucratic decision making and increases the formation of personal, rather than institutional, allegiances.

Formally, political appointments extend to the third echelon in ministries (and to the second level in secretariats) and to the advisers of these people (the so-called *personal de gabinete*). However, ministers and secretaries have found other ways to make political appointments. These range from creating new agencies subject to different civil service provisions to incorporating new line positions that can be filled with temporary personnel to using unmarked budgetary resources to hire "consultants" who perform duties as short-term full-time civil servants. This latter practice has also been quite common within specific programs and projects financed by international agencies such as the World Bank, the Inter-American Development Bank, and the United Nations Development Program.

The parallel bureaucrats are ruled by a much more flexible regime than their bureaucratic peers. The parallel bureaucracy has been expanding

13. One study concluded that the percentage of spending for "consulting" may have been as much as 74 percent of total personnel spending in the then Secretaría de Desarrollo Social (which later became a ministry) and between 40 and 50 percent in the Economics, Labor, and Education Ministries (Ferreres and Capitanich 1999).

Table 6.6. *Distribution of Employment,*
Energy Secretariat, 2000

Mode of Employment	% Employment Contracts
Contratados	63
Hybrid	10
Permanent bureaucrats	12
Internships	3–7
Political appointees	2
World Bank	2

Source: Energy Secretariat (2000).

rapidly since the early 1980s; it was formally regulated by an Executive Order of 1995 (No. 92/95) and modified in 2001 by Decree No. 1184/01. The regime regulated under this executive order is widespread, yet the parallel bureaucracy also appears in other forms, such as personnel hired by international finance institutions or "internships" for university students (Oficina Anticorrupción 2000). Apart from employees hired under Decree No. 1184/01, there are employees hired with funds from international organizations, employees hired for internships, and so on. We were able to obtain complete employment records of both permanent and parallel appointees for the Energy Secretariat of the Ministry of the Economy.[14] The parallel bureaucracy constitutes 78 percent of the total manpower of the secretariat. The exact distribution of employment contracts for the Energy Secretariat is depicted in Table 6.6.

With regard to hiring through international organizations, in a comparison of Latin American countries, Oszlak suggests that "the range [of international hiring] goes from two positions in a small country like Belize, or a very small, irrelevant number, like that reported in Chile, to several hundred (200 in Guatemala, 800 in Uruguay), and thousands in some of the largest countries (Argentina)" (Oszlak 2001: 13). According to estimates of the Office of Employment and Wages of the Public Sector, the total number of personnel with international funding in the national public administration is in the order of 1,200. Yet qualitative studies and survey evidence indicate that public officers perceive the number

14. Near the end of 2001, we were quite close to obtaining similar information for several other government departments (mostly from the Economics Ministry). At that time, the country entered the final stage of the crisis that led to the resignation of President De la Rúa, and all our contacts left their public sector positions.

of consultants to be much larger (Iacoviello, Tommasi, and Zuvanic 2002).[15]

Another mode of temporary employment includes internship agreements with universities. Interns are supposed to be assigned to tasks related to their program of study but are in fact assigned to do administrative and operational work. It is worth noting that in Argentina (especially at the University of Buenos Aires, which concentrates most of these contracts), unlike in the United States, people often are college students for long periods, sometimes into their late thirties.

Key differences between permanent and transitory bureaucrats lie in the appointment and dismissal processes. Appointments of parallel bureaucrats are left to the absolute discretion of the minister or secretary in charge of each agency. Also, permanent bureaucrats enjoy job stability stemming from the Constitution (art. 14bis), but parallel bureaucrats work under short-term contracts, usually from two to six months in length, which tend to be automatically renewed if the minister or secretary in charge is still in office. When the minister or secretary leaves office, all the parallel bureaucrats tend to leave also. (Occasionally, one sees some of these employees shopping for another patron.)

The information gathered about the Energy Secretariat confirms the hypothesis that the parallel bureaucracy rotates much faster than the permanent staff. The average tenure at the secretariat in 1999 was four years for parallel bureaucrats, while that of permanent bureaucrats was almost seventeen years.[16]

Another salient characteristic of the parallel bureaucracy is that its employees receive higher salaries, which allow the incorporation of more qualified personnel than most of those in the permanent bureaucracy. Parallel employees are better educated, on average, than permanent bureaucrats. Indeed, while 49 percent of parallel employees hold university degrees, only 26 percent of career bureaucrats do so (Oficina Nacional de Empleo Público 2003: 39). Parallel bureaucrats command a 10–15 percent premium, on average, although the premium disappears at the lower

---

15. On the dysfunctions created by parallel programs financed by international organizations operating alongside the permanent line programs (often with more qualified and better paid personnel), see, for instance, Peña (2001), Martínez Nogueira (2002), and Acuña and Chudnovsky (2002).

16. And 1999 is a comparison year likely to overestimate the duration of parallel bureaucrats, since it was the last of 10 years of the Menem administration. Contracts tend to expire with administrations. See Bambaci, Spiller, and Tommasi (2002).

Table 6.7. *Salary Scale in Argentina's Public Sector (pesos/month)*

Rank	Parallel Bureaucracy (Decree 92/95)	Permanent Bureaucracy (SINAPA)
General Supervisor	5,400–7,500	2,900–4,900 (executive functions)
Consultant A	3,800–5,000	2,660
Consultant B	2,920–3,640	2,464
Consultant C	1,920–2,590	1,820
Consultant D	1,080–1,730	1,660
Assistant	400–1,000	—

Source: Elaborated by the authors using data in Oszlak (1999) and Executive Decree 92/95.

Table 6.8. *Monthly Salaries of Parallel and Permanent Argentine Bureaucrats, Energy Secretariat, 2000*

	Parallel Staff	Permanent Staff
Average	$2,944	$2,267
Standard deviation	$1,512	$1,445
Maximum	$7,500	$5,880
Minimum	$720	$619
Range	10.42	9.50

Source: Energy Secretariat (2000).

levels (Table 6.7). Our data for the Energy Secretariat shows a slightly larger premium. See Table 6.8.

CIVIL SERVICE POLICY AND REFORM

Building a bureaucracy can be seen as a policy area with some special features in light of the theory presented in Part I of this book. Building an effective and stable bureaucracy requires investments of time and money, as well as consistency. The "objects" of policy are human beings (individually and collectively) and complex organizations. It is commonly argued that in order to produce effective changes in the way a public bureaucracy works, it is necessary to change the "culture" of the organization. That takes time, continuity, coherence, and motivation.[17] On top of that, by its

---

17. None of those things have been present in the reforms attempted recently in Argentina. See Blutman and Mendez Parnes (2003).

very nature, it is an area that invites political opportunism: Government jobs are one of the most common currencies of patronage and clientelism worldwide. Given all these complex Z characteristics, it is not surprising that the Argentine polity has been unable to build up an effective bureaucracy. And, as highlighted throughout the book, the poor quality of its bureaucracy feeds back into the nation's overall policy-making weaknesses.

Civil service "policy" has been a victim first of the democratic instability of most of the twentieth century, and then of the weaknesses of the Argentine Congress and short-term incentives of executives, leading to a weak and incoherent state apparatus. The endless sequence of military and civilian governments from 1930 to 1983 put top public managerial positions into the realm of whimsical and short-lived incumbent regimes. Turnover in top civil service positions was quite high; ineffectiveness was the natural companion of this discontinuity. By the end of the last military dictatorship, professional public management had not taken root in administrative practice (see Oszlak 1999).[18]

Attempts to reform the civil service system have not taken hold even twenty years after the return to democracy. Structural features of the Argentine political system, and in particular the legislators' short tenure in office and their lack of policy interest, have not permitted the development of a bureaucracy that matches the quality of Argentine human capital. In Argentina since the return to democracy, each reform measure has begun with ambitious goals and high expectations, but momentum has

18. The state of the Argentine Civil Service at the return to democracy is well depicted by the following quote from the first secretary of state for the public service of the new democratic period: "[W]e have reached this point because fifty-five years ago we have interrupted the effective operation of democracy in Argentina and because we have not been able, since then, to consolidate it as a universally accepted principle. This perverse 'culture' is the administrative correlate of instability and sectarism, because it is an adaptive answer – not entirely devoid of historical rationality – to a recurrent cycle of aggressions and grievances that our administration has suffered over this long period. . . . Massive dismissals, ideological discrimination, politically biased filters for admission into public office placed in the hands of security services, nepotism, requirements of party affiliation before entrance into public office – we have had everything during these black years of our decline. What else could be expected from a human group so large and so representative of a society in crisis. . . . ? Our civil servants were not apostles nor heroes, but ordinary people, and they maladapted to a situation which was even worse. They are paying – and they are collecting from us – the price of instability and sectarism" (Roulet, 1988, cited in Oszlak, 1999, 296–7). On the impact on the bureaucracy of the military/civilian alternation, see also Repetto, Minteguiaga, and Cruz Olmeda (2004) and Groisman (1991).

waned over time, and each initiative has eventually been distorted or implemented only partially. The aggregation of all these reform efforts has created a view of the Argentine public sector as a "graveyard of projects" where the living and the dead walk alongside one another in the corridors of official buildings.[19]

To illustrate that process, we provide in the rest of the section a quick overview of the main civil service reform initiatives since the return of democracy.

Public sector reform has been on the political agenda since the middle of the twentieth century, and thus it was among the priorities of the new democratic government inaugurated in 1983, which created the Secretaría de la Función Publica (Secretariat of Public Office) to this end. The focus was mainly on increasing the capacity and efficiency of public employees. The major public sector reforms implemented in Argentina came in the 1990s, and they were coupled with other microeconomic reforms, fiscal deficit reduction policies, and a shrinking of the state.

According to Oszlak (2001), Latin American governments have tried four different ways to reform their civil services. They have alternately defined the scope of their respective systems in terms of a small number of key positions, an elite corps, a service-wide career, or an internationally funded, parallel consultants' network. According to Oszlak, Argentina is probably the only country in Latin America that has attempted all four approaches.

The Alfonsín administration (1983–9) gave impetus to a reform with an elite corps approach patterned after France's model of a skilled public sector workforce trained in its Ecole nationale d'administration. It consisted of the creation of the Government Administrators Corps (Cuerpo de Administradores Gubernamentales, CAG). The Administradores Gubernamentales were recruited through a strict competitive system after a complex selection process and a specialized training program. The program was able to attract a number of intelligent, energetic, and committed young professionals. Although we are not aware of complete studies of this initiative, experts agree that its impact, twenty years after its introduction, has been far less than expected. Oscar Oszlak, who was undersecretary of state for administrative reform and advisor to President

---

19. We have heard the expression "graveyard of projects" mainly from Oscar Oszlak, the foremost expert on Argentine public administration. Oszlak (1999) also speaks of the "deformity" of the Argentine civil service, caused by an irrational distribution of posts.

Alfonsín when the CAG was launched, had this to say about the program's results: "It can be safely affirmed that the role of the corps will hardly be as important as it was originally foreseen. Its size has remained fixed at 230, and it appears that it will never reach the targeted 1,000 figure since recruitment of new cadres has been suspended by the present government" (1999: 280).

Oszlak states that "the creation of SINAPA and, especially, the Executive Positions regime seems to have put some limits on the prospects of AGs to be the sole source of supply of top managers for the public sector" (280).[20] The picture got even worse after the Menem administrations (1989–95, 1995–9); the Alianza government (2000–1) did not incorporate any additional cohorts. And in August of 2000, in the context of yet another fiscal adjustment, a program of incentives for early retirement offered a fixed severance package based on years of service. Informal evidence suggests that most of those who left the public sector at that point (45 of the remaining 200) were those with a higher opportunity cost. Some went into the private sector. Others returned to public sector functions as consultants (receiving higher salaries than before).

An attempt with some similarities to the CAG was launched by the Ministry of the Economy in 1995, the so-called Cuerpo de Economistas del Estado (State Economists Corps). Economics Minister Cavallo wanted to develop a professional corps similar to the one in the Foreign Ministry, the Servicio Exterior de la Nación. A school to train this cadre of economists was formed, the Instituto Superior de Economistas de Gobierno (ISEG). The ISEG's objective was to recruit young professionals from the private and public sectors and upgrade their training in different areas of applied economics in order to allow them to take on jobs formulating and implementing national economic policies. The training consisted of a master's program in government economics, which was subcontracted to four universities. The program originally took four semesters spread over a two-year period, but for budgetary and administrative reasons it was later changed to three semesters compressed into 12 months (Harberger 1998). Only three cohorts completed the program before the ISEG was discontinued, and the economists trained by the program

20. The SINAPA initiative (National System of the Administrative Profession, described below) included the creation of 465 executive positions (Cargos con Función Ejecutiva) at the top of the administration.

are serving in different capacities than expected. As of this writing, a few government economists occupy relevant positions in some ministries, particularly those with personal connections to current ministers. Even though their salaries are somewhat higher than those of some of their co-workers (which is a source of some friction), most have a sense of frustration and unfulfilled promises.[21]

After a 1973 attempt to create a public sector–wide career civil service failed, the SINAPA was launched for the same purpose in 1991. One of the main goals of SINAPA was to give greater weight to functional and performance considerations in determining salary levels. This implied a wide departure from the preexisting system, which was full of "additionals" intended to compensate employees' special personal circumstances. The main reason for the preexisting heterogeneity was the permanent need to solve discrete labor conflicts – especially during high inflationary periods – by making small wage and other concessions to a given class or level of civil servants or to employees located in a certain area. Under SINAPA, basic wages for different levels and steps were established on the basis of the functional requirements of the job. In practice, several planned hiring and promotion practices have not materialized fully. SINAPA had too small a quantitative significance to exert a systemic effect: Its total reach is less than a quarter of overall employment in the national public administration, and its size is comparable to that of the temporary personnel (Iacoviello, Tommasi, and Zuvanic 2002).

The last attempt at public sector reform was the Plan de Modernización del Estado led by then–vice president Carlos Alvarez. This plan included novel prescriptions for public administration like the adoption of contracts for performance and the *Carta compromiso con el ciudadano* (documents stating specific commitments of each agency to its citizen-clients). Carlos "Chacho" Alvarez was the leader of the junior coalition partner Frepaso and was given the job in order to provide him with more visibility than the vice president usually has in Argentina. But from the beginning, the project was tainted by turf battles between the vice president's office and the public sector area in the Jefatura de Gabinete (see CEDI 2000). In the end, it was another victim of the country's political and institutional instability: When the vice president resigned, the plan lost political support and left behind only partial and disconnected results.

---

21. This impression is based on personal communications with expert Laura Zuvanic and with government economist Antonio Federico.

Table 6.9. *Organizational Structure of Civil Service Policy in Argentina*

Year	Rule	Agency	Jurisdiction
1973	D-L20,173	Created the National Institute of the Public Administration (INAP)	Office of the president
1977	ED3,981	Created undersecretariat of the public office; placed INAP in its organizational structure	Office of the president
1983		Gave undersecretariat of the public office the rank of national secretariat	National secretariat
1992		Changed jurisdiction of INAP	Office of the president
1993	ED1669	Created a human and organizational resources department in each jurisdiction	Ministries and secretariats
1996	ED660	Transferred the secretariat of public office and INAP to the chief of cabinet	Chief of cabinet
1999	ED20	Replaced the secretariat of public office with the undersecretariat of public office	Secretariat of general coordination, chief of cabinet
2001	ED673, ED889, ED1503	Changed jurisdictional location of the undersecretariat of public office and INAP	Secretariat for the modernization of the state, chief of cabinet
2002	ED78	Transferred the functions of the undersecretariat of public office	Secretariat for the modernization of the state, chief of cabinet

Notes: D-L stands for "decree-law" under military government. ED means Executive Decree.
Source: Elaborated by the authors with data from Iacoviello, Tommasi, and Zuvanic (2002: Section 5.1).

The current administration of President Kirchner does not seem particularly concerned about building capabilities in the state apparatus.

The organizational chart of the national public administration is additional evidence of the "Argentine style" of policy-making in this area. Table 6.9 shows the instability of the very office in charge of civil service policy. Note that all those changes took place by executive decree (without congressional intervention).

CONCLUSION

The description of Argentine policies regarding its civil service provides a nice transition toward the next chapter, in which the characteristics of

Argentine policies are analyzed more broadly. Let us conclude this chapter by listing the characteristics of civil service policy in Argentina:

- Lack of a clear and integrated diagnosis of the problem
- Lack of consensus
- Lack of a clear national policy
- Lack of continuity from administration to administration
- Lack of congressional participation
- Uncoordinated programs and actions by ministries and secretaries within the national government
- Attempts to create arenas for horizontal and vertical articulation and coordination that fail for lack of political interest

Characteristics similar to these will reappear in other policy areas in the next chapter.

7

The Nature of Public Policies in Argentina

We have established in previous chapters several characteristics of the Argentine policy-making environment. Congress is not an important policy arena; presidents tend to have excessive leeway to change policy, except when they face fierce opposition of provincial governors; and nobody has much incentive to invest in long-term policy-making capabilites. Argentina also lacks institutional arrangements, such as a professional bureaucracy or an independent judiciary, that would facilitate enforcement of agreements. These characteristics correspond to what, in the language of Part I of the book, we would describe as a policy-making environment not conducive to cooperation. And, as we established in Proposition 1, a noncooperative policy-making environment can lead to policy volatility, rigid rules, inability to instrument some efficient policy changes, and underinvestment in capacities, all leading to low-quality policies. In this chapter we provide evidence on the characteristics of public policies that fits these predictions.

Previous chapters have already provided some evidence on that regard with respect to policies pertaining to the federal fiscal domain and to civil service policy. This chapter starts with a generic characterization of policies in Argentina, drawing on some international data sets, and then provides vignettes of the process of policy making in some specific policy areas such as international trade negotiations, social policies, pension reform, and regulation of privatized utilities.

GENERAL CHARACTERISTICS OF ARGENTINE POLICIES

In the 1990s, Argentina undertook a wide and profound process of market-oriented reforms. With its ambitious program of macroeconomic stabilization, financial liberalization, privatization, and deregulation,

Argentina became the poster child of the Washington establishment. The cornerstone of that stabilization-cum-structural reform effort was a monetary regime known as "convertibility," which rigidly tied the peso to the dollar at a one-to-one rate. After decades of inward-looking policies, stagnation, and fiscal crises that led to hyperinflation in 1989, Argentina seemed to have found its way. The macroeconomic performance of Argentina for much of the 1990s was very strong, with GDP growth switching from negative in the 1980s to an increase of over 50 percent in the 1991–7 period and inflation coming down from hyperinflation levels (23,104 percent) in 1990 to around zero in 1997.

Despite the promising results in the 1990s, in 1998 the Argentine economy entered a long recession, which exploded into one of the deepest crises in modern economic history in December of 2001. In the end, the 1990s were just one more episode in the long history of hope and despair that characterized Argentina for most of the twentieth century. Most economists who have evaluated the dismal performance of Argentina have pointed to poor economic policies as the culprit of these sad outcomes. We are inclined to agree with that characterization, but instead of blaming the content of economic policies, we blame the characteristics of policies and policy making, including policy instability, inadequate enforcement, inadequate commitment capacities, and an inability to effect necessary adjustments.

Argentine policies are unstable in ways that weaken their credibility in the eyes of economic actors, rendering them far less effective in bringing about desired economic behavior, such as investment, savings, and job creation, and hence desired economic outcomes, such as sustainable growth and employment. Argentine policies are not only unstable but also poorly coordinated within the tiers of the country's federal structure and among ministries, secretaries, and programs of the national government. In many instances, it is also patently clear that the investments in capabilities required to produce effective policies are absent. The Argentine state is, in essence, ineffective in enforcing its policies.

Perhaps the most noticeable characteristic of public policies in Argentina is their instability. One aggregate indicator of policy stability could be constructed from international indexes, such as the Fraser Index of Economic Freedom, which grades a country's economic policy according to market-friendliness. In Figure 7.1, we plot the value of that index from 1970 to 1997 for a small number of countries. In the mid-1970s, Argentina went from being one of the most market-friendly countries in this sample to being the least friendly after the Soviet Union, and then

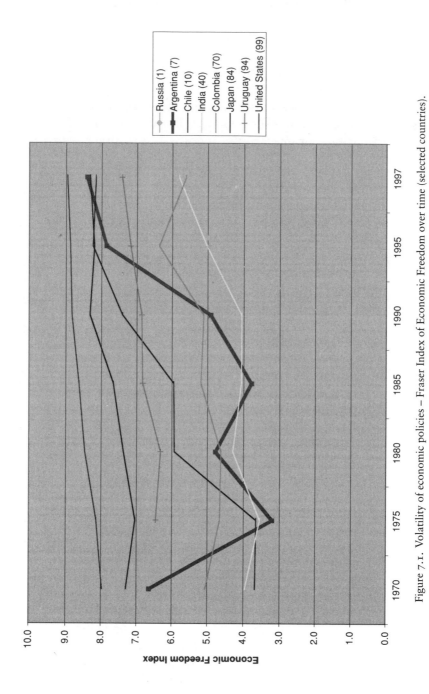

Figure 7.1. Volatility of economic policies – Fraser Index of Economic Freedom over time (selected countries).

Argentina returned to market friendliness during the reform process of the 1990s. (We do not have the data up to the present, but the policies undertaken since the devaluation in January of 2002 make it clear that Argentina's index of market orientation has again started to swing back down, as exemplified in the following section on privatization and regulation.)[1] Looking at the whole sample of 106 countries, Argentina appears as the seventh most volatile according to the coefficient of variation of the Fraser Index over time. Treating countries whose market friendliness goes up and down, like Argentina's, separately from countries like Chile or Russia whose policies moved in just in one direction (toward market liberalization), Argentina ranks as the fourth most unstable.

Argentina shows policy instability not only at this aggregate level but also in its specific policies. In this chapter, we document the volatility of antipoverty programs in the 1990s, describing how large policy changes were made without congressional mandates. Existing welfare programs are often reshuffled (refocusing or discontinuing existing programs and creating new ones) when new ministers or secretaries take office, a frequent event in Argentina. Often, this reshuffling involves substantial tinkering with the geographic distribution of funds.[2]

Another policy area where Argentina has shown volatility in international comparison is fiscal policy (see Mody and Schindler 2004). This policy volatility shortens the time horizons of the economic and social actors, thus reducing policy effectiveness and inducing poor economic and social outcomes.

Businesspeople indicate in international surveys that they view Argentina's policy volatility as very costly for the operation of their businesses (see Figure 7.2). Argentina's business community is reluctant to respond to export-promotion policies because their durability is so uncertain (see Acuña 1991). Similarly, trade policy uncertainty has had a negative impact on the macroeconomic performance of Argentina.[3]

---

1. Lora, Panizza, and Quispe-Agnoli (2004) show Argentina and Venezuela as the two countries in Latin America backsliding from the market-oriented reforms of the 1990s.
2. The average tenure of department heads at the National Secretariat for Social Development is less than a year. Furthermore, the agency has changed from secretariat to undersecretariat to ministry. The position of agency head has been occupied by highly qualified technocrats, by high-profile politicians, by the spouse of one president, and by the sister of another one.
3. Hopenhayn and Neumeyer (2003) argue that trade policy uncertainty was one of the key factors in the poor growth performance of Argentina in the second half of the twentieth century.

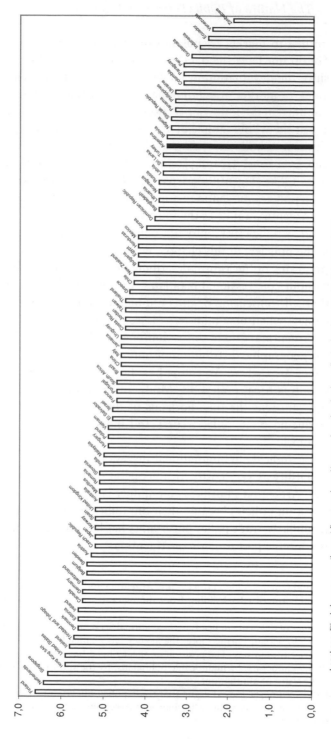

Legal or political changes over the past five years have (1=severely undermined your firm's planning capacity, 7=had no effect)

Figure 7.2. The business view: "Policy volatility is costly" (costs of policy changes). *Source:* Global Competitiveness Report (2001).

Argentina is also a weak enforcer of its policies, at the bottom of the list in its ability to enforce tax collection, Social Security contributions, and payment of minimum wages (see Figures 7.3 and 7.4). This inadequate enforcement also weakens the credibility of Argentine policies. Unlike the case in other countries like Chile,[4] legislation is not a very hard currency for intertemporal policy exchanges in Argentina.

The lack of credibility leads, at times, to the adoption of highly rigid policies. A notable example was the 1991 adoption of the straightjacket monetary mechanism of convertibility, which prevented the authorities from undertaking monetary policies in response to adverse shocks throughout the 1990s.[5] It is paradoxical that one of the few cross-country indicators in which Argentina looked good in the eyes of the international business community was exchange rate stability (see Figure 7.5). An April 2001 survey asked businesspeople (just eight months before the convertibility regime fell and the currency suffered a major devaluation) whether they expected the exchange rate to be volatile, and Argentina ranked the sixth best country by this measure. (After the fact, any measure of exchange rate volatility would have placed Argentina as the most volatile country in the sample.) This suggests that credibility can be temporarily achieved only through very rigid mechanisms. These mechanisms, however, may become very costly under some circumstances.

Another example of Argentina's inability to undertake efficient and flexible policies is provided by the history of fiscal federalism in the country (summarized in Chapter 6). In attempts to protect themselves from the opportunistic behavior of other political actors, national and provincial authorities have introduced all kinds of rigidities into the federal tax-sharing agreement. These rigidities, such as tying specific tax revenues to specific geographic distributions, created numerous microeconomic inefficiencies during the 1980s and 1990s. One of the most recent examples was the 2000 agreement by the national government to transfer fixed nominal amounts to the provinces. In the great economic downturn of 2001, with the convertibility straightjacket in effect and the reluctance of creditors to absorb fresh debt, it became impossible for the national government to honor those intergovernmental commitments. The political disputes over distribution of available fiscal funds and the state's

---

4. See, for instance, Aninat et al. (2004) and Londregan (2002).
5. The details of the adoption of the convertibility regime and the subsequent dynamics throughout the decade that exploded into the 2001–2 economic, social, and political crisis are analyzed by Galiani, Heymann, and Tommasi (2003).

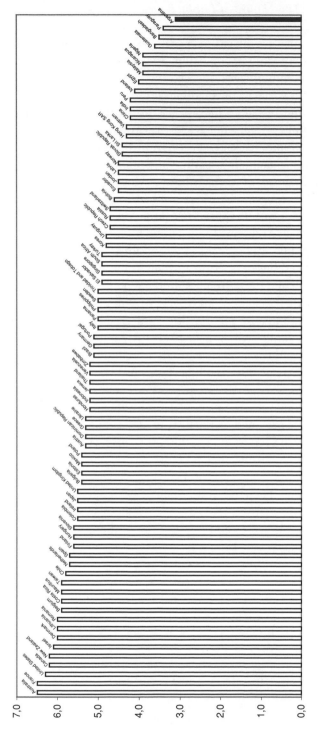

The minimum wage set by law in your country is (1=never enforced, 7=strongly enforced)

Figure 7.3. Minimum wage enforcement.

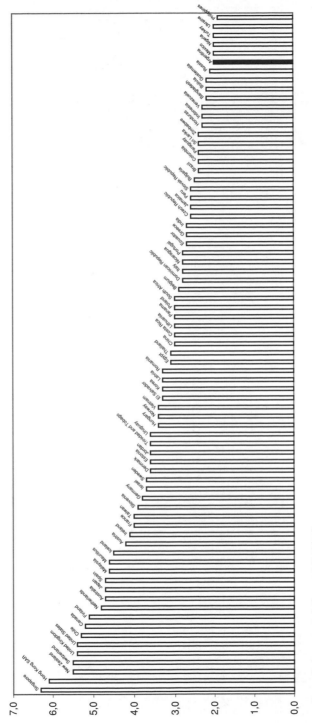

Tax evasion in your country is (1=rampant, 7=minimal)

Figure 7.4. Tax evasion.

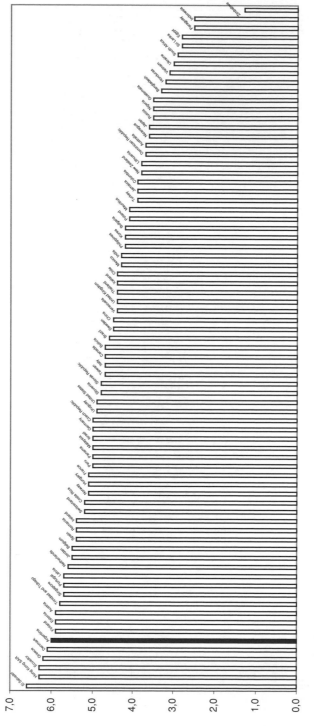

Over the next two years, your country's exchange rate will be (1=very volatile, 7=very stable) [Question asked in February-April 2001]

Figure 7.5. Expected exchange rate volatility.

inability to adjust the fiscal arrangement to the new adverse circumstances are seen as the proximate causes of the Argentine default and crisis of 2001–2. (See Eaton 2003 for references to the international financial press.)

In the next few sections, we describe policy making in Argentina in the areas of trade policy, social policy, pension reform, and utilities privatization and regulation. We draw from assessments of area experts, and we interpret those assessments in light of the framework and language developed in this book.

INTERNATIONAL TRADE NEGOTIATIONS

International trade negotiations are a crucial policy area for Argentina because access to international markets may hold the key to the country's sustained development. Our summary of policy making in this area draws on a recent assessment by one of the foremost Argentine experts in the field, Roberto Bouzas (Bouzas and Pagnotta 2003). As highlighted by Bouzas and Pagnotta, in international trade negotiations and international trade policy more generally, intertemporal capabilities – consensus building, policy consistency, capacity building, and institutionalization – are particularly important. These features, however, are particularly lacking in Argentina.[6]

The Strategy of External Negotiations

Argentina participates in multiple trade negotiations with Mercosur, the World Trade Organization, and the European Union, and within the Americas in the framework of the Free Trade Area of the Americas. Roberto Bouzas and Emiliano Pagnotta describe Argentina's strategy this way:

The strategy of external commercial negotiations by Argentina has had diffuse aims and has been ambiguous. The negotiating position has been guided by multiple, and often contradictory, priorities and interests. This is the result of the

---

6. We might also have included a section on foreign policy more broadly. Several specialists have highlighted the relative weakness (even by Latin American standards) and volatility of Argentine foreign policy. See Russell and Tokatlian (2003) and Lafer (2002) for comparisons of Argentine foreign policy with that of its main regional neighbor, Brazil.

absence of a domestic consensus that ensures the continuity of those aims over time. Worse still, even for those topics on which there is consensus about the importance of the negotiation (as in the case of participation in the OMC), the ability to act in a consistent way has been very limited. (2003: 81)

Institutional Organization

Bouzas and Pagnotta describe the design and execution of international commercial negotiations as highly fragmented, with diverse public offices having overlapping functions with little coordination. They have this to say about the assignment of responsibilities across the three ministries in charge of international commercial negotiations:

The Ministry of the Economy is the executive office with the most extensive responsibilities. These include the administration of a vast scale of instruments of economic policy, such as the design and application of instruments of trade policy (and other related policies), including import duties, quantitative restrictions, special import regimes, measures of commercial exemption, and export duties, as well as measures of fiscal relief for exports. The Ministry of Production and its secretaries are the offices responsible for the application of these instruments, and they also take part in international commercial negotiations. The Ministry of Foreign Affairs is in charge of international commercial negotiations and it designs and implements commercial promotion policies. Other organs linked to the executive also active in the area of trade policy are the National Commission of Foreign Trade, the Federal Administration of Public Revenues, the Investment and Foreign Trade Bank, and the Export-Ar Foundation. (2003: 90–1)

This complex organizational structure requires a high degree of coordination. Instead, according to Bouzas and Pagnotta, "there is no formal deliberative process in the elaboration of these policies." They go on:

The participation of Congress is sporadic and reactive. Although coordination inside the executive branch has changed over time, ... the overlapping of functions, competition across offices, and interbureaucratic struggle have been the rule. This means that the efficiency of the routines and procedures depends strongly on particular circumstances, leadership, and personalities. ... The bureaucratic structures are unstable, and there is high turnover among civil servants, as well as a low level of institutional learning. The high proportion of personnel under temporary contracts conspires against the accumulation of expertise, precisely in an area in which knowledge constitutes a strategic asset. ... The institutional fragility of the policymaking process spreads to the absence of mechanisms for the systematic and organic participation of the private sector, which has promoted lobbying, in a context of a lack of transparent procedures and a general absence of routines. (2003: 91–2)

Highlights of Deficiencies in International Trade Negotiations

Bouzas and Pagnotta's description of policy features and policy making in international trade makes numerous points that are useful for the broader concerns of this book: Coordination among offices is deficient, and competition among agencies is wasteful of time and energy. The assignment of responsibilities is unfocused. As a result, policy implementation is inefficient and ineffective. There is no adequate arena or institutionalized procedure for deliberation, for the creation of consensus, or for the definition of policy direction. There are no formal coordination mechanisms. Congressional intervention is sporadic and haphazard. There are interbureaucratic struggles. Bureaucratic structures change very often. There is a high level of turnover among civil servants and, as a consequence, a low level of institutional learning. Because temporary personnel (*contratados*) fill top policy-making positions, there is little accumulation of institutional experience in an area where knowledge is strategic. There is a lack of effective coordination across levels of government in the federal structure.

SOCIAL POLICY

In the 1980s and 1990s, Argentina faced a steady deterioration of its social conditions; the situation reached catastrophic levels after the fall of convertibility, when the fraction of Argentines living below the poverty line grew to over 50 percent. The complex causes of poverty require the capacity to provide integrated and consistent policies over time rather than ad hoc and temporary fixes. Argentina's public policy apparatus has not responded adequately.

The deterioration in health, education, housing, infrastructure, and employment indicators associated with the increasing rates of poverty and income inequality placed the fight against poverty on the government's agenda. The institutional response has led to dispersion of efforts and the uncoordinated creation of multiple national programs from different government agencies directed toward the poor, greater decentralization of responsibilities related to social services to the provinces and municipalities, and increasing incorporation of civil society organizations in the design, execution, and implementation of social policies. This overall mosaic has tended to be poorly coordinated, unstable, and ineffective (Rodriguez Larreta and Vidal 2001).

Attempts to orient and target social policy to the poor have produced a hybrid social policy system comprising the traditional universal system of social services – in serious decay after numerous economic crises – and an exponential growth of social programs targeted to the poor. The increasing poverty level has generated numerous uncoordinated poverty programs across regions and population segments. Although large – in 1998, these programs involved US$3.9 billion out of US$57 billion in overall social programs – these programs not only did not provide extensive coverage but also were "not adapted to different local realities, as they try to resolve in a centralized manner the particular problems of each region" (Rodriguez Larreta and Vidal 2001: 22). There were fifty-seven poverty alleviation programs alone distributed among seven different ministries. Rodriguez Larreta and Vidal assess the lack of coordination in this way:

To the existence of such a varied supply, we have to add the lack of coordination among the different areas and the limited capacity of the national executive to give a sense of direction to policies and programs. The initiatives in that direction have not had any concrete results. That is the case with the "Social Cabinet," an arena created for the coordination of social policies that convenes all the national ministers concerned with this issue, under the authority of the chief of Cabinet. This initiative, which had the right intentions, was unsuccessful because it lacked political support to become a true social authority that would concentrate all resources and decisions relating to the alleviation of poverty. (2001: 25)

In 1994, the National Secretariat for Social Development was created under the president's office to define and coordinate social policies directed to the poor. But coordination proved an elusive task, and the secretariat was not able to define a strategy or generate coordinated actions even among the twenty-three programs under its own jurisdiction. The overall result has been a failure to respond to the needs of the poor. It is estimated that only 10 percent of the target population is covered by emergency programs. Similarly, unemployment insurance in 2001 covered only 5 percent of the 2.4 million unemployed.

The lack of coordination in the central government is coupled with a process of decentralization toward the provinces. The government has delegated the execution of 70 percent of social programs to provinces and municipalities, programs as varied as education, nutrition, and housing. The vague definition of responsibilities in social policy places high stakes on both horizontal and vertical coordination. Provincial authorities not only implement national policies but also create their own provincial social programs. The ability of the provincial governments to manage all these programs varies widely. The national government created the

Federal Council for Social Development, composed of the social ministers of the twenty-four provinces, to coordinate the actions of the various jurisdictions. Lack of political support caused the failure of the council to achieve its objectives.

A vast majority of the national programs have been created by executive order rather than by law. Congressional actors are not even mentioned in any description of social policy making. Because the programs defined unilaterally by the executive do not include clear and enforceable criteria for the allocation of resources in the different jurisdictions, the political appointee in charge has a high level of freedom to distribute them. As a result, short-term political criteria and lack of transparency taint most of the actions and decisions (see Palanza 2002).

Social spending is supposed to be countercyclical; that is, larger expenditures are required when economic conditions are poor. Braun and Di Gresia (2003), however, find that social spending in Argentina is procyclical, absorbing more spending when economic conditions are good. The elasticity of social spending to the level of aggregate output (an indicator of the state of the economy) is 0.42; that means that when output decreases by \$1 (an economic downturn), social spending is reduced by 42 cents. The comparable elasticity for the United States is −0.75. That means that when U.S. output decreases \$1, social spending is increased by 75 cents. (See Sanguinetti 2002 for a more detailed analysis of the intertemporal properties of social spending in Argentina.) Argentina's procyclical approach to social spending and its failure to adapt social policy to local realities mean that Argentina's social policies are incapable of adjusting adequately to changing geographic or temporal circumstances.

Highlights of Deficiencies of Antipoverty Programs

Policy making to combat poverty suffers from the following characteristics:

- Lack of a clear and integrated diagnosis of the problem
- Lack of a clear national policy
- The discontinuation of preexisting programs by incoming administrations and the creation of new programs in different agencies by new administrations[7]

7. Writing on the social policies of the 1990s, Cortés and Marshall (1998) argue: "As periodically shown by public opinion polls, growing unemployment became a major concern, starting to undermine support for the administration's economic

- A low level of participation by Congress in developing social policies
- Proliferation of programs and of uncoordinated actions across ministries and secretaries within the national government
- Proliferation of programs and of uncoordinated actions across levels of government
- Attempts to create arenas for horizontal and vertical articulation and coordination that do not succeed for lack of political interest
- Inability to focus properly
- Difficulty adapting to different local realities
- Procyclical social spending
- Difficulty adapting the former universalistic social policy strategy to the new strategy of targeting and focusing

REFORM OF THE PENSION SYSTEM

The privatization of the Argentine pension system in 1993 was a salient component of the "reform epic" of Argentina in the 1990s.[8] Pension policy can be characterized at its core as supporting a transaction in which current workers sacrifice current income in exchange for income to be received many years in the future. Because pension policy implies some mandatory behavior on the part of workers and because it holds the potential for opportunistic behavior – with the possible result that you give your money now but do not get your money later – it is difficult to undertake without complex institutional support.[9]

The Argentine pension system in the early 1990s was a public "pay as you go" (PAYG) one. The system had been chronically underfunded

policies. This fostered the highly publicized announcement of a succession of small-scale, short-lived, and continuously redesigned social programs, mostly before elections. In fact, publicity was not matched by the amount of resources allocated to these schemes. Some programs were discontinued without visible reasons, and were replaced by others, that differed slightly. Even those closely monitored by the World Bank had a meager impact, as they were addressed to confined target groups" (10).

8. Tommasi (2004) provides a more general description (and criticism) of the market-oriented reform epic that swept Latin America in the late 1980s and 1990s, as well as a general comment on "market-oriented reforms, the Argentine way." See also Acuña, Galiani, and Tommasi (2005) for a broader analysis of the Argentine reform process of the 1990s.

9. Of course, a pension system has other elements, such as intragenerational redistribution and insurance provided by the people who die early for the people who live longer. But the intertemporal investment described in the text is at its core.

for many decades because of unrealistic parameters, low compliance, and the tendency of successive governments to manipulate its funds politically (see Rofman 2002; Demarco 2004; and Kay 2003a). Analyses in the early 1990s pointed out that PAYG systems create poor incentives for individuals and for the political system. In the words of the labor minister who oversaw the privatization of Chile's pension system (the leading model of the times), "The PAYG social security system . . . destroys, at the individual level, the essential link between effort and reward – in other words, between personal responsibilities and personal rights. Whenever that happens on a massive scale and for a long period of time, the result is disaster" (Piñera 1999, cited in Kay 2003b). Also, it was expected, on the basis of the Chilean experience, that privatization of the pension system would prevent political manipulation of pension funds. (See, for instance, Mesa-Lago's 1994 description of the position of international organizations on this issue.) It was believed that structural reform of the system was necessary to overcome the "institutional weaknesses" that led to very low public confidence in the system (Demarco 2004).

After intense debate, a reform was undertaken in late 1993, including some changes in the parameters, such as increasing employee contribution rates, increasing the minimum retirement age, and, crucially, making changes in the institutional arrangements of the system.[10] The system was organized around two pillars. One would grant a flat benefit of around 28 percent of average wages to those satisfying some age and years-of-contribution requirements. The second pillar offered a choice of either staying in the public PAYG system or switching to a private system of funded individual accounts where individuals accumulate personal contributions (net of some costs). These funds were to be administered by management companies (*Administradoras de Fondos de Jubilaciones y Pensiones*, AFJPs). Most workers joined the privately funded scheme, either by choice (2.3 million workers)[11] or by default assignment – those

---

10. For details on the alternatives considered and the political debates, see Demarco (2004). For a detailed description of the new system, see Rofman (2000).
11. Informal evidence (Ronconi and Tommasi 2003) suggests that the decision to switch to the private system was in some cases not based on higher expected returns but on the cajoling of male workers by the beautiful miniskirted women who constituted the majority of the AFJP's sale force. The sales effort developed by the new AFJPs was very large. In a few months, they created a sale force of almost 30,000 (0.25 percent of the Argentine labor force) and spent more than half a billion dollars on marketing and sales commissions (Rofman 2002).

not exercising an explicit choice, 2.8 million workers, were randomly assigned to one of the AFJPs.[12]

With some minor caveats, then, we can summarize the reform, as most observers do, as a privatization of the pension system. Yet privatization of the pension system did not eliminate the role of the state. The state still has an important role to play in running the first pillar, protecting citizens by regulating the private pension funds, and enforcing compliance with the contributions to the system.

An important determinant of the success of a private pension fund system is the ability of the state to compel workers and employers to contribute to mandatory social insurance programs (Kay 2003b). As Figure 7.6 indicates, of the seven countries listed, Argentina ranks as the worst enforcer of social security contributions. Furthermore, compliance has fallen even among those pension fund participants who have stayed in the system. Figure 7.7 shows that the percentage of formal employees contributing to the pension funds is far lower in Argentina than in Chile, Colombia, Mexico, or Uruguay.

The Argentine state not only failed in its regulatory role, it also failed to restrain itself from expropriation. As indicated by Kay (2003a), the "privatizing" reform did not eliminate political risk. The performance of the system after privatization was no better than it had been before the reform because the Argentine state not only failed to perform its regulatory role but also continued tinkering with people's savings. Since the inception of the system, through regulation, AFJPs relied heavily on having government-issued bonds in their portfolio. But unlike the bonds issued by developed economies, government bonds are not safe assets in Argentina. Not only was the fraction of pension funds invested in government bonds high to begin with, but, through a series of negotiations and unilateral measures, the government forced AFJPs to increase their exposure to government risk during the 2001–2 crisis. Before the default and devaluation of January 2002, the government reduced the mandatory contributions to pension funds. Then it cut benefits by 13 percent and stopped pension fund adjustments. Then it forced the AFJP to accept a debt swap. Then it converted pension fund deposits into treasury notes. With the default and the devaluation of 2002, the government first stopped payment on the debt held by the AFJPs and then converted that debt into

12. A small percentage, close to 15 percent, chose not to belong to the capitalization regime and instead to stay in the previous distributional, or *reparto*, regime.

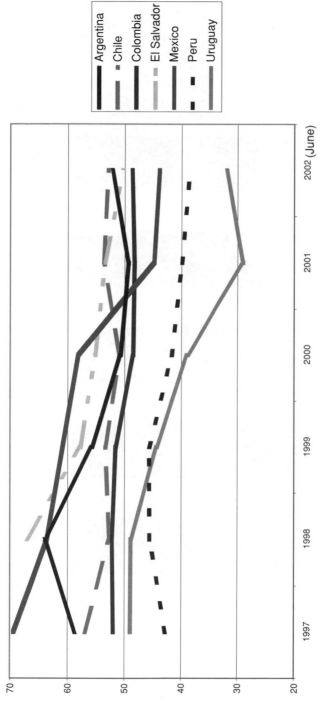

Figure 7.6. Percentage of pension fund affiliates making regular contributions. *Source:* Kay (2003b).

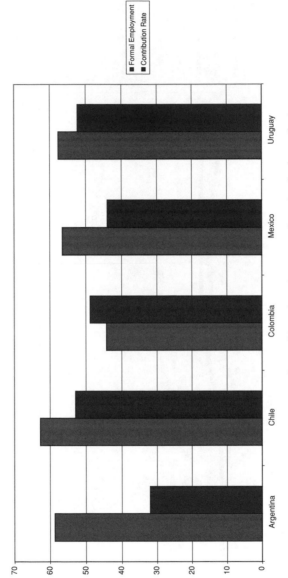

Figure 7.7. Comparison of rate of formal employment and pension fund contribution rate.

pesos. As a consequence, the value of the holdings of AFJPs plummeted (see Kay 2003a: 5).

This episode indicates that the privatization of the pension system did not dramatically change the ability of the government to use the pension system for short-term financial gains.[13] It highlights some permanent characteristics of policies and of the policy-making process in Argentina that are often independent of the content (or title) of the policy in question – whether the system is "public" or "private." These characteristics include most prominently the inability to enforce commitments.

PRIVATIZATION AND REGULATION OF UTILITIES

General Features

Argentina undertook a drastic process of utility privatization and regulatory reform during the 1990s.[14] In the energy sector, Argentina broke up vertically integrated utilities (electricity, gas, and crude oil), creating competitive wholesale markets and separating privatized transportation and distribution companies. It established agencies in gas and electricity to deal with the regulation of distribution and transport. In telecommunications, it founded two large companies and slowly liberalized the market. It privatized airports, postal services, and ports. The provinces joined in this privatization process; many engaged in the privatization of water and electricity distribution services. Some provinces also created specialized regulatory agencies.

The path of reform was rapid, starting in 1989 with the enactment of two basic pieces of legislation: the State Reform Act and the Economic Emergency Act. The former gave the executive, and in particular the area ministries and secretaries, extraordinary powers to privatize public enterprises, while the latter eliminated subsidies and removed barriers to foreign investment. At the same time, Argentina started a process of signing bilateral investment treaties (BITs) with multiple countries. A BIT

---

13. There are several other important dimensions in which the reform did not improve the situation and might have worsened it – for instance, on the fiscal side and in actual and expected future coverage of the elderly. These problems have put the system on the table again for consideration of further reforms. Given the current ideological winds, the resulting reforms are likely to increase the role of the public pillar. See Bulit Goñi (2005) for further criticism.
14. For a detailed analysis of those reforms, see Abdala and Spiller (2000), on which this section is based.

provides investors who are nationals of a foreign country, although not domestic investors, the ability to request arbitration proceedings against Argentina should Argentina undertake unfair, discriminatory, or expropriatory actions against the interests of the foreign investor. The timing of the signing of the BITs is quite illuminating, as most were signed prior to the beginning of the major regulatory reforms of the early 1990s.

The reform process was highly decentralized.[15] The State Reform Act of 1989 set the tone for this decentralization when it delegated to each area ministry the ability to determine the nature of the privatization process. Thus, the privatization commissions normally involved the company's politically appointed manager and the area secretary. Each privatization committee arranged for its own legal and technical support, normally with funding from international organizations, for preparing the regulatory frameworks and undertaking the sale. The high degree of decentralization in the privatization effort, together with the inherent lack of coordination across areas – a key deficiency of Argentine policy making – meant that the privatization processes as well as the resulting regulatory frameworks were highly diverse and idiosyncratic. Although the regulatory frameworks (and the privatizations) of the electricity and natural gas sectors have a high level of coherence, the regulatory frameworks of all other sectors – including airports, ports, trains, highways, the postal service, water, and telecommunications – have little in common. A key noteworthy feature of the privatization and regulatory reform in the energy sector, though, was that a single area secretary, the secretary of energy, undertook it, while ad hoc secretaries undertook the privatization and regulatory reform of all the other sectors.

Institutional Flux in Telecommunications

The design and creation of regulatory agencies was also decentralized. Although the regulatory agencies for gas and electricity were designed in a coherent way and created by law, all the others were designed in an ad hoc fashion by executive decree. As a consequence, their autonomy and political stability were undermined from the start. The telecommunications regulatory agency is probably the best example. The decree creating the National Telecommunications Commission (NTC) was issued on June 22,

---

15. According to Rausch (1995), "Each privatization was modeled according to the peculiarities and sectoral interests and available technical capabilities [of the particular industry in each area]." See also U.S. General Accounting Office (1996).

1990, just before private firms submitted bids for the ENTel companies, and it was established *after* the transfer of ENTel to its private owners. Thus, bidders for the ENTel companies had to prepare their bids without knowing the regulatory capabilities of the agency that would be regulating them. The privatization was directed by the secretary of communications within the Ministry of Public Works, which was not particularly in favor of privatization.

The members of the telecommunications regulatory agency were initially drawn from the group of people in charge of the privatization; its first president was the former secretary of communications. Later, when President Menem named economist Domingo Cavallo as the new minister of the economy, Cavallo merged the ministries of economics and public works and handily removed – as a consequence of disagreements and perceived incompetence – the members of the NTC, naming an acting director of his own choosing in early 1992. In October 1993, a reorganization put the NTC in the jurisdiction of the secretary of public works and communications of the Ministry of Economics and Public Works and curtailed its powers, and the government named new directors. Soon thereafter, the government implemented – without any particular process – a job switch between the president of the commission and the secretary of public works. This state of affairs lasted until mid-1995, when, after another fight between the commission and the secretary of public works and communications, the president of the commission and another commissioner resigned. The government moved fast to intervene once again, removing the remaining three commissioners and again naming its own acting director. Following the threat of litigation from an ombudsman, the government reinstated the removed directors but retained its oversight through the temporary director.

In 1996, the new undersecretary of communications of the Ministry of Economics and Public Works was transferred directly to the presidency with the elevated status of secretary. The newly established secretary of communications then named a new interim director for the commission. The government also merged the commission with its postal service counterpart, creating the National Communications Commission, and in 1997 it named a new board of directors.

Comparing the Telecommunications and Electricity Experiences

The institutional flux of the Communications Commission and the institutional stability of the energy regulatory agencies reflect the power of institutions. Confronted with the ability to intervene at will in conflict resolution processes (at the communications agency), the government implemented the institutional structure that best helped it in the short run, while in those institutional environments with previously existing limitations (in energy) it had to satisfy itself with lobbying and cajoling, with less success. Not surprisingly, the performance of the electricity and gas sector has been hailed throughout the world as an example of successful reform, while the opposite is true of the telecommunications reform.

Investors responded accordingly. During the 1992–7 privatization process, according to the U.S. Energy Information Agency, investors poured more than US$5 billion into acquiring electricity assets in all three segments: generation, transmission, and distribution. The impact on the sector was visible. Nonsupplied electricity, which reached dramatic proportions in the 1988–90 period (it exceeded 600 GWh in January 1989) was completely eliminated by 1995. The extent of competition in the wholesale market and the efficiency gains then ensured that prices fell drastically. Indeed, average wholesale prices, which were very high before the privatization process (upwards of US$70/MWh), fell to below US$25/MWh by the end of 1997.

In contrast, the flawed design of the telecommunications reform and privatization required that strong guarantees be given to investors. The two descendants of the public ENTel were granted exclusive concession agreements, regional monopolies, and a joint monopoly on national and international long-distance phone service. At the same time, the government set very high initial prices. At privatization, new lines were priced at US$2,627 for commercial use and at US$1,050 for residential users, well above costs. These charges gradually fell to US$500 in November 1993, to US$250 in November 1995, and to US$150 in October 1998. Similarly, the price per pulse was increased in 1991, leading to reduced use in the early years of the privatization. With these two assurances in place – monopoly and high prices – the two operators dramatically improved investment and performance.

The 2002 Tariff Freeze and the Role of Bilateral Investment Protection Treaties

The path of reform was drastically reversed in the midst of the economic crisis with the enactment of the Emergency Act of January 6, 2002. The

Emergency Act and its implementation – at both the national and the provincial levels – had drastic consequences for private investors in utilities. Articles 8 through 10 of the Emergency Act froze, in Argentine currency, all utility tariffs (including wholesale prices for natural gas, which were up to then completely deregulated) at the levels prior to the devaluation. Although all other prices have increased drastically since 2002, the tariff freeze has, so far, been maintained.

The tariff freeze was a drastic deviation from the regulatory frameworks instituted in national and provincial regulatory laws and in the respective licenses. The tariff freeze was also very costly for investors, and it forced the exit of several foreign investors from Argentina at substantial losses.[16] The response of private investors is consistent with our analysis of the workings of public policy making. Although the tariff freeze violated multiple contracts signed between the national and provincial government and the various licensees, no major utility or domestic investor appealed the decision to the domestic courts. Instead, foreign investors initiated international arbitration proceedings based on bilateral investment protection treaties that Argentina signed in the early 1990s with both the United States and various European countries. The selection of international arbitration over domestic courts as the arena to obtain a reversal of the tariff freeze is another example of the inability of the Argentine courts to substantially limit the executive's ability to take unilateral actions. In this sense, the signing of the BITs and the development of highly specific regulatory frameworks (either via highly detailed legislation, as in energy, or highly detailed licenses, as in telecommunications and water) reflect the need to create multiple layers of protection against the ability of the executive to alter the rules of the game.

In sum, the utilities privatization case shows some of the key characteristics of Argentine public policy making, among them the lack of coordination across sectors, the ability of the executive to alter the rules of the

---

16. Various foreign investors, such as PSEG, First Energy, Azurix, France Telecom, EDF, and National Grid, sold their holdings in utility operating companies at around 10 percent of their original investments. See, respectively, "AES compra a precio de remate," *El Cronista, http://www.cronista.com*, December 5, 2002; "El agua de Mendoza, de la Enron a capitales nacionales," *Clarín*, January 8, 2004; "Aprueban cambios en Telecom," *El Cronista, http://www.cronista.com*, December 30, 2003; "Edemsa, con nuevo dueño," *La Nación*, July 7, 2004; and "Un comprador con todas las luces," *Revista Fortuna*, August 2, 2004, *http://www. fortuna.uolsinectis.com.ar/edicion_0042/nota_tapa/nota_tapa.htm*.

game, and the need to be restrained by either highly specific legislation (energy) or highly specific concession contracts (telecommunications). In both cases, some credibility was achieved only at the cost of introducing highly rigid policies.

A RECAP: CHARACTERISTICS OF POLICY MAKING AND OF PUBLIC POLICIES IN ARGENTINA

We have provided in this chapter a number of vignettes about policies and policy making in Argentina. In this section, we provide a selective summary of the characteristics highlighted by the policy examples, which we interpret as "stylized facts" consistent with the overall argument of the book. We first list some aspects of the policy-making process and then some features of policies.

The Policy-Making Process

The policy cases narrated in this chapter illustrate some characteristics of the policy-making process. These include deficiencies of the budget process, which gives excessive discretion to some executive actors; insufficient involvement by Congress;[17] instability of the bureaucratic structures in charge of implementation; instability of top bureaucratic personnel; noncooperativeness of the interactions between national authorities and provincial authorities; noncooperativeness of interactions among and within national ministries; provincial governors who appear as relevant actors in national policy; and promises that are not fulfilled.

Characteristics of Policies

Policies in Argentina, then, seem to present the following characteristics: They show a high level of volatility (they often change with low-level political rotation). Paradoxically, other policies are too rigid, not being adjusted when circumstances change. Sometimes they respond to changing circumstances in the wrong direction. They are poorly coordinated. They present poor qualities (in dimensions not captured by the previous points). And they are poorly enforced.

---

17. On the lack of Congressional involvement, see Chapter 3 on the budget, Murillo (2001) on the market-oriented reforms of the 1990s, and Pion-Berlin (1997) on defense policy.

All of these features fit well with the predictions of Proposition 1 (Chapter 2). They are also consistent with our previous analysis of the workings of the political system, where we conclude that the equilibrium of the game among the relevant institutions of public policy decision making in Argentina generates conditions closely resembling those identified in Proposition 2 as conducive to noncooperative policy making and thus generating the conditions for poor policy outcomes.

Concluding Remarks

This book began with the observation that Argentina's policies have shifted dramatically over time, and with the claim that its inability to produce consistent public policies is the reason behind its economic misfortunes. We argued that the deficiencies of Argentine public policies are the outcome of a policy-making process in which key actors have little incentive to cooperate with one another over time, leading to myopical political and policy choices. Argentina has, thus, been unable to steer a consistent path in crucial areas such as economic, social, or international strategies.

Argentina has a national policy-making environment dominated by executives who tend to have too much leeway to pursue whatever policies they fancy, provided they can buy the support of quasi-feudal provincial governors with fiscal largesse. Such a depiction is somewhat surprising for a country that has a basic constitutional structure with separation of powers quite similar to that of the United States. In spite of a common basic constitutional structure, the workings of political institutions in Argentina couldn't be more different than in the United States. The Argentine Congress is neither the arena where key policies are negotiated nor a very attractive place to develop a political career. The Argentine Supreme Court is not a respected institution with the power to act as a real check on executive power. In Argentina, there is no policy delegation to well-staffed independent professional agencies supervised by Congress through the power of the purse. The Argentine president often seeks the support of provincial governors for his national policies, and provincial governors' main objective is to increase the amount of federal funds they obtain to finance provincial public sector activities as well as their political machineries.

As argued in the preceding chapters, each of these peculiar features of the Argentine polity constitutes, in game-theoretic jargon, equilibrium behavior of political actors. This equilibrium behavior, in turn, has developed over time as the outcome of past events and of the incentives provided by the interaction of several "details" of the political rules. Among the "details," we have emphasized the provincial connection to national political careers provided by electoral mechanism that make the province the key arena, as well as the interconnection between provincial and national public finances. These, and other important details, are themselves equilibrium outcomes of past choices. For instance, most key aspects of Argentina's current electoral rules were inherited at the return of democracy in 1983. The earlier choice of such rules has its own history. For example, the overrepresentation of small provinces and the large vertical fiscal imbalances were the result of conscious choices of both prior military dictators and democratically elected presidents. Military dictators saw backward/conservative provinces as their own bastions. Similarly, President Perón created provinces out of sparsely populated national territories, hoping (correctly) to transform them into bastions of his political movement. Although many of these rules do not contribute to inducing national consensus or to generating high-quality public policies, they provide substantial benefits to entrenched political actors. As a consequence, these rules have resisted change.

Those examples relate to the million dollar question that we have been asked repeatedly by audiences, reviewers, and friends: What type of institutional reform would provide a way out for Argentina? Our short answer is that there is no short answer. Designing institutions on paper is not the same as designing institutions in the real world.

Even assuming that the new rules will eventually alter behavior in the desired direction, it is patently clear that modifying basic rules will not be supported by the relevant political actors. We have identified the subnational drag to national policies as a crucial problem. Any change in the direction of reducing the dependence of national legislators from provincial powers seems unlikely given the incentives of current power brokers.

Another important reason is that there could be substantial behavioral inertia due to a number of informal practices that consolidate over time around "the old rules." Colombia had in 1991 a major institutional reform encouraging members of the upper chamber to adopt a more national, programmatic vision. Crisp and Ingall (2002) show that, in spite of that reform, many senators have continued to be elected from geographically concentrated constituencies and have continued to focus on bills with a pork-barrel propensity.

As economists, we started this project out of the frustration of seeing the failure of technocratic approaches to policy making that did not take into account the incentives of political actors. We end this book with a similar note of caution with respect to overly simplified suggestions for political reform.

References

Abdala, Manuel A., and Pablo T. Spiller. 2000. "Instituciones, Contratos y Regulación de Infrastructura en Argentina." Fundación Gobierno y Sociedad, Editorial TEMAS, Buenos Aires.

Abuelafia, Emmanuel, Sergio Berensztein, Miguel Braun, and Luciano Di Gresia. 2005. "Who Decides on Public Expenditures? A Political Economy Analysis of the Budget Process: The Case of Argentina." Mimeo, Cippec-IADB.

Acemoglu, Daron. 2005. "Constitutions, Politics and Economics: A Review Essay on Persson and Tabellini's 'The Economic Effect of Constitutions'." *Journal of Economic Literature* 43: 1025–48.

Acuña, Carlos H. 1991. "La relativa ausencia de exportaciones industriales en la Argentina. Determinantes políticos y sus consecuencias sobre la estabilidad y el tipo de democracia esperables." *Realidad Económica* 100: 9–38.

Acuña, Carlos H., and Mariana Chudnovsky. 2002. "Salud: Análisis de la Dinámica Político-Institucional y Organizacional del Área Materno Infantil (Con Énfasis en el Programa Materno Infantil y Nutrición, PROMIN)." Working Paper 61. Center for Studies of Institutional Development, Fundación Gobierno y Sociedad, Buenos Aires.

Acuña, Carlos H., Sebastián Galiani, and Mariano Tommasi. 2005. "Understanding Reforms. The Case of Argentina." Paper prepared for the Global Research Project on "Understanding Reform," Global Development Network, July.

Afifi, A. A., and Virginia Clark. 1996. *Computer-Aided Multivariate Analysis*, 3rd ed. New York: Chapman and Hall.

Alesina, Alberto. 1988. "Credibility and Policy Convergence in a Two-Party System with Rational Voters." *American Economic Review* 78 (4): 796–805.

Alesina, Alberto, and Allan Drazen. 1991. "Why Are Stabilizations Delayed?" *American Economic Review* 81 (December): 1170–88.

Alston, Lee J., and Andrés Gallo. 2005. "The Erosion of Rule of Law in Argentina, 1930–1947: An Explanation of Argentina's Slide from the Top Ten." Mimeo, University of Colurado at Boulder. Available at: *http://www.colurado.edu/ibs/EB/alston/paper.html*

Alston, Lee J., Marcus Andrés Melo, Bernardo Mueller, and Carlos Pereira. 2004. "Political Institutions, Policymaking Processes and Policy Outcomes in Brazil." Paper written for the project "Political Institutions, Policymaking Processes and Policy Outcomes" of the Latin American Research Network, Inter-American Development Bank.

Alter, Veronica. 2000. "Es de Difícil Cumplimiento la Ley de Acceso a la Información." *La Nación*, July 11.

Amadae, S. M., and Bruno Bueno de Mesquita. 1999. "The Rochester School: The Origins of Positive Political Theory." *Annual Review of Political Science* 2: 269–95.

Ames, Barry. 1995. "Soft Theory, Hard Evidence: Rational Choice and Empirical Investigation in Brazil." Paper prepared for the Twenty-Ninth International Congress of the Latin American Studies Association, Washington, DC, September 28–30.

———. 2001. *The Deadlock of Democracy in Brazil*. Ann Arbor: University of Michigan Press.

Aninat, Cristóbal, John Londregan, Patricio Navia, and Joaquín Vial. 2004. "Political Institutions, Policymaking Processes, and Policy Outcomes in Chile." Paper written for the project "Political Institutions, Policymaking Processes and Policy Outcomes" of the Latin American Research Network, Inter-American Development Bank.

Archer, R. P., and Matthew Soberg Shugart. 1997. "The Unrealized Potential of Presidential Dominance in Colombia." In Scott Mainwaring and Matthew Soberg Shugart, eds., *Presidentialism and Democracy in Latin America*, 110–59. New York: Cambridge University Press.

Ardanaz, Martín. 2004. "El federalismo fiscal en la reforma constitucional de 1994: Un caso de estudio en la teoría de los costos de transacción." Trabajo de Licenciatura, Universidad de San Andrés, August.

Ardanaz, Martín, Marcelo Leiras, and Mariano Tommasi. 2005. "Beyond Plaza de Mayo: Provincial Party Bosses in Argentina." Mimeo, Universidad de San Andrés.

Bambaci, Juliana, Pablo T. Spiller, and Mariano Tommasi. 2001. "Bureaucracy and Public Policy in Argentina" Mimeo, Center of Studies for Institutional Development (CEDI), Fundación Gobierno y Sociedad.

Baron, David P. 1996. *Business and Its Environment*. New York: Prentice Hall.

Baron, David P., and John A. Ferejohn. 1989. "Bargaining in Legislatures." *American Political Science Review* 83: 1181–206.

Bednar, Jenna. 2003. "On the Inevitability of Shirking." Mimeo, University of Michigan, March.

Benedetti, Paolo F. 1999. "Aspectos Institucionales de la Administración Pública: Implicancias para la Argentina." Working Paper 22. Center of Studies for Institutional Development, Fundación Gobierno y Sociedad.

Benton, Allyson. 2003. "Presidentes Fuertes, Provincias Poderosas: La Economía Política de la Construcción de Partidos en el sistema Federal Argentino." *Política y Gobierno* (Mexico) 10: 103–37.

Bergara, Mario, Barak Richman, and Pablo T. Spiller. 1999. "Judicial Politics and the Econometrics of Preferences." Working Paper 18. Center of Studies for Institutional Development, Buenos Aires.

References

Best, H., and M. Cotta. 2000. *Parliamentary Representatives in Europe, 1848–2000: Legislative Careers and Recruitment in Eleven European Countries.* New York: Oxford University Press.

Bidart Campos, Germán J. 1982. *La Corte Suprema.* Buenos Aires: Allende y Brea.

Bill Chavez, Rebecca. 2003. "The Construction of the Rule of Law in Argentina: A Tale of Two Provinces." *Comparative Politics* 35 (4): 417–37.

Bird, Richard M. 1996. "Descentralización Fiscal: una Revisión." *Descentralización Fiscal y Regímenes de Coparticipación Impositiva.* Seminario Internacional, Facultad de Ciencias Económicas de la Universidad Nacional de la Plata, June 29.

Blutman, Gustavo, and Soledad Mendez Parnes. 2003. "Reformas Administrativas del Estado y Cultura Organizacional." Paper presented at the Second Argentine Congress on Public Administration, Córdoba, November.

Boix, Carles. 2005. "The Fiscal Consequences of Presidentialism." Paper prepared for Workshop on Economic Consequences of Political Institutions, Duke University, April 1–2.

Bonifacio, José Alberto, and Graciele Falivene. 2002. "Análisis Comparado de las Relaciones Laborales en la Administración Pública Latinoamericana: Argentina, Costa Rica, México y Perú." Working Paper. Regional Policy Dialogue, Red de Transparencia y Gestión de la Política Pública, CLAD.

Botana, Natalio. 1993. "El federalismo liberal en Argentina, 1852–1930." In Marcello Carmagnani, coord., *Federalismos Latinoamericanos: México, Brasil, Argentina*, 224–61. Mexico City, Mexico: Fondo de Cultura Económica.

Botana, Natalio, and Ana María Mustapic. 1991. "La Reforma Constitucional frente al Régimen Político Argentino." In D. Nohlen and Liliana De Riz, comps., *Reforma Institucional y Cambio Político*, 45–92. Buenos Aires: CEDES-Legasa.

Bouzas, Roberto, and Emiliano Pagnotta. 2003. *Dilemas de la Política Comercial Externa Argentina.* Buenos Aires: Fundación OSDE / Universidad de San Andrés.

Braun, Miguel, and Luciano Di Gresia. 2003. "Towards Effective Social Insurance in Latin America: The Importance of Countercyclical Fiscal Policy." Working Paper 487. Research Department, Inter-American Development Bank.

Braun, Miguel, and Mariano Tommasi. 2004. "Subnational Fiscal Rules: A Game Theoretic Approach." In G. Kopits, ed., *Rules Based Fiscal Policy in Emerging Markets: Background, Analysis, and Prospects*, 183–97. Palgrave: McMillan.

Buchanan, James M., and Gordon Tullock. 1962. *The Calculus of Consent: Logical Foundations of Constitutional Democracy.* Ann Arbor: University of Michigan Press.

Bulit Goñi, Luis G. 2005. "Control y Regulación. Políticas y Agencias para la Seguridad Social Argentina." Tesis de Maestría, Maestría en Administración y Políticas Públicas, Universidad de San Andrés.

Calvo, Ernesto, and Juan Manuel Abal Medina, eds. 2001. *El Federalismo Electoral Argentino: Sobrerrepresentación, reforma política y gobierno dividido en la Argentina.* Buenos Aires: Eudeba.

References

Calvo, Ernesto, and Juan Pablo Micozzi. 2004. "The Governor's Backyard: A Bayesian Model to Estimate the Seat-Vote Properties of Subnational Electoral Reforms." Paper prepared to be presented at the 62nd Annual Conference of the Midwest Political Science Association, Chicago, April 15–18.

Calvo, Ernesto, and María Victoria Murillo. 2004. "Who Delivers? Partisan Clients in the Argentine Electoral Market." *American Journal of Political Science* 48 (4): 742–58.

2006. "The New Iron Law of Argentine Politics?" In Steven Levitsky and María Victoria Murillo, eds., *Argentine Democracy: The Politics of Institutional Weakness*, 207–28. College Park: Pennsylvania State University Press.

Calvo, Guillermo A. 1989. "Incredible Reforms." In Guillermo Calvo et al., eds., *Debt, Stabilization, and Development*, 217–34. New York: Basil Blackwell.

1996. *Money, Exchange Rates, and Output.* Cambridge, MA: MIT Press.

Carey, John M. 1996. *Term Limits and Legislative Representation.* New York: Cambridge University Press.

Carey, John M., and Matthew Soberg Shugart. 1992. *Presidents and Assemblies: Constitutional Design and Electoral Dynamics.* New York: Cambridge University Press.

1998. *Executive Decree Authority.* New York: Cambridge University Press.

Carlsson, I., and J. Mark Payne. 2002. "Public Management and Transparency Network: Cross-Country Comparisons of Public Employment and Pay of 26 Latin American and Caribbean Countries." Working Paper. Inter-American Development Bank, Washington, DC.

Carrió, A. 1996. *La Corte Suprema y su Independencia.* Buenos Aires: Abeledo Perrot.

Castilla, Luis Miguel. 2002. "Finance Minister Turnover and Fiscal Outcomes: New International Evidence." Mimeo, Corporación Andina de Fomento.

Cayuso, Susana G., and María Angélica Gelli. 1988. "Ruptura de la Legitimidad Constitucional: La Acordada de la Corte Suprema de Justicia de la Nación de 1930." Cuadernos de Investigaciones (1). Instituto de Investigaciones Jurídicas y Sociales "Ambrosio L. Gioja." Facultad de Derecho y Ciencias Sociales, Universidad de Buenos Aires.

CEDI. 1999. Consensos Básicos sobre Relaciones Fiscales Federales y Coparticipación (rapporteur notes taken by Matías Iaryczower and Mariano Tommasi at the Forum on Fiscal Institutions), *Cuaderno de Opinión* (Discussion Paper) 4. Center of Studies for Institutional Development, Fundación Gobierno y Sociedad, Buenos Aires.

2000. "Notas sobre el Plan de Modernización del Estado" (Iaryczower and Mariano Tommasi at the Forum on Fiscal Institutions), *Cuaderno de Opinión* (Discussion Paper) 9. Center for Studies of Institutional Development, Fundación Gobierno y Sociedad, Buenos Aires.

Cooter, Robert D. 2000. *The Strategic Constitution.* Princeton, NJ: Princeton University Press.

Cooter, Robert D., and Tom Ginsburg. 1996. "Comparative Judicial Discretion: An Empirical Test of Economic Models." *International Review of Law & Economics* 16: 295–313.

References

Cornelius, Peter, Klaus Schwab, and Michael E. Porter. 2003. *The Global Competitiveness Report 2002–2003*, World Economic Forum. Cambridge, MA: Oxford University Press.

Cornelius, Wayne. 2000. "Politics in Mexico." In Gabriel A. Almond, G. Bingham Powell Jr., Kaare Ström, and Russell J. Dalton, *Comparative Politics Today: A World View*, 7th ed. New York: Addison Wesley Longman.

Cortés, Rosalía, and Adriana Marshall. 1998. "Growth Strategy Requirements and Institutional Barriers in the Restructuring of Social Policy – The Case of Argentina." Paper prepared for delivery at the 1998 meeting of the Latin American Studies Association, Chicago, September 24–26.

Cowhey, Peter, and Mathew D. McCubbins. 1995. *Structure and Policy in Japan and the United States*. New York: Cambridge University Press.

Cox, Gary W., and Mathew D. McCubbins. 2001. "The Institutional Determinants of Economic Policy Outcomes." In Stephen Haggard and Mathew D. McCubbins, eds., *Presidents, Parliaments and Policy*, 21–63. New York: Cambridge University Press.

Crisp, Brian F. 2000. *Democratic Institutional Design: The Powers and Incentives of Venezuelan Politicians and Interest Groups*. Stanford, CA: Stanford University Press.

Crisp, Brian, and Rachael Ingall. 2002. "Institutional Engineering and the Nature of Representation: Mapping the Effects of Electoral Reform in Colombia." *American Journal of Political Science* 46 (4): 733–48.

Cuevas, Alfredo. 2003. "Reforming Intergovernmental Fiscal Relations in Argentina." IMF Working Paper, March.

Cukierman, Alex, and Mariano Tommasi. 1998a. "When Does It Take a Nixon to Go to China?" *American Economic Review* 88 (1): 180–97.

1998b. "Credibility of Policymakers and Economic Reforms." In Federico Sturzenegger and Mariano Tommasi, eds., *The Political Economy of Economic Reforms*. Cambridge, MA: MIT Press.

Danesi, Silvina. 2004. *A Dieciocho Años de Democracia, la Gestión en la Honorable Cámara de Diputados de la Nación*. Tesis de Maestría. Maestría en Administración y Políticas Públicas, Universidad de San Andrés.

de Figueiredo, Rui J. P. 2002. "Electoral Competition, Political Uncertainty, and Policy Insulation." *American Political Science Review* 96 (2): 321–33.

De Luca, Miguel. 2004. "Political Recruitment of Presidents and Governors in the Argentine Party-Centered System." Prepared for the symposium "Pathways to Power: Political Recruitment and Democracy in Latin America," Graylyn International Conference Center, Wake Forest University, Winston-Salem, NC, April 3–4.

De Luca, Miguel, Mark P. Jones, and María Inés Tula. 2002. "Back Rooms or Ballot Boxes? Candidate Nomination in Argentina." *Comparative Political Studies* 35: 413–36.

Demarco, Gustavo. 2004. "The Argentine Pension System Reform and International Lessons." In Kurt Weyland, ed., *Learning from Foreign Models in Latin American Policy Reform*, 81–109. Baltimore: Johns Hopkins University Press.

References

Desposato, Scott W. 2003. "Comparing Group and Subgroup Cohesion Scores: A Nonparametric Method with an Application to Brazil." *Political Analysis* 11 (3): 275–88.

Díaz-Cayeros, Alberto, and Beatriz Magaloni. 2001. "Party Dominance and the Logic of Electoral Design in the Mexican Transition to Democracy." *Journal of Theoretical Politics* 13 (3): 271–93.

Diermeier, Daniel, Michael P. Keane, and Antonio M. Merlo. 2005. "A Political Economy Model of Congressional Careers." *American Economic Review* 95 (1): 347–73.

Dixit, Avinash K. 1996. *The Making of Economic Policy: A Transaction-Cost Politics Perspective.* Cambridge, MA: MIT Press.

2003. "Some Lessons from Transaction-Cost Politics for Less-Developed Countries." *Economics and Politics* 15 (2): 107–33.

Dixit, Avinash K., Gene Grossman, and Faruk Gul. 2000. "The Dynamics of Political Compromise." *Journal of Political Economy* 108 (3): 531–68.

Drazen, Allan. 2000. *Political Economy in Macroeconomics.* Princeton, NJ: Princeton University Press.

Eaton, Kent. 2004. *Politics beyond the Capital: The Design of Subnational Institutions in South America.* Stanford, CA: Stanford University Press.

Ekmekdjian, Miguel A. 1999. *Tratado de Derecho Constitucional: Constitución de la Nacion Argentina, comentada, y anotada con legislación, jurisprudencia y doctrina.* Buenos Aires: Depalma.

Epstein, Lee, and Jack Knight. 2000. "The Role of Constitutional Courts in the Establishment and Maintenance of Democratic Systems of Government." Paper presented at the annual meeting of the American Political Science Association, Washington, DC.

Epstein, Lee, and Sharyn O'Halloran. 1999. *Delegating Powers: A Transaction Cost Politics Approach to Policy Making under Separate Powers.* New York: Cambridge University Press.

Etchemendy, Sebastián. 2002. "Constructing Reform Coalitions: The Politics of Compensations in the Argentine Path to Economic Liberalization." *Latin American Politics and Society* 43: 1–35.

Evans, Peter B. 1995. *Embedded Autonomy: States and Industrial Transformation.* Princeton, NJ: Princeton University Press.

2004. "Development as Institutional Change: The Pitfalls of Monocropping and Potentials of Deliberation." *Studies in Comparative International Development* 38 (4): 30–53.

Fearon, James D. 1999. "Electoral Accountability and the Control of Politicians: Selecting Good Types versus Sanctioning Poor Performance." In Adam Przeworski, Bernard Manin, and Susan Stokes, eds., *Democracy, Accountability, and Representation,* 29–54. New York: Cambridge University Press.

Ferejohn, John A. 1999. "Accountability and Authority: Toward a Theory of Political Accountability." In Adam Przeworski, Bernard Manin, and Susan Stokes, eds., *Democracy, Accountability and Representation.* New York: Cambridge University Press.

References

Ferreres, Orlando, and Jorge Capitanich. 1999. "Relaciones laborales y costo salarial en el sector público Argentino." Publication 15. Buenos Aires: Fundación Norte y Sur.

Figueiredo, Argelina C., and Fernando Limongi. 2000. "Presidential Power, Legislative Organization, and Party Behavior in Brazil." *Comparative Politics* 32 (2): 151–70.

Fudenberg, Drew, and Eric Maskin. 1986. "The Folk-Theorem in Repeated Games with Discounting and with Incomplete Information." *Econometrica* 54: 533–56.

Fudenberg, Drew, and Jean Tirole. 1991. *Game Theory*. Cambridge, MA: MIT Press.

Furubotn, Eirik G., and Rudolf Richter. 1998. *Institutions and Economic Theory: The Contribution of the New Institutional Economics*. Ann Arbor: University of Michigan Press.

Galiani, Sebastián, Daniel Heymann, and Mariano Tommasi. 2003. "Great Expectations and Hard Times: The Argentine Convertibility Plan." *Economia: Journal of the Latin American and Caribbean Economic Association* 3 (2): 109–60.

Garay, A. F. 1995. "La independencia del Poder Judicial." *El Derecho*, January 2.

Gely, Rafael, and Pablo T. Spiller. 1990. "A Rational Choice Theory of Supreme Court Statutory Decisions with Applications to the *State Farm* and *Grove City* Cases." *Journal of Law, Economics and Organization* 6: 263–300.

———. 1992. "The Political Economy of Supreme Court Constitutional Decisions: The Case of Roosevelt's Court Packing Plan." *International Review of Law and Economics* 12: 45–67.

Gibson, Edward L. 2004. "Subnational Authoritarianism: Territorial Strategies of Political Control in Democratic Regimes." Paper prepared for delivery at the 2004 Annual Meeting of the American Political Science Association, September 2–5, Chicago.

Gibson, Edward L., and Ernesto Calvo. 2000. "Federalism and Low-Maintenance Constituencies: Territorial Dimensions of Economic Reform in Argentina." *Studies in Comparative International Development* 35 (3): 32–55.

González, Christian Y., David Rosenblatt, and Steven B. Webb. 2002. "Stabilizing Intergovernmental Transfers in Latin America: A Complement to National/Subnational Fiscal Rules?" Paper prepared for the IMF/World Bank Conference on Rules-Based Fiscal Policy in Emerging Market Economies, Oaxaca, Mexico, February 14–16.

Graham, Lawrence. 1998. "Transients and Careerists in Latin America." In Ali Farazmad, ed., *Modern Systems of Government: Exploring the Role of Bureaucrats and Policymakers*. Thousand Oaks, CA: Sage.

Granado, María José. 2003. "Comentario a Spiller-Tommasi 2003 y a Tommasi 2002." Mimeo, Magister en Economía, Universidad Nacional de Tucumán, December.

Green, E., and R. Porter. 1984. "Non-cooperative Collusion under Imperfect Price Information." *Econometrica* 54: 975–94.

References

Grindle, Merilee. 1996. *Challenging the State: Crisis and Innovation in Latin America and Africa*. New York: Cambridge University Press.

Groisman, Enrique. 1991. *Políticas Administrativas para el Sistema Democrático*. Buenos Aires: Centro Editor de América Latina.

Harberger, Arnold C. 1998. "Letter to a Younger Generation." *Journal of Applied Economics* 1 (1): 1–31. Buenos Aires: CEMA.

Hardin, Russell. 1997. "Economic Theories of the State." In Dennis C. Mueller, ed. *Perspectives on Public Choice*, 21–34. Cambridge: Cambridge University Press.

Helmke, Gretchen. 2000. "Checks and Balances by Other Means: Strategic Defection and the 'Re-Relection' Controversy in Argentina." Paper presented at the Annual Meeting of the American Political Science Association, Washington, DC.

——— 2002. "The Logic of Strategic Defection: Court-Executive Relations in Argentina under Dictatorship and Democracy." *American Political Science Review* 96 (2): 291–303.

Henisz, Witold J. 2000. "The Institutional Environment for Economic Growth." *Economics and Politics* 12: 1–31.

Hopenhayn, Hugo A., and Pablo A. Neumeyer. 2003. "The Argentine Great Depression, 1975–1990." Mimeo, August. Available at: *http://200.32.4.58/~paneumeyer/Argentina.pdf*

Huber, John D., and Nolan McCarty. 2001. "Legislative Organization, Bureaucratic Capacity and Delegation in Latin American Democracies." Paper prepared for the Conference on Brazilian Political Institutions in Comparative Perspective, St. Antony's College, Oxford University, May 28–29.

Huber, John D., and C. Shipan. 2002. *Deliberate Discretion? The Institutional Foundations of Bureaucratic Autonomy*. New York: Cambridge University Press.

Hungerford, Thomas. 1991. "GATT: A Cooperative Equilibrium in a Noncooperative Trading Regime?" *Journal of International Economics* 31: 357–69.

Iacoviello, Mercedes, and Laura Zuvanic. 2004. "Síntesis del Diagnóstico Institucional de Sistema de Servicio Civil: El caso Chile." Mimeo, Inter-American Development Bank, Washington, DC.

Iacoviello, Mercedes, Mariano Tommasi, and Laura Zuvanic. 2002. "Diagnóstico Institucional de Sistemas de Servicio Civil: Caso Argentina." Regional Policy Dialogue, Inter-American Development Bank.

Iaryczower, Matías, Pablo T. Spiller, and Mariano Tommasi. 2002. "Judicial Decision-Making in Unstable Environments: The Argentine Supreme Court, 1936–1998." *American Journal of Political Science* 46 (4): 699–716.

Inter-American Development Bank. 2005. *The Politics of Policies: Economic and Social Progress in Latin America and the Caribbean 2006 Report*. Washington, DC: Inter-American Development Bank and Harvard University.

Iversen, T., and D. Soskice. 2002. "Political Parties and the Time Inconsistency Problem in Social Welfare Provision." Paper presented at the Annual Meeting of the Public Choice Society, San Diego, March 22–24.

Jones, Mark P. 2001. "Political Institutions and Public Policy in Argentina. An Overview of the Formation and Execution of the National Budget." In

Stephen Haggard, and Matthew D. McCubbins, eds., *Presidents, Parliaments and Policy*. New York: Cambridge University Press.

2002. "Explaining the High Level of Party Discipline in the Argentine Chamber of Deputies." In Scott Morgenstern and Benito Nacif, eds., *Legislative Politics in Latin America*. New York: Cambridge University Press.

2004. "The Recruitment and Selection of Legislative Candidates in Argentina." Prepared for the symposium "Pathways to Power: Political Recruitment and Democracy in Latin America," Graylyn International Conference Center, Wake Forest University, Winston-Salem, NC, April 3–4.

Jones, Mark P., and Wonjae Hwang. 2005. "Provincial Party Bosses: Keystone of the Argentine Congress." In Steven Levitsky and María Victoria Murillo, eds., *Argentine Democracy: The Politics of Institutional Weakness*. College Park: Pennsylvania State University Press.

Jones, Mark P., Sebastián Saiegh, Pablo T. Spiller, and Mariano Tommasi. 2001. "Keeping a Seat in Congress: Provincial Party Bosses and the Survival of Argentine Legislators." Paper presented at the Annual Meeting of the American Political Science Association, San Francisco, 2001.

2002. "Amateur Legislators, Professional Politicians: The Consequences of Party-Centered Electoral Rules in Federal Systems." *American Journal of Political Science* 46 (3): 656–69.

Jones, Mark P., Pablo Sanguinetti, and Mariano Tommasi. 2002. "Voters as Fiscal Liberals." Unpublished manuscript. Michigan State University.

Juárez, Carlos Edward. 1995. "The Political Economy of Economic Policy Reform in Colombia: Technocratic Bureaucracy and Business-Government Relations, 1966–1992." Ph.D. dissertation, Department of Political Science, UCLA.

Kay, Stephen J. 2003a. "Pension Reform and Political Risk." Paper prepared for the Latin American Studies Association 24th International Congress, Dallas, March 27–29.

2003b. "State Capacity and Pensions." Paper prepared for the Latin American Studies Association 24th International Congress, Dallas, March 27–29.

Kopits, George. 2001. "Fiscal Rules: Useful Policy Framework or Unnecessary Ornament." Paper presented at the Research Department Public Finance Workshop "Fiscal Rules," Bank of Italy, Perugia, Italy, February 1–3.

Krehbiel, Keith. 1991. *Information and Legislative Organization*. Ann Arbor: University of Michigan Press.

Kydland, Finn E., and Edward C. Prescott. 1977. "Rules Rather Than Discretion: The Inconsistency of Optimal Plan." *Journal of Political Economy* 85 (3): 473–91.

Lafer, Celso. 2002. *La identidad internacional de Brasil*. Buenos Aires: Fondo de Cultura Económica.

Latinobarómeter. 2001. "Latinobarometer: Latin American Public Opinion." Available at: *http://www.latinobarometro.org*

Lehoucq, Fabrice. 1996. "The Institutional Foundations of Democratic Cooperation in Costa Rica." *Journal of Latin America Studies* 28 (2): 329–55.

Lehoucq, Fabrice, Francisco Aparicio, Allyson Benton, Benito Nacif, and Gabriel Negretto. 2004. "Political Institutions, Policymaking Processes, and Policy Outcomes in Mexico." Paper written for the project "Political Institutions,

Policymaking Processes and Policy Outcomes" of the Latin American Research Network, Inter-American Development Bank.

Lehrer, E. 1989. "Lower Equilibrium Payoffs in Two-Player Repeated Games with Non-Observable Actions." *International Journal of Game Theory* 18: 57–89.

Levitsky, Steven. 2003. *Transforming Labor-Based Parties in Latin America: Argentine Peronism in Comparative Perspective.* New York: Cambridge University Press.

Levy, Brian, and Pablo T. Spiller. 1994. "The Institutional Foundations of Regulatory Commitment: A Comparative Analysis of Telecommunications Regulation." *Journal of Law, Economics, and Organization* 10 (2): 201–46.

(eds.). 1996. *Regulations, Institutions, and Commitment: Comparative Studies of Telecommunications.* Political Economy of Institutions and Decisions Series. Cambridge: Cambridge University Press.

Lindauer, David L., and Lant Pritchett. 2002. "What Is the Big Idea? The Third Generation of Development Advice." *Economia: Journal of the Latin American and Caribbean Economic Association* 3 (1): 1–39.

Llanos, Mariana. 2003. "Los Senadores y el Senado en Argentina y Brasil: Informe de una encuesta." Working Paper 10. Institute für Iberoamerika-Kunde, Hamburg, February.

Londregan, John B. 2000. *Ideology and Legislative Institutions in Chile's Transition towards Democracy.* New York: Cambridge University Press.

2002. Appointment, Reelection, and Autonomy in the Senate of Chile. In Scott Morgenstern and Benito Nacif, eds., *Legislative Politics in Latin America.* New York: Cambridge University Press.

Londregan, John, and James Snyder. 1994. "Comparing Committee and Floor Preferences." *Legislative Studies Quarterly* 19: 233–66.

Lora, Eduardo, Ugo Panizza, and Myriam Quispe-Agnoli. 2004. "Reforms Fatigue: Symptoms, Reasons and Implications." *Economic Review*, Federal Reserve Bank of Atlanta, Second Quarter.

Mainwaring, Scott, and Timothy R. Scully. 1995. *Building Democratic Institutions: Party Systems in Latin America.* Stanford, CA: Stanford University Press.

Martinelli, César, and Mariano Tommasi. 1997. "Sequencing of Economic Reforms in the Presence of Political Constraints." *Economics and Politics* 9 (2): 115–31.

Martínez Nogueira, Roberto. 2002. "Las Administraciones Públicas Paralelas y la Construcción de Capacidades Institucionales: Gestión por proyectos y las unidades ejecutoras." *Revista del CLAD Reforma y Democracia*, No. 24 (October).

Mas-Colell, A., M. Whinston, and J. Green. 1995. *Microeconomic Theory.* Oxford: Oxford University Press.

Masnatta, Héctor. 1997. "Magistratura y Política." *La Ley*, April 1.

Mayhew, David. 1974. *Congress: The Electoral Connection.* New Haven, CT: Yale University Press.

References

McCubbins, Mathew D., Roger Noll, and Barry R. Weingast. 1989. "Structure and Process, Politics and Policy: Administrative Arrangements and the Political Control of Agencies." *Virginia Law Review* 75 (2): 431–82.

Meinhold, Stephen S., and Steven A. Shull. 1998. "Policy Congruence between the President and the Solicitor General." *Political Research Quarterly* 51: 527–32.

Mesa-Lago, Carmelo. 1994. *Changing Social Security in Latin America*. Boulder, CO: Lynne Rienner.

Miller, Jonathan M. 1997. "Judicial Review and Constitutional Stability: A Sociology of the U.S. Model and Its Collapse in Argentina." *Hastings International and Comparative Law Review* 77: 151–62.

Miller, Jonathan M. 2001. "Evaluating the Argentine Supreme Court Under President Alfonsín and Menem (1983–1999)." *Southwestern Journal of Law and Trade in the Americas* 7: 369.

Mody, Ashoka, and Martin Schindler. 2004. "Argentina's Growth: A Puzzle?" Mimeo, Research Department, International Monetary Fund.

Moe, Terry M. 1987. "An Assessment of the Positive Theory of Congressional Dominance." *Legislative Studies Quarterly* 12: 475–520.

1990a. "The Politics of Structural Choice: Toward a Theory of Public Bureaucracy." In Oliver Williamson, ed., *Organization Theory: From Chester Barnard to the Present and Beyond*. New York: Oxford University Press.

1997. "The Positive Theory of Public Bureaucracy." In Dennis C. Mueller, ed., *Perspectives on Public Choice*. Cambridge: Cambridge University Press.

Moe, Terry M., and William G. Howell. 1999. "The Presidential Power of Unilateral Action." *Journal of Law, Economics, and Organization* 15 (1): 132–79.

Molinelli, N. Guillermo. 1999. "La Corte Suprema de Justicia de la Nación frente a los poderes políticos, a través del control de constitucionalidad, 1983–1998." Instituto de Investigaciones, Ambrosio Giojia, Facultad de Derecho, Facultad de Buenos Aires, 1999.

Molinelli, N. Guillermo, Valeria Palanza, and Gisella Sin. 1999. *Congreso, Presidencia y Justicia en Argentina: Materiales para su Estudio*. Buenos Aires: Temas/Fundación Gobierno y Sociedad.

Monaldi, Francisco, Rosa Amelia González, Richard Obuchi, Michael Penfold, and Eduardo Zambrano. 2004. "Political Institutions, Policymaking Processes, and Policy Outcomes in Venezuela." Paper written for the project "Political Institutions, Policymaking Processes and Policy Outcomes" of the Latin American Research Network, Inter-American Development Bank.

Montecinos, Verónica. 2003. "Economic Policy Making and Parliamentary Accountability in Chile." Paper 11, Democracy, Governance and Human Rights Program UNRISD, Geneva, Switzerland.

Morello, Augusto M. 1996. "El Servicio de Justicia que Languidece." *El Derecho*, March 4.

Morgenstern, Scott. 1998. "The U.S. Model and Latin American Legislatures." Mimeo, Duke University.

Morgenstern, Scott, and Benito Nacif, eds. 2002. *Legislative Politics in Latin America*. New York: Cambridge University Press.

References

Morón, Eduardo, and Cynthia Sanborn. 2004. "The Pitfalls of Policymaking in Peru: Actors, Institutions and Rules of the Game." Paper written for the project "Political Institutions, Policymaking Processes and Policy Outcomes" of the Latin American Research Network, Inter-American Development Bank.

Morrow, James D. 1994. *Game Theory for Political Scientists*. Princeton, NJ: Princeton University Press.

Murillo, María Victoria. 1997. "Union Politics, Market-Oriented Reforms and the Reshaping of Argentine Corporatism." In Douglas Chalmers et al., eds., *The New Politics of Inequality in Latin America: Rethinking Participation and Representation*, 72–94. Oxford: Oxford University Press.

2001. *Labor Unions, Partisan Coalitions, and Market Reforms in Latin America*. New York: Cambridge University Press.

2002. "Political Bias in Policy Convergence: Privatization Choices in Latin America." *World Politics* 54 (4): 462–93.

Nacif, Benito. 2002. "Understanding Party Discipline in the Mexican Chamber of Deputies: The Centralized Party Model." In Scott Morgenstern and Benito Nacif, eds., *Legislative Politics in Latin America*, 254–86. New York: Cambridge University Press.

Nelson, Joan M., and Mariano Tommasi. 2001. "Politicians, Public Support and Social Equity Reforms." Working Paper 51. Center of Studies for Institutional Development, Fundación Gobierno y Sociedad.

Nino, Carlos S. 1992. *Fundamentos de Derecho Constitucional*. Buenos Aires: Astrea.

Novaro, Marcos. 2000. "La Jefatura del Gabinete de Ministros en Argentina y sus capacidades de coordinación y control." *Revista "Política y Gestión"* No. 1, pp. 81–108. Ediciones HomoSapiens, Buenos Aires, Noviembre.

Oficina Anticorrupción, Ministerio de Justicia. 2000. "Estudio exploratorio sobre la transparencia en la Administración Pública Argentina: 1998–1999." Dirección Nacional de Planificación de Políticas de Transparencia, Oficina Anticorrupción, Ministerio de Justicia, República Argentina, August.

Oficina Nacional de Empleo Público. 2003. "Algunas Caracteristicas Significativas de las Personas Contratadas por la Administracion Pública Nacional Bajo el Regimen del Decreto No. 1.184/01 Durante el Año 2.002." Jefatura de Gabinete, May.

Ornstein, Norman J., Thomas E. Mann, and Michael J. Malbin. 1998. *Vital Statistics on Congress, 1997–1998*. Washington, DC: American Enterprise Institute.

Oszlak, Oscar. 1999. "The Argentine Civil Service: An Unfinished Search for Identity." *Research in Public Administration* 5: 267–326.

2001. "Sistemas de Servicio Civil en América Latina y el Caribe. Situación Actual y Desafíos Futuros." Working Paper. Regional Policy Dialogue, Inter-American Development Bank, Washington DC.

Palanza, María Valeria. 2002. "¿Qué Hizo el Congreso en Política Social Durante la Década de los '90?" Working Paper 70. Center for Studies of Institutional Development, Fundación Gobierno y Sociedad.

References

2005. "Legislative Oversight and Inter-Branch Relations in Separation of Powers Systems: Evidence from Argentina." Mimeo, Department of Politics, Princeton University.

Palmer, Matthew S. R. 1995. "Toward an Economics of Comparative Political Organization: Examining Ministerial Responsibility." *Journal of Law, Economics, and Organization* 11 (1): 164–88.

Pearce, David. 1992. "Repeated Games: Cooperation and Rationality." In *Advances in Economic Theory, 6th World Congress*, 132–74. New York: Cambridge University Press.

Peña, Marcos. 2001. "La economía política de los créditos del Banco Mundial y del Banco Interamericano de Desarrollo en el Estado Nacional argentino durante la década del 90." *Boletín Informativo Techint* 305 (January–March): 53–81.

Pereira, Carlos, and Bernardo Mueller. 2004. "The Cost of Governing: Strategic Behavior of the President and Legislators in Brazil's Budgetary Process." *Comparative Political Studies* 37 (7): 781–815.

Pereira, Carlos, Eduardo Leoni, and Lucio Renno. 2001. "Strategies for Surviving Politically: Political Career Choice in the Brazilian Chamber of Deputies." Mimeo, Oxford University.

Persson, Torsten, and Guido Tabellini, eds. 1994. *Monetary and Fiscal Policy*. Cambridge, MA: MIT Press.

2000. *Political Economics: Explaining Economic Policy*. Cambridge, MA: MIT Press.

2003. *The Economic Effect of Constitutions*. Cambridge, MA: MIT Press.

Petracchi, Enrique S. 1987. "Control Judicial en la Argentina." *La Ley*, E-709.

Piñera, Jose. 1999. Statement by Jose Piñera, testimony before the House Committee on Ways and Means, February 11. Available at: *http://waysandmeans. house.gov/legacy.asp?file=legacy/fullcomm/106cong/2-11-99/2-11pine.htm*

Pion-Berlin, David. 1997. *Through Corridors of Power: Institutions and Civil-Military Relations in Argentina*. University Park: Pennsylvania State University Press.

Polsby, Nelson W. 1968. "The Institutionalization of the U.S. House of Representatives." *American Political Science Review* 62: 144–68.

Poole, Keith T., and Howard Rosenthal. 1991. "Patterns of Congressional Voting." *American Journal of Political Science* 35: 228–78.

Pritchett, Lant. 2004. "Reform Is Like a Box of Chocolates: Understanding the Growth Disappointments and Surprises." Mimeo, Harvard University.

Ramseyer, Mark J., and Eric B. Rasmusen. 1997. "Judicial Independence in a Civil Law Regime: The Evidence from Japan." *Journal of Law, Economics and Organization* 13: 259–86.

Ramseyer, J. Mark, and Frances McCall Rosenbluth. 1993. *Japan's Political Marketplace*. Cambridge, MA: Harvard University Press.

Rauch, James E., and Peter B. Evans. 1999. "Bureaucratic Structure and Bureaucratic Performance in Less Developed Countries." Discussion Paper 99–06. University of California at San Diego.

Rausch, A. 1995. "La Regulación en la Argentina: Acerca de su Diseño e Implementación." Presentado en la conferencia Sobre Post-Privatización en América Latina, PNUD – Gobierno Argentino.

References

Remmer, Karen L., and François Gelineau. 2003. "Subnational Electoral Choice." *Comparative Political Studies* 36 (7): 801–22.

Remmer, Karen, and Erik Wibbels. 2000. "The Subnational Politics of Economic Adjustment: Provincial Politics and Fiscal Performance in Argentina." *Comparative Political Studies* 33: 419–51.

Repetto, Fabián, Analía Minteguiaga, and Juan Cruz Olmeda. 2004. "La Política de la Reforma Administrativa Argentina." Mimeo, Center for Studies of Institutional Development, Fundación Gobierno y Sociedad.

Rock, David. 1987. *Argentina, 1516–1982*. Berkeley: University of California Press.

Rodriguez, Jesús, and Alejandro Bonvecchi. 2004. "El Papel del Poder Legislativo en el Proceso Presupuestario: La Experiencia Argentina." Serie macroeconomía para el desarrollo No. 32, CEPAL, Santiago, Chile.

Rodríguez Larreta, Horacio, and María Eugenia Vidal. 2001. *Plan Social Nacional*. Buenos Aires: Grupo Sophia.

Rodrik, Dani. 1989. "Credibility of Trade Reform: A Policy Maker's Guide." *World Economy* 12 (1): 1–16.

——— 1995. "Taking Trade Policy Seriously: Export Subsidization as a Case Study in Policy Effectiveness." In Jim Levinsohn, Alan V. Deardoff, and Robert M. Stern, eds., *New Directions in Trade Theory*. Ann Arbor: University of Michigan Press.

——— 2006. "Goodbye Washington Consensus, Hello Washington Confusion?" Mimeo, January. Harvard University. Available at: *http://ksghome.harvard.edu/~drodrik/papers.html*

Rofman, Rafael. 2000. "The Pension System in Argentina Six Years after the Reform." Social Protection Discussion Paper 15. World Bank, Washington, DC.

——— 2002. "The Pension System and the Crisis in Argentina: Learning the Lessons." Mimeo.

Ronconi, Lucas, and Mariano Tommasi. 2003. "Pension Policy in Argentina." Mimeo, Center for Studies of Institutional Development, Fundación Gobierno y Sociedad.

Rosenbluth, Frances, and Michael Thies. 2000. "Politics in Japan." In Gabriel A. Almond and G. Bingham Powell, gen. eds., *Comparative Politics Today: A World View*, 7th ed. New York: Addison Wesley Longman.

Rossi, Gloria. 1998. "La formación de acuerdos en la Cámara de Diputados del Congreso argentino." Thesis, Universidad de San Andrés, Buenos Aires, Argentina.

Rotemberg, Julio J., and Garth Saloner. 1986. "A Supergame-Theoretic Model of Price Wars during Booms." *American Economic Review* 76: 390–407.

Roulet, J. 1988. *El Estado Necesario*. Buenos Aires: Centro de Participación Política.

Rundquist, Paul S., and Clay H. Wellborn. 1994. "Building Legislatures in Latin America." In Lawrence D. Longley, ed., *Working Papers on Comparative Legislative Studies*, 387–406. Appleton, WI: Research Committee of Legislative Specialists of the IPSA.

References

Russell, Roberto, and Juan Gabriel Tokatlian. 2003. *El Lugar de Brasil en la Política Exterior Argentina*. Buenos Aires: Fondo de Cultura Económica.

Sabatier, Paul A., ed. 1999. *Theories of the Policy Process*. Boulder, CO: Westview Press.

Saiegh, Sebastián M. 2005. "The Role of Legislatures in the Policymaking Process." Paper prepared for Workshop on State Reform, Public Policies and Policymaking Processes, Inter-American Development Bank, Washington DC, February 28–March 2.

Saiegh, Sebastián, and Mariano Tommasi. 1998. "Argentina's Federal Fiscal Institutions: A Case Study in the Transaction-Cost Theory of Politics." Working Paper 11. Center for Studies of Institutional Development, Universidad de San Andrés.

Salzberger, Eli, and Paul Fenn. 1999. "Judicial Independence: Some Evidence from the English Court of Appeal." *Journal of Law and Economics* 42 (2): 831–47.

Samuels, David J. 2000. "The Gubernatorial Coattail Effect: Federalism and Congressional Elections in Brazil." *Journal of Politics* 62 (1): 240–53.

———. 2003. *Ambition, Federalism, and Legislative Politics in Brazil*. New York: Cambridge University Press.

Samuels, David J., and Richard Snyder. 2001. "The Value of a Vote: Malapportionment in Comparative Perspective." *British Journal of Political Science* 31 (3): 651–71.

Sanguinetti, Juan. 2002. "Los Determinantes Políticos e Institucionales de las Políticas Sociales: Un análisis de los Procedimientos Presupuestarios." Working Paper 65. Center for Studies of Institutional Development, Fundación Gobierno y Sociedad.

Sawers, Larry. 1996. *The Other Argentina: The Interior and National Development*. Boulder, CO: Westview Press.

Scartascini, Carlos, and Ernesto Stein. 2005. "El Rol del Legislativo en el Proceso Presupuestario: Un Análisis Comparativo." Paper presented at the 17th Seminario Regional de Política Fiscal, CEPAL, Santiago de Chile, January 24–27.

Schneider, Ben Ross. 1993. "The Career Connection: A Comparative Analysis of Bureaucratic Preferences and Insulation." *Comparative Politics* 25 (3): 331–50.

Schwartz, Gerd, and Claire Liuksila. 1997. "Argentina." In Teresa Ter-Minassian, ed., *Fiscal Federalism in Theory and in Practice*, 387–422. Washington, DC: International Monetary Fund.

Segal, Jeffrey A. 1989. "Supreme Court Support for the Solicitor General: The Effect of Presidential Appointments." *Western Political Quarterly* 43 (1): 137–52.

———. 1997. "Separation-of-Power Games in the Positive Theory of Congress and Courts." *American Political Science Review* 91: 28–44.

Shah, Anwar. 1994. "The Reform of Intergovernmental Fiscal Relations in Developing and Emerging Market Economies." World Bank Policy and Research Series No. 23, Washington, DC.

Shepsle, Kenneth A. 1978. *The Giant Jigsaw Puzzle*. Chicago: University of Chicago Press.

References

Shepsle, Kenneth A., and Mark S. Bonchek. 1997. *Analyzing Politics: Rationality, Behavior and Institutions.* New York: Norton.

Shepsle, Kenneth A., and Barry R. Weingast. 1995. *Positive Theories of Congressional Institutions.* Ann Arbor: University of Michigan Press.

Shugart, Matthew Soberg, and Stephan Haggard. 2001. "Institutions and Public Policy in Presidential Systems." In Stephan Haggard and Matthew D. McCubbins, eds., *Presidents, Parliaments, and Policy.* New York: Cambridge University Press.

Sikkink, Kathryn. 1993. "Las Capacidades y la Autonomía del Estado en Brasil y la Argentina. Un Enfoque Neoinstitucionalista." *Desarrollo Económico* 32 (128): 543–74.

Snyder, Susan K., and Barry R. Weingast. 2000. "The American System of Shared Powers: The President, Congress and the NLRB." *Journal of Law, Economics and Organization* 16: 269–305.

Spiller, Pablo T. 1996. "A Positive Political Theory of Regulatory Instruments: Contracts, Administrative Law or Regulatory Specificity?" *USC Law Review* 69: 477–515.

Spiller, Pablo T., and Mariano Tommasi. 2003. "The Institutional Foundations of Public Policy: A Transactions Approach with Application to Argentina." *Journal of Law, Economics, and Organization* 19 (2): 281–306.

Spiller, Pablo T., and Santiago Urbiztondo. 1994. "Political Appointees vs. Career Civil Servants: A Multiple Principals Theory of Political Bureaucracies." *European Journal of Political Economy* 10: 465–97.

Spiller, Pablo T., Ernesto Stein, and Mariano Tommasi. 2003. "Political Institutions, Policymaking Processes and Policy Outcomes: An Intertemporal Transactions Framework." Mimeo, Research Department, Inter-American Development Bank. Available at: *http://www.iadb.org/res/politicalinstitutions*

Sribney, Bill. 1998. *Advantages of the Robust Variance Estimator.* FAQ, Stata Corporation. Available at: *http://www.stata.com/support/faqs/stat/robust_var.html*

Stein, Ernesto, and Mariano Tommasi. 2005. "Democratic Institutions, Policymaking Processes, and the Quality of Policies in Latin America." Paper presented at the International Seminar "Una Nueva Agenda de Desarrollo Económico para América Latina," Fundación CIDOB, Salamanca, Spain, October 7–8.

Strøm, Kaare. 1997. "Rules, Reasons, and Routines: Legislative Roles in Parliamentary Democracies." In Thomas Saalfeld and Wolfgang C. Muller, eds., *Members of Parliament in Western Europe: Roles and Behaviour,* 155–74. London: Frank Cass.

Sturzenegger, Federico, and Mariano Tommasi, eds. 1998. *The Political Economy of Reform.* Cambridge, MA: MIT Press.

Tanzi, Vito. 1996. "Fiscal Federalism and Decentralization: A Review of Some Efficiency and Macroeconomic Aspects." In Michael Bruno and Boris Pleskovic, eds., *Annual World Bank Conference on Development Economics, 1995,* 295–316. Washington, DC: World Bank.

Ter-Minassian, Teresa, ed. 1997. *Fiscal Federalism in Theory and Practice.* Washington, DC: International Monetary Fund.

References

Tommasi, Mariano. 2002. "Fiscal Federalism in Argentina and the Reforms of the 1990s." Working Paper 147. Center for Research on Economic Development and Policy Reform, Stanford University.

—— 2004. "Crisis, Political Institutions, and Policy Reform: The Good, the Bad, and the Ugly." In Bertil Tungodden, Nicholas Stern, and Ivar Kolstad, eds., *Toward Pro-Poor Policies: Aid, Institutions, and Globalization*. Annual World Bank Conference on Development Economics – Europe 2003, 135–64. New York: World Bank and Oxford University Press.

Tommasi, Mariano, and Pablo T. Spiller. 2000. *Las fuentes institucionales del desarrollo argentino: Hacia una agenda institucional*. Buenos Aires: UNPD-Eudeba.

Tsebelis, George. 2002. *Veto Players: How Political Institutions Work*. Princeton, NJ: Princeton University Press.

Uña, Gerardo, Gisell Cogliandro, Nicolás Bertello, and Juan Labaqui. 2005. "El Congreso y el Presupuesto Nacional: Desempeño y Condicionantes de su Rol en el Proceso Presupuestario." Mimeo, Fundación Konrad Adenauer.

Urrutia, Miguel. 1991. "On the Absence of Economic Populism in Colombia." In Rudiger Dornbusch and Sebastian Edwards, eds., *The Macroeconomics of Populism in Latin America*. Chicago: University of Chicago Press.

U.S. General Accounting Office (GAO). 1996. "Privatization Practices in Argentina." Report prepared by the General Accounting Office in response to a request by U.S. Rep. Scott Klug. GAO/AIMD-96-55 (March).

Waxman, Seth P. 1998. "Presenting the Case of the United States as It Should Be: The Solicitor General in Historical Context." *Journal of Supreme Court History* 1998 (2): 3–25.

Weaver, Kent, and Bert Rockman, eds. 1993. *Do Institutions Matter? Government Capabilities in the United States and Abroad*. Washington, DC: Brookings Institution.

Weingast, Barry R. 1995. "The Economic Role of Political Institutions: Market-Preserving Federalism and Economic Development." *Journal of Law, Economics and Organization* 11 (1): 1–31.

Weingast, Barry R., and W. Marshall. 1988. "The Industrial Organization of Congress: Or, Why Legislatures, Like Firms, Are Not Organized as Markets." *Journal of Political Economy* 96 (1): 132–63. Translated into Spanish in Sebastián Saiegh and Mariano Tommasi, comp., *La Nueva Economía Política: Racionalidad e instituciones*. Buenos Aires: Eudeba.

Weingast, Barry R., and Mark Moran. 1983. "Bureaucratic Discretion or Congressional Control? Regulatory Policymaking by the Federal Trade Commission." *Journal of Political Economy* 91: 765–800.

Wibbels, Erik. 2003. "Bailouts, Budget Constraints, and Leviathans: Comparative Federalism and Lessons from the Early U.S." *Comparative Political Studies* 36 (5): 475–508.

Williamson, Oliver E. 2000. "Economic Institutions and Development: A View from the Bottom." In Mancur Olson and Satu Kahkonen, eds., *A Not-So-Dismal Science: A Broader View of Economies and Societies*, 92–118. Oxford: Oxford University Press.

References

World Bank. 1996. *Argentina: Provincial Finances Study; Selected Issues in Fiscal Federalism.* Report No. 15487-AR.

———. 1998. *Argentina: The Fiscal Dimensions of the Convertibility Plan.* Washington, DC: World Bank.

———. 2001. *Peru: Institutional and Governance Review.* Poverty Reduction and Economic Management Unit, Latin America and the Caribbean.

Wynia, Gary W. 1995. "Argentina's New Democracy: Presidential Power and Legislative Limits." In David Close, ed., *Legislatures and the New Democracies in Latin America*, 71–88. Boulder, CO: L. Rienner Publishers.

Ziulu, Adolfo G. 1998. *Derecho Constitucional.* Buenos Aires: De Palma.

Index

Index